VMware Cookbook

VMware Cookbook

Ryan Troy and Matthew Helmke

O'REILLY®

Beijing · Cambridge · Farnham · Köln · Sebastopol · Taipei · Tokyo

VMware Cookbook

by Ryan Troy and Matthew Helmke

Published by O'Reilly Media, Inc., 1005 Gravenstein Highway North, Sebastopol, CA 95472.

O'Reilly books may be purchased for educational, business, or sales promotional use. Online editions are also available for most titles (*http://my.safaribooksonline.com*). For more information, contact our corporate/institutional sales department: (800) 998-9938 or *corporate@oreilly.com*.

Editor:	Andy Oram	**Indexer:**	Lucie Haskins
Production Editor:	Sumita Mukherji	**Cover Designer:**	Karen Montgomery
Copyeditor:	Rachel Head	**Interior Designer:**	David Futato
Proofreader:	Sada Preisch	**Illustrator:**	Robert Romano

Printing History:

October 2009:   First Edition.

RepKover™

This book uses RepKover™, a durable and flexible lay-flat binding.

ISBN: 978-0-596-15725-8

[M]

1255441618

Table of Contents

Preface xi

1. **VMware Infrastructure Installation** 1
    1.1 What Is VMware Infrastructure 3?   2
    1.2 What Is VMware vSphere 4.0?   3
    1.3 VMware ESX 3.x/4.x Configuration Maximums   5
    1.4 VMware ESX 3.x Server Overview   11
    1.5 VMware ESX 3.x Installation   12
    1.6 VMware ESXi 3.5 Overview   21
    1.7 VMware ESXi 3.5 Installation   22
    1.8 VMware vCenter Server 2.x Overview   27
    1.9 vCenter Server 2.x Installation   27
    1.10 VMware vCenter Client 2.x Overview   36
    1.11 vCenter Client 2.x Installation   36
    1.12 License Server Overview   37
    1.13 License Server (vCenter 2.x) Installation   37
    1.14 vConverter Overview   38
    1.15 vConverter Installation   38
    1.16 VMware ESX 4.0 Installation   42

2. **Storage** 55
    2.1 Comparing ESX Storage Options   55
    2.2 Storage Device Naming Scheme   56
    2.3 Creating a Network for a Software iSCSI Initiator   57
    2.4 Configuring Software iSCSI   59
    2.5 Configuring a Hardware iSCSI Initiator   62
    2.6 Configuring iSCSI in Windows Virtual Machines   64
    2.7 Opening Firewall Ports for an ESX iSCSI Software Initiator   68
    2.8 Multipathing with iSCSI   69
    2.9 Adding Fibre Channel Storage in ESX   72
    2.10 Raw Device Mapping in Virtual Machines   73

2.11 Creating a Port to Access NFS Datastores   74
2.12 Configuring ESX to Use NFS   77
2.13 Creating a VMFS Volume in vCenter   78
2.14 Performing a Storage Rescan   79
2.15 Creating a VMFS Volume via the Command Line   80
2.16 Viewing the Files That Define a VMFS Volume   81
2.17 Extending a VMFS Volume   82
2.18 Reading VMFS Metadata   83
2.19 Renaming a VMFS Volume Label from the Command Line   84
2.20 Manually Creating and Aligning a VMFS Partition   85
2.21 Creating a Diagnostic Partition   86
2.22 Removing Storage Volumes from ESX   87
2.23 Determining Whether a VMFS Datastore Is on a Local or SAN Disk 88
2.24 Adjusting Timeouts When Adding Storage in vCenter   89
2.25 Setting Disk Timeouts in Windows   89

3. Networking 91
3.1   Understanding Differences Between ESX 3.5 and ESXi 3.5 in
      Network Support   91
3.2   Configuring ESX Network Ports and Firewall   92
3.3   Creating a vSwitch for Virtual Machines   95
3.4   Removing a Virtual Switch   97
3.5   Adding VMotion to Enable Virtual Machine Migration   98
3.6   Creating a Service Console Network via the CLI   101
3.7   Checking Connectivity Using vmkping   103
3.8   Modifying the Speed of a Network Adapter   104
3.9   Choosing Network Elements That Protect Security   105
3.10 Setting the Basic Level 2 Security Policy   106
3.11 Ethernet Traffic Shaping   109
3.12 Using Multiple Gateways   111
3.13 Load Balancing and Failover   112
3.14 Creating a Jumbo Frame VMkernel Interface for iSCSI   116
3.15 Enabling Jumbo Frames on a vSwitch   117
3.16 Enabling Jumbo Frames on a Virtual Machine   118
3.17 Changing the Service Console IP Address   118
3.18 Using the Command Line to Locate Physical Ethernet Adapters   120
3.19 Changing the Ethernet Port Speed via the Command Line   121
3.20 Restoring a Service Console via the CLI   122

4. Resource and vCenter Management 125
4.1   Understanding Virtual Machine Memory Use Through
      Reservations, Shares, and Limits   126
4.2   Configuring Virtual Machine CPU Limits   128

  4.3 Configuring Virtual Machine CPU Shares   129
  4.4 Configuring Virtual Machine CPU Reservations   131
  4.5 Setting Up Resource Pools   132
  4.6 Understanding Resource Pools   134
  4.7 Expandable Reservations in Resource Pools   136
  4.8 Creating a Cluster   138
  4.9 Adding Hosts to a Cluster   141
  4.10 Enabling DRS in a Cluster   144
  4.11 Understanding Cluster States and Warnings   148
  4.12 Reconfiguring HA on a Host   149
  4.13 Using ESX 4.x CPU/RAM Hot Add/Hotplug Support   151
  4.14 Surviving a vCenter Server Failure or Outage   151

5. Useful Command-Line Tools **155**
  5.1 Entering Maintenance Mode via the Command Line   155
  5.2 Displaying Server Information   156
  5.3 Viewing the ESX Version   157
  5.4 Changing the Virtual Disk from BusLogic to LSI Logic   158
  5.5 Hiding the VMware Tools Icon   160
  5.6 Emptying a Large Virtual Machine Logfile   161
  5.7 Viewing Disk Partitions via the Console   161
  5.8 Monitoring CPU Usage   162
  5.9 Monitoring Memory   164
  5.10 Monitoring Storage Performance   168
  5.11 Monitoring Network Usage   169
  5.12 Managing Virtual Switches   171
  5.13 Generating a Logfile for VMware Support   173
  5.14 Checking ESX Patches   175
  5.15 Enabling NTP in vCenter   176
  5.16 Enabling NTP via the Command Line   179
  5.17 Changing the ESX Server's Time   180
  5.18 Using TCP Wrappers   181
  5.19 Restarting the vCenter Agent   182
  5.20 Unregistering a Virtual Machine via the Command Line   183
  5.21 Registering a Virtual Machine via the Command Line   183
  5.22 Finding Virtual Machine Snapshots   183
  5.23 Renaming a Virtual Machine via vCenter   184
  5.24 Renaming a Virtual Machine via the Command Line   185
  5.25 Using Host Files   186
  5.26 Setting ESX Options Using the Command Line   186
  5.27 Configuring Authentication Choices Using the Command Line   188
  5.28 Manipulating the Bootloader   189
  5.29 Manipulating the Crash Dump Partition   190

    5.30 Configuring a Firewall on the Command Line   192
    5.31 Managing ESX Driver Modules   193
    5.32 Configuring Storage Multipathing   194
    5.33 Managing NFS Mounts   196
    5.34 Managing Disk Volumes with ESX4   197
    5.35 Configuring Ethernet Adapters   198
    5.36 Rescanning Host Bus Adapters   199
    5.37 Managing ESX4 Add-ons from the Command Line   199
    5.38 Managing Resource Groups from the Command Line   201
    5.39 Managing VMkernel Network Routes   202
    5.40 Configuring Software iSCSI Options   203
    5.41 Configuring Hardware iSCSCI Options   204
    5.42 Upgrading Your Version of VMware   205
    5.43 Displaying vmhba Names with Associated Mappings   206
    5.44 Managing SCSI Device Mappings with ESX4 vSphere   207
    5.45 Managing VMkernel Ports   208
    5.46 Managing vswif Console Network Settings   209

 6. General Security 213
    6.1   Enabling SSH on ESXi   213
    6.2   Enabling Direct root Logins on Your ESX Server   214
    6.3   Adding Users and Groups   215
    6.4   Allowing or Denying Users the Use of SSH   217
    6.5   Turning on the MOTD for Console Users   219
    6.6   Changing the root Password via the Console   219
    6.7   Recovering a Lost root Password   220
    6.8   Disabling Direct root Console Logins   222
    6.9   Securing the GRUB Bootloader Menu   224
    6.10 Disabling USB Drive Mounting   225
    6.11 Opening and Closing Firewall Ports via the Console   225
    6.12 Checking Default ESX Ports   228
    6.13 Turning on SNMP for Remote Administration   229
    6.14 Using SNMP Version 3   231
    6.15 Using sudo   232
    6.16 Configuring sudo   233
    6.17 Tracking Users via the CLI   235
    6.18 Configuring Active Directory Authentication   238
    6.19 Setting a Maximum Number of Failed Logins   240
    6.20 Limiting Access to the su Command   241
    6.21 Setting User Password Aging   241
    6.22 Disabling Copy and Paste   246
    6.23 Disabling Disk Shrinking on Virtual Machines   246
    6.24 Disabling Unneeded Devices   247

    6.25 Preventing Unwanted Device Additions and Removals   248
    6.26 Disabling VMware Tools Settings Override   248

7. **Automating ESX Installation** **251**
    7.1 Enabling Scripted Install Support on ESX   251
    7.2 Using the Scripted Installer   252
    7.3 Enhancing the Kickstart Configuration   257
    7.4 Copying the CD-ROM to Facilitate NFS Installations   266
    7.5 Advanced Install Scripting Using %pre   266
    7.6 Advanced Install Scripting Using %post   267
    7.7 Using the ESX Deployment Appliance   269

Index **271**

Preface

VMware is one of those products that many of us, including this book's authors, have been reading about for years. Ryan had the opportunity to become involved with and architect a virtualized environment a few years ago. After researching several options, he became particularly interested in and impressed by VMware's enterprise virtualization platform. As time passed and he worked directly with VMware's products in a production environment, he became even more enthused.

Matthew and Ryan have worked together on several projects in the past. In the summer of 2008, the two of us decided we would like to write a book together. We tossed around ideas and decided to write on VMware's ESX platform, because it impressed us so. Since Matthew was already an established writer and also technologically proficient, although new to this specific software, we decided that Ryan would do the technical writing and Matthew would concentrate his efforts on making sure it all came across clearly and accurately. As we mention later in the Acknowledgments, Dell was kind enough to lend us some equipment for testing while writing, and the two of us got together and began experimenting.

We are genuinely delighted by VMware as a company, and have found its employees very kind and helpful. We have also become sold on its products. Using VMware's platform in a production environment has been everything it is advertised to be: it has made system administration easier, made the use of resources more efficient and cost-effective, and quite frankly been a lot of fun. If this weren't the case, like all true geeks (in the best sense of the word), we would find something else to play with. So far, we haven't.

This book encompasses many of the most useful and interesting recipes we have discovered while using the platform in production, as well as some cool tricks we encountered while testing and playing. We believe that anyone who's using the VMware platform will find this book useful, and we hope it helps you enjoy VMware as much as we do.

Audience

This book is intended for system administrators who have some experience with VMware ESX, ESXi, or vSphere. Throughout the book we've tried to appeal to beginners and also include a generous amount of complex recipes for advanced users. We believe this book will be a solid reference guide for any system administrator, regardless of his level of knowledge. We hope you enjoy it!

Organization of This Book

This book is made up of seven chapters:

- Chapter 1, *VMware Infrastructure Installation*, covers installation details for ESX and ESXi. It includes instructions for 3.x and the steps that worked for 4.0 at the time the book was written.

- Chapter 2, *Storage*, covers partitions, iSCSI and NFS configuration, and other choices reflecting local or external data storage.

- Chapter 3, *Networking*, covers communications at multiple levels, including configuration of virtual switches, software and hardware adapters, Ethernet frame sizes, and more.

- Chapter 4, *Resource and vCenter Management*, shows you how best to apportion memory and CPU resources through clustering, shares, hot add/hotplug support, and other options.

- Chapter 5, *Useful Command-Line Tools*, presents miscellaneous commands that can rescue you in a pinch and help you keep apprised of your servers' functioning.

- Chapter 6, *General Security*, covers a range of access issues, such as how to control which users have access to each level of the system and how to set up firewalls, networking, and remote access to your desired level of security.

- Chapter 7, *Automating ESX Installation*, introduces the configuration files used to control basic networking options, startup activities, and other aspects of the system you'll want to automate in order to make it easier to replicate virtual machines.

Along the way, you'll also find plenty of pointers and advice on good programming practices and tips that may help you find and solve hard-to-detect programming errors. There are also plenty of links to websites containing further details on the topics covered.

Font Conventions

This book uses the following typographical conventions:

Italic
> Used for email addresses, URLs, filenames, pathnames, and emphasizing new terms when they are first introduced

`Constant width`
> Used for the contents of files and for commands and their output

`Constant width bold`
> Used in code sections to show commands or text that would be typed by the user, and, occasionally, to highlight portions of code

`Constant width italic`
> Used for replaceable items and some comments in code sections

 Indicates a tip, suggestion, or general note relating to the nearby text.

 Indicates a warning or caution relating to the nearby text.

Using Code Examples

This book is here to help you get your job done. In general, you may use the code in this book in your programs and documentation. You do not need to contact us for permission unless you're reproducing a significant portion of the code. For example, writing a program that uses several chunks of code from this book does not require permission. Selling or distributing a CD-ROM of examples from O'Reilly books *does* require permission. Answering a question by citing this book and quoting example code does not require permission. Incorporating a significant amount of example code from this book into your product's documentation *does* require permission.

We appreciate, but do not require, attribution. An attribution usually includes the title, author, publisher, and ISBN. For example: "*VMware Cookbook*, by Ryan Troy and Matthew Helmke. Copyright 2010 Ryan Troy and Matthew Helmke, 978-0-596-15725-8."

If you feel your use of code examples falls outside fair use or the permission given above, feel free to contact us at *permissions@oreilly.com*.

We'd Like to Hear from You

Every recipe in this book has been tested on various platforms, but occasionally you may encounter problems. The information in this book has also been verified at each step of the production process. However, mistakes and oversights can occur and we will gratefully receive details of any you find, as well as any suggestions you would like to make for future editions. You can contact the author and editors at:

> O'Reilly Media, Inc.
> 1005 Gravenstein Highway North
> Sebastopol, CA 95472
> (800) 998-9938 (in the United States or Canada)
> (707) 829-0515 (international or local)
> (707) 829-0104 (fax)

We have a web page for this book, where we list errata, examples, and any additional information. You can access this page at:

> *http://www.oreilly.com/catalog/9780596157258*

To comment or ask technical questions about this book, send email to the following address, mentioning the book's ISBN (9780596157258):

> *bookquestions@oreilly.com*

For more information about our books, conferences, Resource Centers, and the O'Reilly Network, see our website at:

> *http://www.oreilly.com*

Safari® Books Online

Safari Safari Books Online is an on-demand digital library that lets you easily search over 7,500 technology and creative reference books and videos to find the answers you need quickly.

With a subscription, you can read any page and watch any video from our library online. Read books on your cell phone and mobile devices. Access new titles before they are available for print, and get exclusive access to manuscripts in development and post feedback for the authors. Copy and paste code samples, organize your favorites, download chapters, bookmark key sections, create notes, print out pages, and benefit from tons of other time-saving features.

O'Reilly Media has uploaded this book to the Safari Books Online service. To have full digital access to this book and others on similar topics from O'Reilly and other publishers, sign up for free at *http://my.safaribooksonline.com*.

Acknowledgments

Ryan: I would like to thank my wife, Holly, for her continued support and always-sound advice while I work on projects, which require me to be engulfed in concentration. Without her dedication and interest in my projects they probably wouldn't become realities. I want to thank my coauthor, Matthew Helmke, for his words of wisdom, great ideas, and never-ending copyediting; you are a true rock star. I'd also like to say thanks to my family, friends, and coworkers for supporting me during the writing of this book—your consistent interest helped keep me motivated.

Matthew: I would like to thank my wonderful wife, Heather, for her consistently supportive attitude and encouragement. Without that, I wouldn't even try to take on big projects like this book. My kids didn't help in the project directly, but they did put up with me asking them to be quiet at odd times while I was writing something that required my full attention, and they are incredibly wonderful kids—I love you, Saralyn, Sedona, and Philip! I want to thank Ryan Troy for the opportunity to collaborate on this and other projects and also for the hospitality he and Holly showed me during my visit. I freely and gratefully acknowledge that there is no way this book could/would have been written without Ryan. Finally, I would like to thank all my computer geek friends around the world who were genuinely excited when they discovered I was involved in a book project with O'Reilly—I'm so glad to have people like you in my life with whom I can share my joy as well as my enjoyment of this topic.

Together, we would like to thank all those who helped us make this a better book than it would have been without their assistance: our editor, Andy Oram, and all of the staff at O'Reilly, who have been kind and attentive from the moment we first submitted our book proposal; the wonderful people at Dell who lent us a rack of Dell PowerEdge servers, Cisco switches, and a Dell EqualLogic iSCSI array to use for testing as we wrote the book; the people who helped with the book's tech review, including Paul Jahnz, Cathy Leik, Guillermo Amodeo, David Deeths, John S. Howard, and Beth Cohen; and finally, the people at VMware for allowing us to be a part of the beta cycle for 4.0 and for making such cool software that we found ourselves excited to learn it and use it and write about it.

## CHAPTER 1

VMware Infrastructure Installation

Before we can begin serving the main recipes of our cookbook, we have to make sure that all of our readers understand the terms we'll use in the rest of the book, and that you have all the necessary components installed. This book aims to be useful for both new and seasoned VMware ESX users. Because of the nature of this cookbook, we will assume from time to time that you have advanced knowledge and understanding of how the products work.

Virtualization provides a way for multiple operating systems to be installed on the same physical hardware. By using virtual technology, we can consolidate hardware and instantly build quality assurance and test environments. This is a tremendous breakthrough, as it allows underutilized equipment to do more than sit around idle, as well as allowing developers and administrators to test and use multiple software configurations and packages that require different operating systems on the same piece of equipment, without having to purchase, set up, and maintain multiple computers. This savings makes the accounting department and managers happy and gives the technology lovers an opportunity to do all the things they want or need to do at the same time.

A typical IT scenario goes something like this: you have lots of servers in your rack or collection of racks. Most of them only run at about 10–15% of their capacity the majority of the time, but you let that happen because you want to keep their various functions and operating systems isolated from one another. This provides some security, both because if one server is compromised it does not necessarily mean that access has been granted to others, and because a problem with one piece of software will not cause other parts of your IT infrastructure to go down as you deal with it.

Virtualization helps you make better use of those physical resources, without compromising the original intent of keeping services isolated. Instead of installing your operating system directly on your hardware, you instead begin with a *virtualization layer*: a stripped-down OS designed to schedule access to network, disk, memory, and CPU resources for guest OSs, the same way that those guest OSs control that scheduling for their applications. Most virtualization platforms limit themselves to specific hardware and present a specific set of virtual components to the operating systems installed on top of them. This provides a very stable and consistent presentation to the operating systems you install and allows them to be moved much more easily.

Once you've installed and configured the virtualization layer, you can partition the physical hardware and assign it to discrete operating system instances that you install on top of the virtualization layer. These virtual installations operate exactly as they would normally. They are not aware of the presence of other virtual installations that exist on the same hardware. Each acts as if it is installed on a predefined piece of equipment by itself, with the virtualization layer controlling what the virtual installation sees and how it interacts with other equipment outside its control. Basically, the virtual installation looks, feels, acts, and is administered exactly the same as a standard installation from the inside, but may be manipulated and configured easily and alongside others from the outside.

Here is the coolest part: virtualization, as provided by sophisticated systems like VMware, also allows you to pool the resources of several physical machines and then divide them up however you want or need. If you have 10 physical servers, each with four processors, 4GB of RAM, and an 80GB hard drive, you can segment those resources to provide a small and low-powered server for your in-house email, a powerful and high-memory processor for the number crunchers in accounting, multiple load-balanced servers for your web server, a separate server for your database, and so on, each with a configuration of memory, disk space, processor power, and so on specific for its needs. Then, if you discover that one virtual server has more resources than it really needs and another doesn't have enough, you can change the configuration quickly, easily, and without taking your servers offline! You can take a physical server offline for maintenance without losing access to any of your virtual servers and their functions. You can move resources in and out and around your pool as needed, and even automatically. These are the sorts of things we will discuss in this book.

There are many companies that provide powerful and stable virtualization platforms, but we have found VMware's offerings to be wonderfully stable, flexible, easy to set up and maintain, and well supported. We like VMware. If you are reading this book, you probably do, too, but chances are you want to make better use of its potential than you are doing now—either that, or you have been asked to set it up or maintain it and you are wondering how to get started. Whatever your reason, if you use VMware at all, we hope you will find this book useful and practical.

1.1 What Is VMware Infrastructure 3?

VMware, Inc., is a company headquartered in Palo Alto, California, with over 7,500 employees and about 120,000 customers, including 100% of the Fortune 100. In 2007, it had revenues of over $1.33 billion. VMware is a rapidly growing company that began in 1998 and now has over 20,000 partnerships with companies ranging from somewhat small to extremely large.

VMware Infrastructure 3 (VI3) is easily the most widely used virtualization platform today. It is well tested and has been used in applications ranging from very small, localized installations with just a handful of servers to exceptionally large server farms in major corporations. It is robust, scalable, easy to administer, and flexible. It is also small and fast, which means the virtual installations running on top of it have more processor power and other resources available to them than they would if they were using some of the more resource-heavy virtualization software available.

Unlike some of the other hosted virtualization products you may be familiar with, including the company's well-known VMware Server, VMware Infrastructure 3 does not require any other operating system. Most virtualization platforms begin with a Linux/Unix, Mac OS X, or Windows platform; install their product on top of it; and then begin segmenting the resources from there. This is how a developer may run a copy of Windows on top of her laptop's base installation of Linux, perhaps using a product like VMware Server, Xen, or VirtualBox. VI3 is designed to be installed on bare metal, as the base operating system. This design choice eliminates a layer of software between the virtual installations and the hardware and results in faster, smoother performance.

The platform is composed of several major products, including ESX, ESXi, vCenter Server, and vCenter Converter. VMware recently changed the names of its VirtualCenter Server (now vCenter Server) and VMware Infrastructure client (now vCenter client); however, the products themselves haven't been changed to reflect the new names. We will use the new terminology within the book and reference the versions when appropriate. The remainder of this chapter will introduce these key pieces of technology within the virtualization environment.

1.2 What Is VMware vSphere 4.0?

In June 2009 VMware launched ESX 4.0, which now falls under the vSphere 4.0 suite of products. vSphere 4.0 encapsulates both vCenter and ESX 4.0, along with other products that we don't discuss in this book. This new release not only brings incremental improvements but takes the virtualization platform to a whole new level by letting you think in terms of complete installations or deployments instead of managing your site server by server. Throughout the book we'll lightly reference ESX 4.0 in relevant chapters to explain the differences between versions 3.x and 4.x. However, it's worth mentioning that ESX 4.0 is a completely new product:

- ESX4 is 64-bit, as compared to the 32-bit versions of ESX 3.x.
- ESX4 supports more hardware and more virtual machines.
- The new version sets the bar for commercial virtualization products even higher, with new features such as fault tolerance, vShield, distributed switches, and much more.

For a complete list of new features, please visit the following website:

http://vmware.com/support/vsphere4/doc/vsp_40_new_feat.html

Here are 10 features we feel are worth highlighting:

vCenter server linked mode
> This mode allows you to connect multiple vCenter servers in a "linked" fashion. Doing this allows them to share licenses and roles and provides them with an "overview" of the entire virtual environment.

Host profiles
> Host profiles are provided in Enterprise Plus to make it easy to push a template of an already existing ESX host to a new server. This feature is a huge benefit, as it means you no longer need to manually configure networks, storage, and so on in your new ESX Servers.

Performance, graphs, and events
> CPU, memory, storage, and networking graphs are now displayed on one central page. In additional to improved graphs, customers will benefit from improved event messages, alarm settings, and error reporting.

Storage VMotion within vCenter
> You can initiate a storage VMotion within the vCenter client. This takes away the need for the command-line management or third-party plug-ins that were popular with the ESX 3.x versions.

Enhanced VMotion
> Enhanced VMotion Compatibility (EVC) allows customers to initiate VMotion between Intel FlexMigration and AMD-V Extended Migration technologies. In essence, this means you can now move a running server between hosts using different CPU technologies.

Virtual machine hot add support
> You can add CPU and memory resources to an existing virtual machine without having to reboot.

Virtual machine hardware improvements
> Virtual machines can now scale up to eight virtual SMP processors and up to 255GB of RAM. vSphere supports IDE devices, Serial Attached SCSI (SAS), and VMXNET Generation 3 network support.

Physical node improvements
> Physical hosts can now have up to 1TB of memory, 64 logical CPUs, and 320 virtual machines. The 64-bit architecture of ESX4 allows greater memory capacity, better performance, and seamless hardware support compared to previous releases.

Storage improvements
> ESX 4.0 brings a huge set of improvements to the realm of storage within ESX. Thin provisioning for virtual disks enables virtual machines to utilize storage on an as-needed basis, eliminating a major source of wasted space on a storage area

network (SAN). The VMFS Volume Grow feature allows you to dynamically grow a Virtual Machine File System without interrupting the running virtual machines. There is also enhanced support for NFS and iSCSI software initiators, which now supply support for jumbo frames on 1GB or 10GB local networks.

Distributed switch

A distributed switch is provided on Enterprise Plus to let customers create a virtual switch for all their ESX hosts to connect to and utilize. This helps reduce network maintenance and allows virtual machines to be moved to any host using VMotion without having to worry about network connections.

As we mentioned earlier, this is only a small subset of the new features available in vSphere 4.0.

1.3 VMware ESX 3.x/4.x Configuration Maximums

VMware's vSphere (ESX 4.x) and Virtual Infrastructure (ESX 3.x) products have limits within which they can operate. We feel it is important to include this information so that you have it at your disposal prior to installing ESX/ESXi 3.x/4.x or vCenter. These values can be crucial when planning your virtual environment, and we suggest you read through them to become familiar with the different maximums. We've tried to include all relevant, publicly provided values from VMware in Tables 1-1 through 1-16, but you may notice a "-" when we could not find a matching reference between the two versions of ESX.

Table 1-1. Virtual machine maximums

Value/item	Maximum	
	ESX 3.5	ESX 4.0
Number of virtual CPUs per virtual machine	4	8
SCSI adapters per virtual machine	4	4
Devices per SCSI adapter	15	15
SCSI targets per virtual machine	60	60
SCSI disk size	2TB	2TB
Size of RAM per virtual machine	64GB	255GB
Virtual machine swap file size	64GB	255GB
Number of NICs per virtual machine	4	10
Number of IDE devices per virtual machine	4	4
Number of IDE controllers per virtual machine	1	1
Number of floppy devices per virtual machine	2	2
Number of parallel ports per virtual machine	3	3
Number of serial ports per virtual machine	4	4

Value/item	Maximum	
	ESX 3.5	ESX 4.0
Number of remote consoles to a virtual machine	10	40
VMDirectPath PCI/PCIe devices per virtual machine	-	2
VMDirectPath SCSI targets per virtual machine	-	60

Table 1-2. General storage maximums

Value/item	Maximum	
	ESX 3.5	ESX 4.0
VMFS block size	8MB	8MB
Max I/O size (before splits)	32MB	32MB
Raw device mapping size	2TB	2TB
Recommended number of hosts that can share a VMFS volume while running virtual machines against that volume	32	64
Number of hosts per cluster	32	32
Number of VMFS volumes configured per server	256	256
Number of extents per VMFS volume	32	32
Number of HBAs (host bus adapters of any type)	16	8
Number of targets per HBA (iSCSI HBA)	15 (64)	256

VMFS2 file stores are not supported in ESX4.0, but are fully supported in ESX 3.0–ESX 3.5. Please refer to the ESX 4 documentation on converting your VMFS2 datastore if you are upgrading your ESX software to the latest version.

Table 1-3. Storage VMFS2 maximums

Value/item	Maximum	
	ESX 3.5	ESX 4.0
Extent size	2TB (100MB min)	2TB
Volume size	64TB	64TB
File size (block size = 1MB)	456GB	456GB
File size (block size = 8MB)	3.5TB	2TB
File size (block size = 64MB)	28.5TB	27TB
File size (block size = 256MB)	64TB	64TB
Files per volume	256+(64 × number of additional extents)	256+(64 × number of additional extents)

Table 1-4. Storage VMFS3 maximums

Value/item	Maximum ESX 3.5	ESX 4.0
Extent size	2TB	
Volume size	64TB (2TB × 32 extents)	64TB
Volume size (block size = 1MB)	~50TB	-
Volume size (block size = 2MB)	64TB	-
Volume size (block size = 4MB)	64TB	-
Volume size (block size = 8MB)	64TB	-
File size (block size = 1MB)	256GB	256GB
File size (block size = 2MB)	512GB	512GB
File size (block size = 4MB)	1TB	1TB
File size (block size = 8MB)	2TB	2TB
Files per directory	~30,000	~30,000
Directories per volume	~30,000	~30,000
Files per volume	~30,000	~30,000

Table 1-5. Storage Fibre Channel maximums

Value/item	Maximum ESX 3.5	ESX 4.0
LUNs (logical unit numbers) per server	256	256
LUN size	2TB	2TB
Number of paths to a specific LUN	32	32
Number of total paths on a server	1,024	1,024
LUNs concurrently opened by all virtual machines	256	256
LUN IDs	256	256
HBAs per host	8	8
Targets per HBA	256	256
HBA ports	16	16

Table 1-6. Storage NAS maximums

Value/item	Maximum ESX 3.5	ESX 4.0
Default number of NAS (network attached storage) datastores	8	8
Number of NAS datastores	32 (requires changes to advanced settings)	64 (requires changes to advanced settings)

Table 1-7. Storage hardware iSCSI maximums

Value/item	Maximum	
	ESX 3.5	ESX 4.0
LUNs per server	256	256
LUNs concurrently used	-	256
Dynamic targets per port	-	64
Static targets per port	-	61
Total targets (static + dynamic must not exceed this number)	-	256
Paths to LUN	-	8
Total paths	-	1,024

Table 1-8. Storage software iSCSI maximums

Value/item	Maximum	
	ESX 3.5	ESX 4.0
LUNs per server	256	256
LUNs concurrently used	-	256
Targets	64	-
Ethernet ports bound with the software iSCSI stack	-	8
Total targets (static + dynamic must not exceed this number)	-	256
Paths to LUN	-	8
Total paths	-	1,024

Table 1-9. CPU maximums

Value/Item	Maximum	
	ESX 3.5	ESX 4.0
Number of virtual CPUs per server	192	512
Number of virtual machines per server	170	320
Number of HT (hyper-threading) logical processors per host	32	64
Number of virtual CPUs per core	8	20

Table 1-10. Memory maximums

Value/Item	Maximum	
	ESX 3.5	ESX 4.0
Size of RAM per ESX Server	256GB	1TB
Maximum RAM allocated to the service console by default	800MB	800MB

Value/Item	Maximum	
	ESX 3.5	ESX 4.0
Minimum RAM allocated to the service console by default	400MB	400MB
Swap files	1	1

Table 1-11. Networking maximums

Value/Item	Maximum	
	ESX 3.5	ESX 4.0
Physical e100 NICs	26	-
Physical e1000 NICs (PCI-x)	32	32
Physical e1000 NICs (PCI-e)	32	32
Physical Broadcom NICs	20	-
igb 1GB Ethernet ports (Intel)	-	16
tg3 1GB Ethernet ports (Broadcom)	-	32
bnx2 1GB Ethernet ports (Broadcom)	-	16
Forcedeth 1GB Ethernet ports (NVIDIA)	-	2
Scio 10GB Ethernet ports (Neterion)	-	4
nx_nic 10GB Ethernet ports (Net-XEN)	-	4
ixgbe Oplin 10GB Ethernet ports (Intel)	-	4
bnx2x 10GB Ethernet ports (Broadcom)	-	4
Number of PCI VMDirectPath devices per host	-	8
Number of port groups per standard switch	512	512
Number of NICs in a team	32	-
Number of Ethernet ports	32	-
Number of virtual NICs per virtual switch	1,016	-
Number of virtual switches per host	127	248
Number of port groups (VLANs)	4,096	4,096

Table 1-12. Networking vNetwork distributed switch maximums (4.0 only)

Value/Item	Maximum	
	ESX 3.5	ESX 4.0
Total virtual switch ports per host (vDS and vSS ports)	-	4,096
Distributed virtual network switch ports per vCenter	-	6,000
Distributed groups per vCenter	-	512
Distributed switches per vCenter	-	16
Hosts per distributed switch	-	64

Table 1-13. Resource pool HA cluster maximums

Value/Item	Maximum	
	ESX 3.5	ESX 4.0
Hosts per high availability (HA) cluster	32	32
Virtual machines per HA cluster	-	1,280
Virtual machines per host in HA cluster	-	100
Failover hosts per cluster	4	4
Failover as percentage of cluster	50.00%	50.00%

Table 1-14. Resource pool DRS cluster maximums

Value/Item	Maximum	
	ESX 3.5	ESX 4.0
Hosts per distributed resource scheduler (DRS) cluster	-	32
Virtual machines per DRS cluster	-	1,280
Virtual machines per host in DRS cluster	-	256

Table 1-15. Resource pool maximums

Value/Item	Maximum	
	ESX 3.5	ESX 4.0
Resource pools per ESX host	512	4,096
Children per resource pool	256	1,024
Tree depth per resource pool	12	12
Tree depth per resource pool in a DRS cluster	10	10
Resource pools per cluster	128	512

Table 1-16. vCenter maximums

Value/Item	Maximum	
	ESX 3.5	ESX 4.0
Number of virtual machines powered on (32-bit)	2,000	2,000
Hosts per vCenter server (32-bit)	200	200
Registered virtual machines (32-bit)	-	3,000
Hosts per vCenter server (64-bit)	-	300
Number of virtual machines powered on (64-bit)	-	3,000
Registered virtual machines (64-bit)	-	4,500
Linked vCenter servers	-	10
Hosts in linked-mode environment	-	1,000

Value/Item	Maximum	
	ESX 3.5	ESX 4.0
Powered-on virtual machines in linked mode	-	10,000
Registered virtual machines in linked mode	-	15,000
Concurrent vSphere client connections (32-bit)	20	15
Concurrent vSphere client connections (64-bit)	-	30
Hosts per datacenter	50	100

See Also

Recipes 1.5, 1.7, 1.11, and 1.16

1.4 VMware ESX 3.x Server Overview

VMware ESX Server is the foundation for every other piece of the virtualization package. It is the *hypervisor*, or main software layer that installs on the bare metal and allows everything above it to communicate with the hardware, to allow virtualization. When you install VMware ESX Server, you are actually installing two main components: the VMkernel and the Service Console.

The VMkernel is the base on which all other software in the package is built: the operating system. For those familiar with Linux, this would be the equivalent of (and is built from) the Linux kernel, without any other software.

The Service Console (or COS) is an alternative means of communicating with and configuring the VMkernel using standard Linux and VMware-specific commands to modify and adjust parameters. Typically, management will be done via the vCenter client; however, there may be cases where you find you can accomplish things more easily with the command line or need to use it because you can't access vCenter.

VMware has designed ESX Server to run only on specific pieces of hardware and has removed support for any kinds of devices it is not interested in, thereby reducing the kernel code. What remains is a stripped-down, fast kernel and tool package with little to no extra overhead. This is one of the things that gives VMware an advantage over other virtualization technologies that require installation on top of a standard operating system, which will be filled with drivers and features you won't need.

It's important to verify the hardware on which you will be running your virtualized environment, as VMware doesn't directly support smaller desktop-related hardware. However, everything that a server needs is well supported. This is a sleek operating system designed to put as little as possible between the virtual machines and the hardware.

1.5 VMware ESX 3.x Installation

Installation of ESX 3.5 is pretty straightforward if you are familiar with installing Linux, and especially Red Hat, as VMware has taken Red Hat's default installer and made a few modifications.

ESX 4.0 and ESXi 4.0 can now be installed and virtualized within VMware Workstation and VMware Fusion. This allows you to install, test, and get a feel for the product before implementing it on physical hardware.

Before you get started installing ESX, you should verify that your hardware is fully compatible by visiting the following URL—you will notice that ESX 3.5 has a wider range of hardware support than its newer relative, ESXi:

http://www.vmware.com/resources/compatibility/search.php?action=base&device Category=server

The ESXi ISO image is available for download at *http://www.vmware.com/download/vi/*.

ESX Server has the following hardware requirements (refer to Tables 1-1 through 1-16, shown previously, for configuration maximums):

- At least two processors chosen from among the 1500MHz Intel Xeon and later, AMD Opteron (32-bit), 1500MHz Intel ViiV, or AMD A64 X2 dual-core processors (be sure to check the latest specs to confirm)
- 1GB RAM minimum
- One or more Ethernet controllers (we recommend a minimum of four ports for the Service Console, VMkernel, Virtual Machine Network, etc.)
- Direct attached storage (DAS) or network attached storage (NAS)

 To avoid possible data loss make sure to remove any attached storage, such as Fibre Channel, DAS, or iSCSI disks, before the initial installation of ESX.

The installer has a couple of modes:

Graphical mode
> The recommended method for installation. It uses a mouse and a graphical interface to guide you through the installation. This is the method we will be using for our installation as we continue in this section.

Text mode
> A text-only mode for installing ESX; this option is normally used when you have mouse or video problems in the graphical installer.

To begin the installation, make sure your server is set to boot off the CD-ROM. This can be accomplished by changing the settings in your server's BIOS. Next, follow these steps:

1. Upon booting from the CD-ROM, you will be presented with a screen that allows you to choose your installation method. Pressing the Enter key accepts the default graphical installer. By typing **esx text**, you can invoke the text-mode installer (Figure 1-1).

   The installer will begin to load, displaying another screen that will allow you to test the CD-ROM media for errors. If you want to test the media, use the Tab key to highlight the Test button; otherwise, select the Skip button to continue the installation (Figure 1-2).

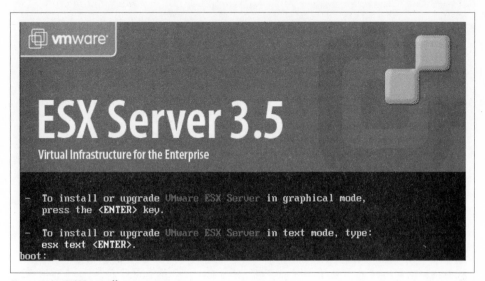

Figure 1-1. ESX installation screen

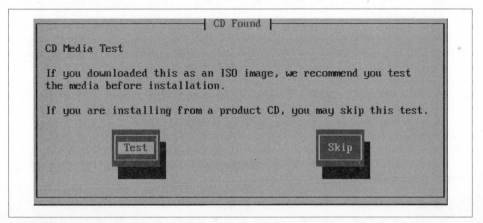

Figure 1-2. CD-ROM media test

2. A welcome screen will be presented. Click the Next button to proceed to the keyboard configuration (Figure 1-3), where you will select the default keyboard layout. Click Next to continue.

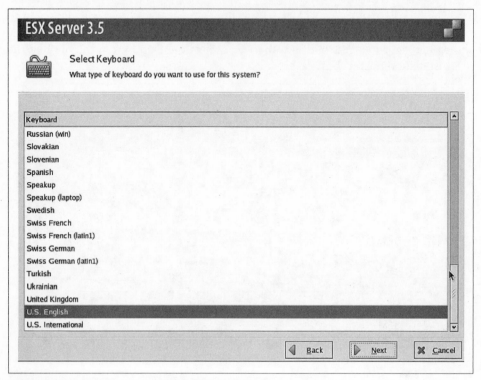

Figure 1-3. Keyboard selection during ESX installation

3. The mouse configuration menu now appears, allowing you to select the mouse type for your ESX Server (Figure 1-4). Accepting the default here is OK because the mouse will not be used at any point after the initial installation. Proceed by clicking the Next button.

4. The installer will begin to search for already installed versions of ESX (Figure 1-5). If one is found, you will be given the following options:

Upgrade

This option can be used for upgrading an existing ESX Server; however, it's not recommended. Using Update Manager inside vCenter, as discussed in Chapter 5, is a much safer method.

Install

This will install a clean version of ESX and erase any existing installations, including all configuration settings and data.

If this is the first time the disk has been used, the installer will also give you a warning to initialize an empty disk.

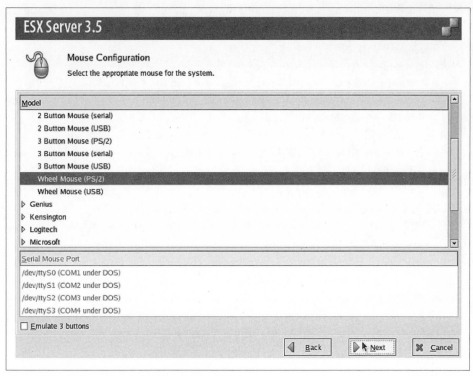

Figure 1-4. Mouse selection during ESX installation

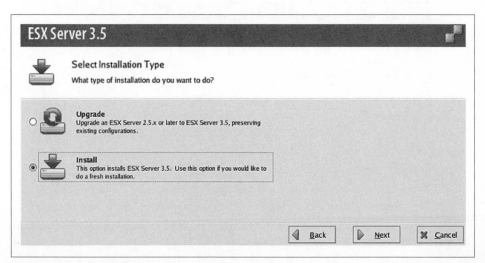

Figure 1-5. Option to choose Install or Upgrade

5. The ESX license agreement will appear. Read the license agreement, select "I accept the terms of this license agreement," and click Next.

6. The partition options screen (Figure 1-6) will appear, allowing you to configure the ESX Server's partitions.

You have two options here:

Recommended
> Configures the default ESX partitions based on the hard drive size. This is the recommended method, unless you specifically need to set your partitions for a more customized install.

Advanced
> Allows you to specify all the partition settings and sizes based on your hard drive size (Table 1-17).

 The values in Table 1-17 are general best practices, and you may adjust them higher than the listed values if you have more space available.

Choose the disk on which ESX will be installed, and leave the "Keep virtual machines and the VMFS (virtual machine file system) that contains them" button checked. This is primarily used when installing on top of another ESX installation, to preserve any existing virtual machines and their data. Click the Next button to see the finalized disk partition configuration, then click the Next button to continue.

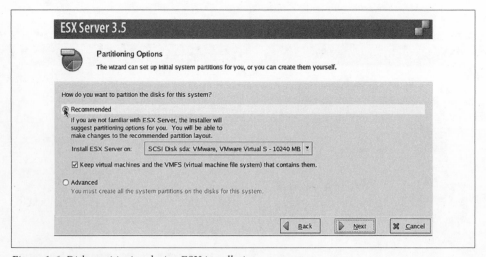

Figure 1-6. Disk partitioning during ESX installation

To avoid possible data loss make sure to remove any attached storage, such as Fibre Channel, DAS, or iSCSI disks, before the initial installation of ESX.

Table 1-17. Disk partitioning sizes

Mount point	Type	Size	Notes
Swap	Swap	544MB	Allows the service console to use disk-based memory when the physical memory isn't available.
/boot	ext3	100MB	Holds the ESX Server's kernel bootloader images. In ESX 3.x, the bootloader is GRUB.
/	ext3	10GB[a]	Holds the operating system, configuration files, and third-party applications.
/var	ext3	2GB[b]	Storage for logfiles.
None	vmkcore	100MB	Holds the dump files for the VMkernel and is required for support.
/vmfs	vmfs		Holds virtual machine *vdmk* files.[c]

[a] The / partition should not be smaller than 5GB. To be on the safe side, we recommend setting this value to 10GB.

[b] The /var partition should not be set lower than 500MB, although we think a safer setting would be 2GB.

[c] The /vmfs partition doesn't need to be configured on a local disk, unless you do not have any SAN attached storage. However, it is often convenient to have a local /vmfs file store for testing, generally a local /vmfs partition will use the remainder of space on the local drive.

7. The bootloader window (Figure 1-7) will load, giving you options for how the ESX Server will boot. There are three options here:

    From a drive (install on the MBR of the drive)
    The first disk will be selected. If you change this, it's important that you select the first disk listed in the BIOS. Checked by default, this is the option that will be used on most ESX installations.

    From a partition
    This option will be used for legacy installations where the BIOS is stored on the master boot record.

    Boot Options
    Allows you to enter specific kernel parameters to be loaded on reboot of the ESX Server.

    As mentioned previously, we recommend using the default selections for the bootloader configuration. As a side note, if you decide you need to use the Back or Next buttons during the installation, ensure that the default selection stays checked. Click the Next button to continue.

8. The network configuration section of the installation (Figure 1-8) allows you to specify the network and address type that will be used on the ESX Server. This screen is broken up into four different sections:

    Network Interface Card
    The network interface that your ESX Server's management network will use. We like to use the first interface on the server or add-on card, mainly because

when you are managing a large number of physical hosts it is easier to remember which interface is being used on each one.

Network Address and Host name
You have the option to use DHCP for your ESX Server, but this is not recommended. By default, you will be asked for a static IP address. Fill in the rest of the network fields as necessary.

VLAN Settings
This allows you to specify whether your ESX Server will be on a specific VLAN. If you are unsure, ask your network team for this information.

"Create a default network for virtual machines"
This option is enabled by default. You must uncheck it because your virtual machines will be placed on the same network as your service console/ management network.

After entering the appropriate network information, click the Next button to continue.

From the next screen (Figure 1-9), select the time zone in which your ESX Server is located. Continue by pressing the Next button.

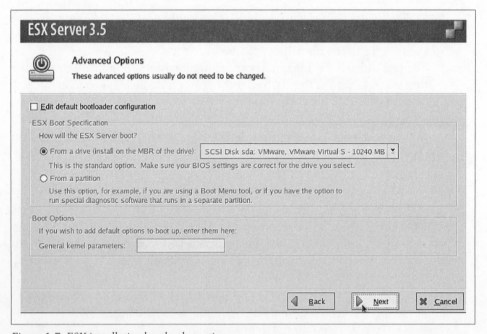

Figure 1-7. ESX installation bootloader options

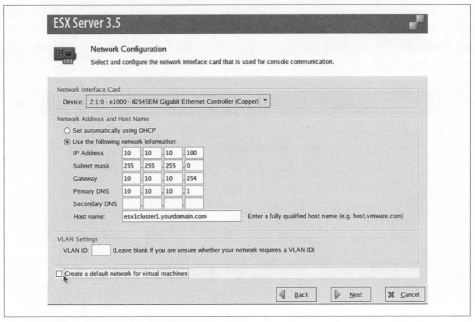

Figure 1-8. Networking settings during ESX installation

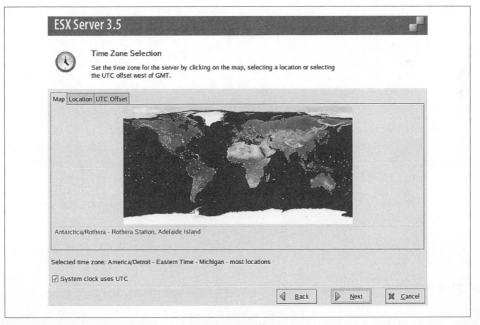

Figure 1-9. Time zone configuration during ESX installation

9. A new window (Figure 1-10) will appear, asking you to set your root password. Enter your root password and set up any additional accounts you might need on your ESX Server, pressing the Next button to continue. (For more information on account usage in ESX, see Chapter 7.)

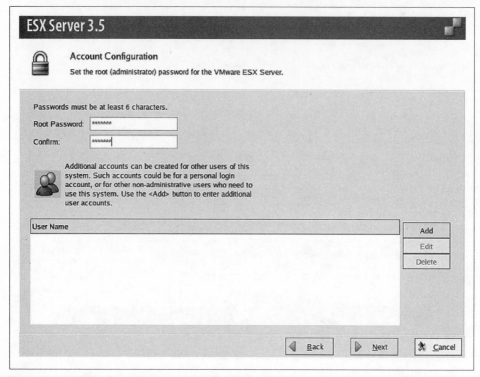

Figure 1-10. Setting the root user's password

10. The final window to appear in the installation is the summary (Figure 1-11). This is the last chance you have to make any changes to the installation settings you previously configured, so look over the details carefully. If everything looks OK, press the Next button to begin the installation.

When all is complete, click the Finish button and the installer will exit and eject the CD-ROM.

See Also

Recipes 1.3 and 1.7

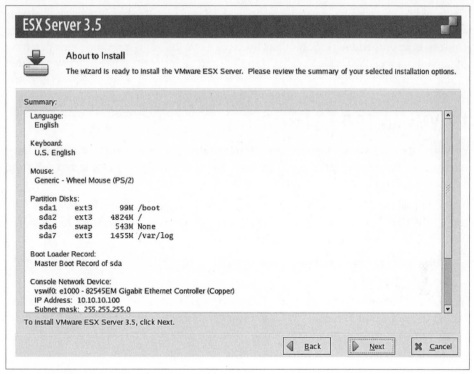

Figure 1-11. Installation summary

1.6 VMware ESXi 3.5 Overview

ESXi is a newer form of the technology that strips down the ESX Server even further, to the absolute bare minimum possible. It does not include or rely upon a service console and can perform its hypervisor duties with an installation that takes up a mere 32MB of disk space. In ESX Server, the service console runs on top of the hypervisor alongside the installed virtual machines. In ESXi, the hypervisor is all you install on your hardware. This allows for very fast hardware additions to existing pools. Want to add a new server to your rack? No problem. Hook it up, power it on, install ESXi, set your root password and networking details, take a minute or two to configure the virtual network, and you're all set. This is an amazingly quick way to create or expand an existing ESX hardware cluster.

Even more exciting than the installable version of ESXi is the embedded version. It is now possible to buy hardware that is preconfigured with ESXi installed on it. This completely eliminates the installation step and speeds up the configuration process. Companies like Dell, which graciously allowed us to borrow some of its equipment as we were writing this book, are now selling servers that require only a little more than racking, cabling, and powering on to expand your VMware cluster.

The benefits of using ESXi over the standard ESX product are that it's extremely light-weight and installs quickly, it can be purchased on some servers from Dell and other vendors as an embedded option, it has no service console, and it requires less patching and maintenance. ESXi is also available for free and includes the basic functions needed to start a virtual environment.

1.7 VMware ESXi 3.5 Installation

VMware customers who have received a preinstalled OEM version of ESXi may have vendor-specific customizations and drivers. These versions will be different from the downloadable version on VMware's website.

Before you get started installing ESXi, you should verify that your hardware is fully compatible by visiting the following URL, as VMware's ESXi product has a much smaller compatibility list than its older ESX model:

http://www.vmware.com/resources/compatibility/search.php?action=base&device Category=server

ESX 4.0 and ESXi 4.0 can now be installed and virtualized within VMware Workstation and VMware Fusion. This allows you to install, test, and get a feel for the products before implementing them on physical hardware.

As of Update 3, ESXi has the following hardware requirements:

- 1500MHz Intel Xeon and later models or AMD Opteron (32-bit mode) for ESXi
- 1500MHz Intel Xeon and later models or AMD Opteron (32-bit mode) for Virtual SMP
- 1500MHz Intel Viiv or AMD A64 X2 dual-core processors
- 1GB of RAM minimum
- Broadcom NetXtreme 570x Gigabit controllers or Intel PRO 100/1000 adapters
- Basic SCSI adapters—Adaptec Ultra160, Ultra320, LSI Logic Fusion-MPT, or most NCR/Symbios SCSI controllers
- RAID adapters—Dell PercRAID (Adaptec RAID and LSI MegaRAID) or IBM ServeRAID controllers

This list represents the minimum requirements to install ESXi, but many more devices are available. To ensure complete compatibility, search for your specific hardware at the aforementioned URL.

The ESXi ISO image is available for download at *http://www.vmware.com/download/ esxi/*.

VMware has a done a great job of streamlining the installation of ESXi. If you are familiar with installing ESX, this will be a breeze. After booting to the installation CD-ROM, you'll notice a blue screen titled "ThinESX Installer" that looks similar to the bootloader in Linux.

Once the initial boot has completed, the installer will present a couple of options: you can choose to cancel the installation, upgrade an existing installation, or perform a fresh ESXi installation (Figure 1-12). Once you have selected the appropriate installation type, you will be shown the EULA. Press F11 to accept and continue the installation.

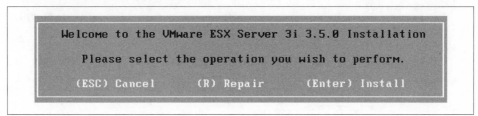

Figure 1-12. ESXi initial installation

Select the disk on which you wish to install ESXi. Typically, this will be a local disk. Also, make sure you have disconnected all your SAN and direct-attached storage, to prevent any accidental data removal. Once you've selected the disk, the installation will begin and will take only a few minutes. When it is complete, remove the CD-ROM and reboot the system.

Unlike a normal ESX installation, ESXi requires a little more configuration after the initial install, because the only thing being configured during installation is the disk on which the hypervisor is going to be installed. Once the new ESXi server has been rebooted, you will notice a screen that is similar to the ESX console screen but with two new options: F11 to reboot the system and F2 to manage the system.

To begin configuration, make sure you have a keyboard and monitor plugged into the ESXi server. Press F2 to access the menu-based configuration utility, which will be the main screen in which all ESXi configuration will take place (Figure 1-13).

Configure Root Password

This is the first option that will need to be configured, as it is not set by default. The password you set here will be the default for the "root" user account (Figure 1-14).

Configure Lockdown Mode

This is disabled by default. If enabled, it prevents users from logging into the ESXi server remotely as the root user.

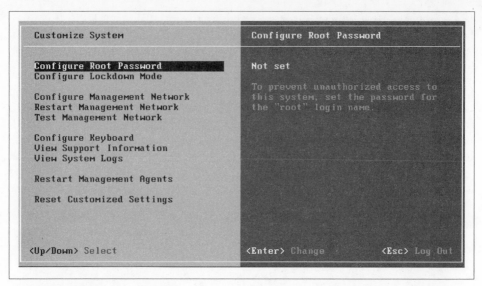

Figure 1-13. ESXi management menu

Figure 1-14. Changing the password

Lockdown mode provides a valuable extra layer of security, but it can prove inconvenient for one function that is common on ESXi: managing user accounts. These can be managed via vCenter though, so if you enable lockdown mode it's a good idea to set up an administrative account that lets you add and remove user accounts remotely through the vCenter client. VMware also offers a remote command-line interface (RCLI) that can perform user account functions, called *vicfg-user*. This allows you to centrally manage your ESX and ESXi servers from the command line if you choose. For more information on the RLCI utility, see the VMware website at *http://www.vmware.com*.

Configure Management Network

By default, ESXi will be configured to use the Dynamic Host Configuration Protocol (DHCP) and will automatically attempt to configure the IP address. However, you can bypass this and set your network to use a static IP address using the tools provided in the Management Network interface. Using a static IP address is recommended.

As shown in Figure 1-15, the management network offers a few options to configure your ESXi server.

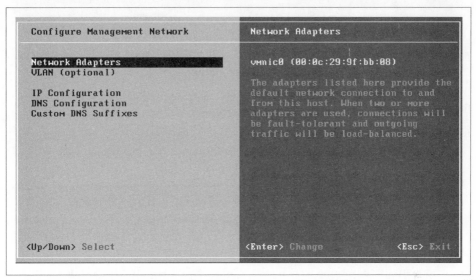

Figure 1-15. Management network configuration

The Network Adapters option allows you to select which network adapter to use for the service console IP address, if you have more than one interface available; the interfaces will be labeled *vmnic0*, *vmnic1*, etc.

You also have the option to configure your service console IP address to use a specific VLAN. This is an optional setting.

The next option on the list is IP Configuration. Here, you have the option to configure DHCP or a static IP address. Choosing the latter will allow you to enter the basic information needed, such as the IP address, subnet mask, and gateway (Figure 1-16).

The management network configuration screen also provides options to set up your DNS servers and DNS suffixes:

Restart Management Network
> Making changes to a static IP address or renewing a DHCP lease on the network may require a restart of the management network.

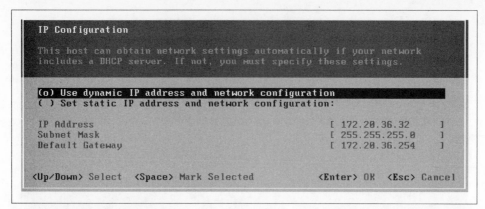

Figure 1-16. IP Configuration screen

Test Management Network

    Testing the management network will allow you to ping different hosts and resolve DNS entries.

Configure Keyboard

    ESXi supports different keyboard layouts: English is the default, but you can select from French, German, Russian, and Japanese.

View Support Information

    No configurable options are available in this menu; however, it provides a general location for your ESXi server's license key, serial number, and SSL footprint, and the URL to VMware's support website.

View System Logs

    There are three options available here for viewing log entries. As shown in Figure 1-17, you can view system messages, config, and management agent (*hostd*) logs.

Restart Management Agents

    From time to time it may be necessary to restart the management agents on the ESXi host without restarting the server itself. If the management agents are restarted, all remotely connected clients (such as vCenter clients and the vCenter server) will be disconnected.

    It's important to note that in your vCenter server the host will show up disconnected while the management network restarts; however, your virtual machines will continue to be unaffected.

Reset Customized Settings

    Resetting the customized settings will reset all the variables on the ESXi server to factory defaults.

To further configure the ESXi server, you can use the vCenter client.

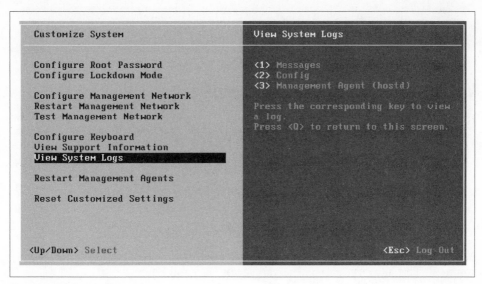

Figure 1-17. System logs

See Also

Recipe 1.3

1.8 VMware vCenter Server 2.x Overview

There comes a point as networks grow when it becomes unwieldy to manage each server individually. For some of us, that happens right around the time the second box is added, because we want to use our time for more interesting things than repetitive procedures and maintenance. VMware vCenter provides a central location for managing all of the virtual machines on your VMware network. It is licensed and sold separately and requires a dedicated Windows server or a Windows virtual machine and a database (Oracle or Microsoft SQL Server). Once installed and configured, it will make the system administrator's life much easier. vCenter provides a way to distribute resources, manage users, move virtual machines from one piece of physical hardware to another (while still running!), schedule tasks, and much more.

1.9 vCenter Server 2.x Installation

To get started, download vCenter Server from *http://vmware.com/download/vi/*.

The vCenter Server installation is pretty straightforward. During the course of the installation you will be asked to enter some required information and make some crucial decisions about your environment. We will walk you through those steps in this section.

It's worth mentioning that if you plan to install your vCenter database on the same server as your vCenter server, the system server requirements will be larger.

VMware vCenter 2.x Server Requirements

- One of the following: Windows 2000 Server with SP4 Update Rollup 1, Windows XP Pro with SP2, Windows 2003 Server with SP1 and SP2 (all releases except 64-bit), or Windows 2003 Server R2
- 2.0GHz or faster Intel or AMD X86 processor
- 2GB or more of RAM
- Minimum 560MB of disk space (2–4GB recommended)
- 10/100/1000 Ethernet Adapter (Gigabit recommended)

VMware vCenter can also be installed inside a virtual machine within the ESX environment. This allows you to take advantage of DRS and HA.

VMware vCenter 2.x Server Database Requirements

The vCenter Server requires one of the following databases:

- Microsoft SQL Server 2000 Standard with SP4
- Microsoft SQL Server 2000 Enterprise with SP4
- Microsoft SQL Server 2005 Standard with SP1 or SP2
- Microsoft SQL Server 2005 Enterprise with SP1 or SP2
- Microsoft SQL Server 2005 Express with SP2 (not recommended for production)
- Oracle 9i Release 2 Standard: apply patch 9.2.0.8.0 to server and client
- Oracle 9i Release 2 Enterprise: apply patch 9.2.0.8.0 to server and client
- Oracle 10g Release 1 Standard (10.1.0.3.0)
- Oracle 10g Release 1 Enterprise (10.1.0.3.0)
- Oracle 10g Release 2 Standard (10.2.0.1.0): apply patch 10.2.0.3.0 to server and client, then apply patch 5699495
- Oracle 10g Release 2 Enterprise (10.2.0.1.0): apply patch 10.2.0.3.0 to server and client, then apply patch 5699495

The vCenter Server offers a few download options: you may download an ISO image that can be burned to DVD, or a ZIP file that can be extracted on the server on which you wish to install vCenter Server. Once you have chosen your installation method, follow these steps:

1. Either insert the CD-ROM and let *autorun.exe* start the installation, or manually run the *autorun.exe* located in the ZIP file that you downloaded. A screen similar to Figure 1-18 will appear. Click Next to continue.

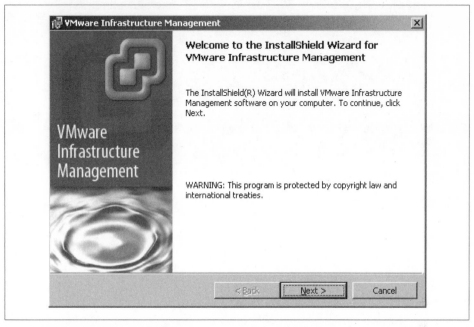

Figure 1-18. vCenter Server installation

2. The introduction page tells you the benefits of vCenter Server. Once you have read these, click Next to continue.

3. Read the license agreement and accept it by clicking "I accept the terms in the license agreement." The circle next to this statement will now show a dot. Click Next to continue the installation.

4. You will now be prompted to enter information about your company (Figure 1-19). When you're done, click Next to continue.

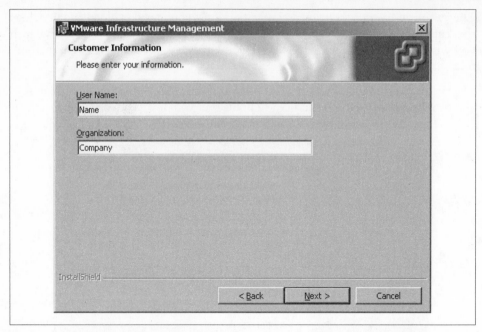

Figure 1-19. Entering company information

5. Now that the basic elements of the installation have been taken care of, you must decide what pieces of the application to install. You have three different options, as shown in Figure 1-20 (the names are different in the installer, because although VMware has changed the product names, as of this writing the installers have not been updated to reflect these changes):

Install VMware Infrastructure Client (vCenter client)
> This option will install only the vCenter client (formerly known as the VI client), without installing the vCenter server pieces. This option is appropriate for a desktop or workstation that you will use to manage the vCenter server. The client is automatically installed with the next option.

Install VirtualCenter Server (vCenter Server)
> This is the recommended installation: it includes the VI client (vCenter client), VirtualCenter Server (vCenter Server), Update Manager, and VMware Converter Enterprise for VirtualCenter Server (vCenter Converter).

Custom installation
> This option allows you to install any combination of the four pieces mentioned: VI client (vCenter client), VirtualCenter Server (vCenter Server), Update Manager, and VMware Converter Enterprise for VirtualCenter Server (vCenter Converter).

Once you have chosen the method of installation you wish to use, click the Next button to continue.

Figure 1-20. Choosing the vCenter installation type

6. You are now ready to choose the database method (Figure 1-21). vCenter Server supports Microsoft SQL Server 2005 Express (MSDE), Microsoft SQL Server 2000, Microsoft SQL Server 2005, and Oracle 10g. Refer to the database requirements list for the exact versions.

   For production installations, VMware recommends that you do not use the Microsoft SQL Server Desktop Engine (MSDE) that is included with the installation, as it's only suitable for 5 hosts and 50 virtual machines.

   Assuming the installation will be in a production environment, select the "Use an existing database server" option and fill in the necessary fields with your database's information, keeping in mind the following:

   • You must set up ODBC connections before you use Microsoft SQL Server or Oracle. This can be accomplished in the Control Panel on Windows.

   • The data source name (DSN) must be a system DSN.

   • If you are using a local SQL server with Windows NT authentication, make sure to leave the username and password fields blank. Otherwise, enter the username and password.

Once you have entered your information successfully, press the Next button to continue the installation.

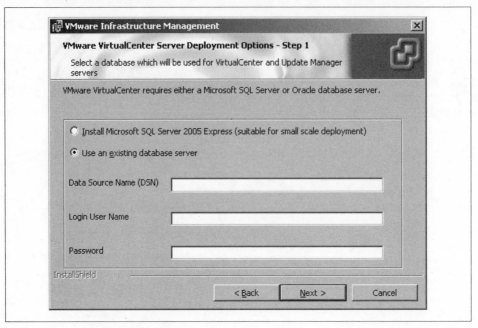

Figure 1-21. vCenter database selection

7. Next, you'll need to select a license server. There are a couple of options here (Figure 1-22). If you plan to use vCenter Server in evaluation mode for 60 days, select the "I want to evaluate VirtualCenter Server" option. This will install the full product, which can be changed from evaluation mode to a licensed product after installation, if required.

To use a license file, first uncheck the evaluation mode checkbox. The default path of *C:\Program Files\VMware\VMware License Server\Licenses\vmware.lic* will appear, allowing you to browse to select your license file. Press Next to continue.

If you plan to use a license server, uncheck the "Use an Existing License Server" option, select the edition of vCenter Server that you purchased, and press Next to continue. If this is the first time you are installing a vCenter server, the license server has not yet been installed and you will be prompted with a warning stating "Unable to connect to license server...." Press OK to continue the installation.

If you choose to do a custom installation, proceed to step 8; otherwise, skip to step 9.

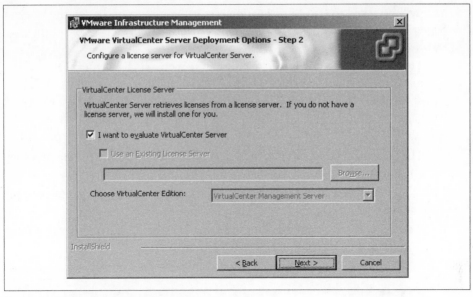

Figure 1-22. License server configuration

8. If you selected the custom installation option, you will be allowed to modify the ports in which the vCenter Server applications run (Figure 1-23). Modify these or accept the defaults, and click Next to continue the installation.

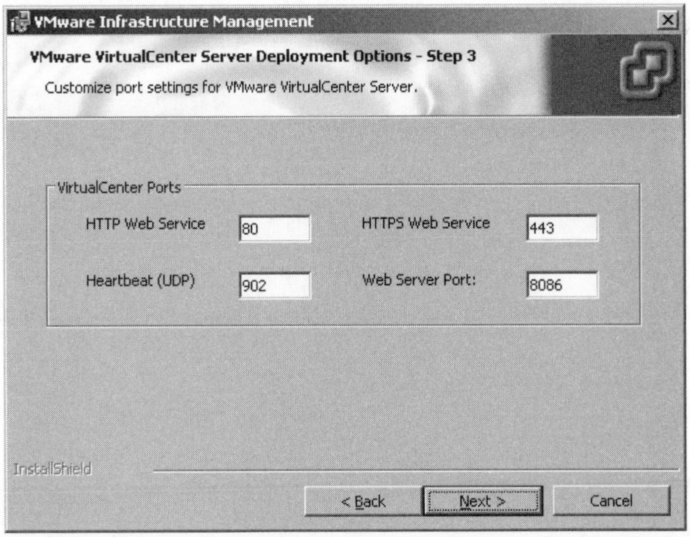

Figure 1-23. Custom install only, changing ports

9. You will be asked to enter information about the system on which the vCenter Server components are going to be installed (Figure 1-24):

VC Server IP
> The IP address or domain name of the system on which vCenter Server will be installed. Normally, both options will appear in the drop-down menu.

VC Server Port
> This value can be changed only during a custom installation.

Administrator login/password
> The login/password with which to log into Windows on the system on which you are installing vCenter Server.

Once you've entered the appropriate values, click the Next button to continue the installation.

If you chose to do a custom installation, proceed to step 10; otherwise, skip to step 12 to continue the installation.

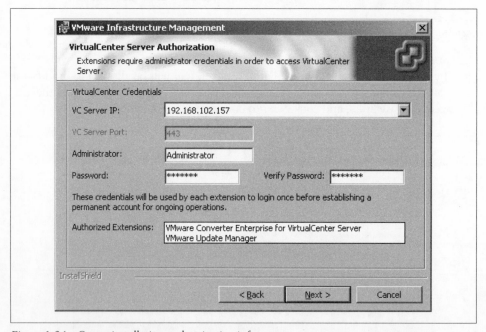

Figure 1-24. vCenter installation authentication info

10. During a custom installation, you will be asked to enter information for the VMware Update Manager. You can use the same database as the one you used earlier for the vCenter server, or a separate database (Figure 1-25). When you are satisfied with the settings, click the Next button to continue the installation.

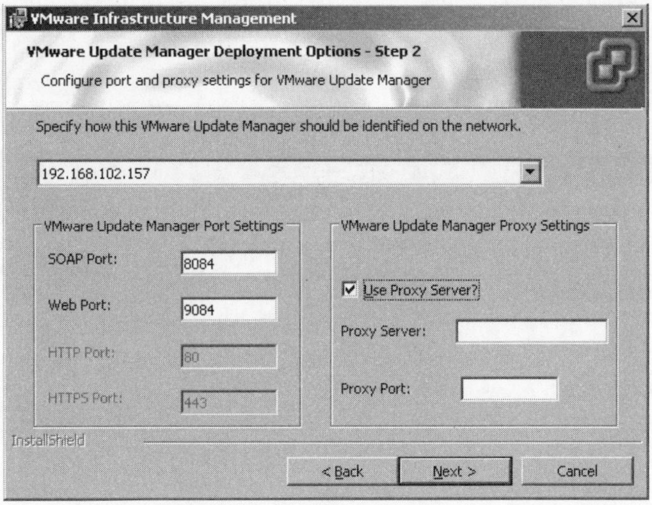

Figure 1-25. Custom installation Update Manager settings

11. After configuring the Update Manager settings, if you are doing a custom installation, you will be asked to enter information for the Converter piece of vCenter (Figure 1-26).

Enter your port and IP information or accept the defaults, and click Next to continue the installation.

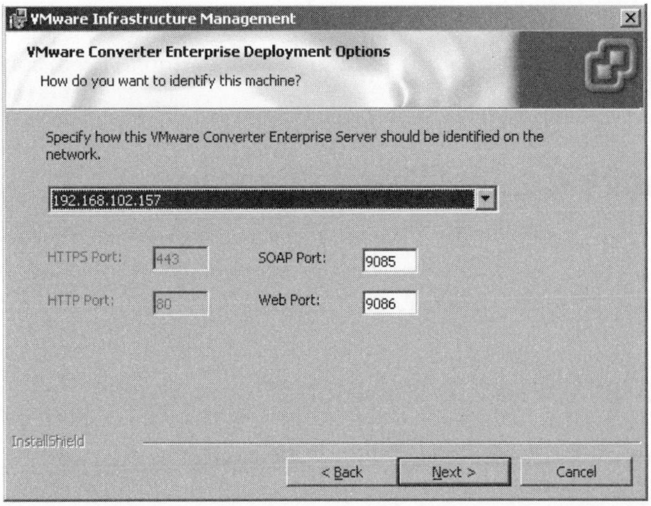

Figure 1-26. Custom installation Converter settings

12. Click the Install button (Figure 1-27) to start the installation. During the installation process each piece will be installed, along with .NET if it is missing from your server.

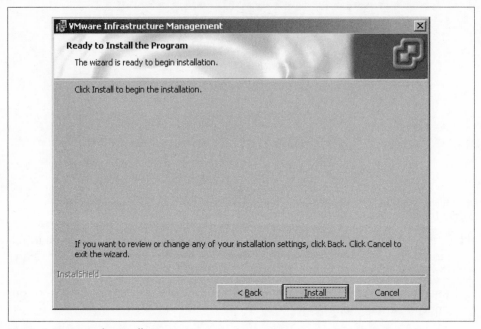

Figure 1-27. Begin the installation

After the installation has completed, click the Finish button to begin configuring your ESX Servers.

1.10 VMware vCenter Client 2.x Overview

The vCenter client (formerly the VMware Infrastructure client) is used to manage individual ESX hosts as well as to provide an administration interface to the vCenter server. It is included with the vCenter Server download.

1.11 vCenter Client 2.x Installation

vCenter client requirements are:

- One of the following 32-bit operating systems:
  — Windows 2000 Server with SP4 Update Rollup 1
  — Windows XP Professional with SP2

—Windows 2003 Server with SP1 and SP2

—Windows 2003 Server R2

—Windows Vista Business

—Windows Vista Enterprise

- .NET Framework 2.0 (this is included with the VCenter client installer)
- 266MHz Intel or AMD X86 processor
- 256MB RAM minimum (2GB recommended)
- 150MB storage space for the basic installation (additional space is required if you will be storing your virtual machine templates locally)
- 10/100/1000 Ethernet adapter (Gigabit recommended)

The vCenter client is normally installed along with the vCenter Server installation. However, it is possible to install the vCenter client by itself on other computers by going to *https://youresxserver/client/VMware-viclient.exe* and downloading the client installer. Once you've downloaded it, run the application. The installation is very intuitive.

1.12 License Server Overview

It is possible to manage your VMware licenses on each machine individually using host-based licenses. However, it is much more convenient, especially as networks grow large, to set up one VMware license server as a repository and use it to manage your licenses, allowing them to float between hosts. Doing so also opens up new options that are not available when using individual host-based licenses, such as using VMotion to move virtual machines from one physical host to another. In particular, a license server enables the distributed resource scheduler and high availability features in ESX and vCenter.

1.13 License Server (vCenter 2.x) Installation

The license server has the following requirements:

- One of the following: Windows 2000 Server with SP4 Update Rollup 1, Windows XP Pro with SP2, Windows 2003 Server with SP1 and SP2 (all releases except 64-bit), or Windows 2003 Server R2
- 266MHz or faster Intel or AMD X86 processor
- 256MB RAM minimum (512MB recommended)
- 25MB hard drive space for a basic installation
- 10/100/1000 Ethernet adapter (Gigabit recommended)

If you use the VMware Infrastructure installer, it will automatically install the license server for you. However, it is possible to install the license server on another server. To install this piece, navigate to the *\vpx* folder on the installation CD and run the *VMware-licenseserver.exe* file to begin the installation.

The installer will begin. Accept the license agreement and continue the installation by clicking the Next button. You will be prompted for your license file; either enter the path or use the Browse button to navigate to its location. Click Install to begin the installation. When finished, click Finished to complete the license server install.

1.14 vConverter Overview

vConverter is a free application available from VMware that allows you to transform your physical servers into virtual servers easily, moving them from their own machine(s) into your VMware system. There are two ways this can be done. In a *cold migration*, you power down a server and convert it while it is offline. With vConverter, though, you can also perform a *hot migration*, which allows you to convert and migrate a live, operating server while it is in use. VMware Converter also allows you to take older virtual machines and migrate them into a new network while upgrading them to the current version.

1.15 vConverter Installation

The installation of vConverter is pretty straightforward.

vCenter Converter Standalone 4.x components (client, server, and agent) can be installed on the following platforms:

- Windows 2000 with SP4
- Windows XP Professional (32-bit and 64-bit)
- Windows 2003 (32-bit and 64-bit)
- Windows Vista (32-bit and 64-bit)
- Windows Server 2008 (32-bit and 64-bit)
- Red Hat Enterprise Linux 4.0 (32-bit and 64-bit)
- Red Hat Enterprise Linux 5.0 (32-bit and 64-bit)
- SuSE Linux Enterprise Server 10 (32-bit and 64-bit)
- Ubuntu 6.x
- Ubuntu 7.x (32-bit and 64-bit)

The vCenter Converter Standalone 4.x server and agent components (without client support) can also be installed on the following platforms:

- Red Hat Enterprise Linux 3.0
- SuSE Linux Enterprise Server 8
- SuSE Linux Enterprise Server 9 (32-bit only)
- Ubuntu 5.x

vConverter can be downloaded from the following URL (registration is required to download, and you will have two options—one for supported Windows platforms and one for supported Linux platforms):

> *http://vmware.com/download/converter*

VMware has done a great job of porting the familiar Windows-side GUI to the Linux version of the tool, allowing you the same "feel" with whichever version you prefer.

Installation on Windows

To install vConverter on Windows:

1. Download the Windows executable.
2. Run the installer, clicking Next at the introduction screen.
3. Accept the license agreement by checking "I accept the terms in the license agreement" and clicking Next to continue.
4. Choose the directory in which to install the files. The installer will default to *C:\Program Files\VMware\VMware vCenter Converter Standalone*. Once you're satisfied, click Next to continue the installation.
5. Select the type of installation you want to do. There are two options here, as shown in Figure 1-28:

   Local installation
   > This installs vCenter Converter on the server. It allows you to create and manage conversion tasks from this local server only.

   Client-Server installation (advanced)
   > This option sets up a client/server model for vCenter Converter. Here, you can install the individual client, server, and/or agent pieces on the local server (Figure 1-29).

   If you choose "Local installation," proceed to step 7; otherwise, continue to step 6.

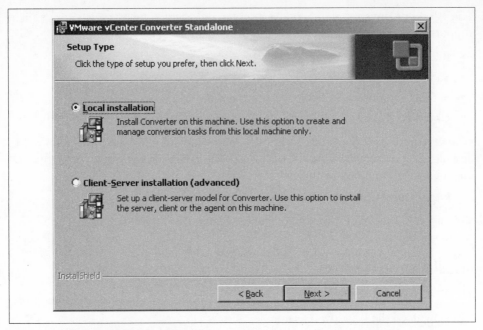

Figure 1-28. vCenter Converter setup types

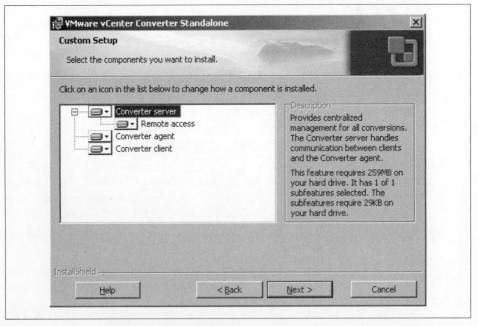

Figure 1-29. vCenter Converter custom setup

6. The advanced installation choice gives you the option to specify which ports vCenter Converter will use (Figure 1-30). The defaults are:

- HTTPS Service Port—443
- HTTP Service Port—80
- Agent Service Port—9089

When you are satisfied with the ports, click Next to continue the installation.

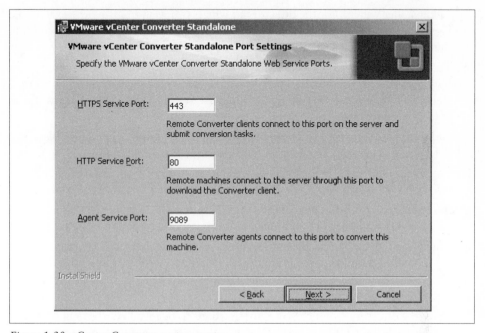

Figure 1-30. vCenter Converter custom ports

7. You are now ready to proceed with the installation. Click Install to continue.
8. When the installation has completed, you will have the option to automatically launch the vCenter Converter client. Click the Finish button to complete the install.

Installation on Linux

On each of the various Linux distributions we have tested, we have found that the default options worked well. Here are the steps to follow:

1. Download the Linux-based installer.
2. Extract the *tar* file by running `tar xvzf Vmware-converter*.tar.gz`. This will produce a directory called *vmware-converter-distrib*.
3. Change to the *vmware-converter-distrib* directory.
4. Run the *vmware-install.pl* file as *root* (you can switch to the *root* user or use `sudo`).

5. You will be presented with the license agreement. Press the space bar to read through it. When asked, type **yes** to agree and press Enter to continue the installation.

6. After accepting the license agreement, you will be asked if you wish to install the vCenter Converter Standalone client. The default is Yes, so you can press Enter.

7. You will be asked if you wish to install the vCenter Converter Standalone server. Again, the default is Yes, so you can press Enter to continue.

8. The installer will ask for the directory in which you wish to install the executable files. The default is */usr/bin*; however, you can change this if required by entering the path. Press Enter to accept either the default or your custom path.

9. You will now be asked where the VMware vCenter Converter Standalone library files should be installed. The default is */usr/lib/vmware-vcenter-converter-standalone*; however, you can enter a different directory if you prefer. Press Enter when you're ready to move to the next step.

10. Next, the installer will ask if you wish to create the path for the library files. The default is Yes, so you can press Enter to continue the installation.

11. Enter the path that contains the *init* directories for *rc0.d* and *rc6.d*. The default is */etc*. Press Enter to accept the default, or after entering a custom path if required.

12. Enter the path to the system's *init* scripts. The default is */etc/init.d*. Press Enter to accept the default, or after entering a custom path if required.

13. You have the option to enable remote access in vCenter Converter Standalone. The default is No, but you can change this to Yes if you wish to allow other vCenter Converter clients to connect to this instance. Press Enter to accept the default, or after changing the value.

14. Enter the directory in which you want the icons to be installed (the default is */usr/share/icons*). Press Enter to accept the default, or after entering a custom path.

15. Enter the directory that contains your *.desktop* menu entry files (the default is */usr/share/applications*). Press Enter to accept the default, or after entering a custom path.

The installation will now begin.

Once the installation has completed, you can check the System Tools menu in your X11 windows environment or launch the client from the command line by running the *vmware-converter-client* application.

1.16 VMware ESX 4.0 Installation

Like ESX 3.5, this new version is easy to install. If you have previously installed ESX 3.5, you will notice that the installer has received an upgrade: it's a little more user-friendly and has a more polished look. ESX 4.0 also uses an upgraded version of the Red Hat Linux platform: Red Hat Enterprise 5.x.

Before you get started installing ESX 4.0, you should verify that your hardware is fully compatible by visiting the following URL:

http://www.vmware.com/resources/compatibility/search.php?action=base&device Category=server

The ESX ISO image is available for download at *http://www.vmware.com/download/vi/*.

ESX 4.0 is based on a 64-bit hardware platform, so unlike the previous version, which would run only as 32-bit, you can only install on a 64-bit platform. VMware suggests the following as the minimum requirements for the ESX Server 4.x installation:

- A processor that supports 64-bit installations (e.g., all AMD Opterons, and the Intel Xeon 3000/3200, 3100/3300, 5200/5400, 7100/7300 and 7200/7400).
- 2GB RAM minimum.
- One or more Ethernet controllers (we recommend a minimum of four). VMware suggests Intel or Broadcom-based controllers, but you may check the hardware compatibility list for other options.
- Local, Hardware iSCSI, or SAN storage.

 To avoid possible data loss make sure to remove any attached storage, such as Fibre Channel, DAS, or iSCSI disks, before the initial installation of ESX.

The installer has the same graphical and text install modes as 3.5 and includes three other options for initializing the installation:

Install ESX in graphical mode
> The recommended method for installation. It uses a mouse and a graphical interface to guide you through the installation. This is the method we will be using for our installation as we continue this section.

Install ESX in text mode
> A text-only mode for installing ESX. This option is normally used when you have mouse or video problems in the graphical installer.

ESX Scripted Install using USB ks.cfg
> This allows you to build a custom kickstart script and launch it from a USB storage device.

ESX Scripted Install to first disk
> This is a default installation included on the ESX 4.0 media, and it cannot be customized. The default password for the installation is *mypassword*.

ESX Scripted Install to first disk (overwrite VMFS)
> This is a default installation included on the ESX 4.0 media, and it cannot be customized. This option will delete any VMFS storage you may have, removing any

virtual machines at the same time. The default password for the installation is *mypassword*.

To begin the installation, make sure your server is set to boot from the CD-ROM. This can be accomplished by changing the settings in your server's BIOS.

When you boot the ESX4 CD-ROM, you will notice a new installation screen (Figure 1-31) with the options we just mentioned.

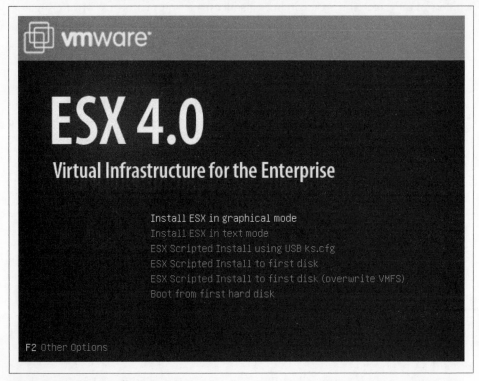

Figure 1-31. ESX4 installation menu

Here are the installation steps:

1. We are going to install using the graphical mode, since this will be the most widely used option. When you begin the installation, you will notice that the look and feel of the installer is a little more polished than in previous releases.

2. Once the installation has begun, you will be presented with a welcome screen instructing you to check your hardware to ensure it's compatible with ESX4. To continue the installation, click the Next button and accept the license agreement by checking the box. Then click Next again.

3. You will now be presented with the option to select which keyboard layout you want to use during the installation and afterward. Typically, you will select your language here (Figure 1-32). Click Next to continue the installation.

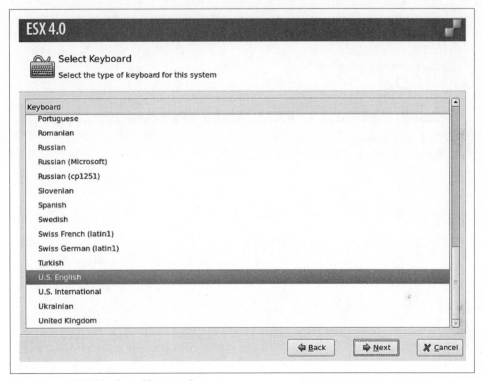

Figure 1-32. ESX4 keyboard layout selection

4. The next screen is new in ESX 4.0; it lets you load custom drivers for your hardware. This can be beneficial if the hardware you are using isn't compatible with ESX 4.0 out of the box (Figure 1-33).

If you need drivers that are not already installed, you have to install them at this screen. You will not be able to install them later.

If you have no drivers to install, click the Next button to continue the installation. To add a custom driver, click Yes and then the Add button and select the driver from your media. When you are finished, click Next to continue the installation.

The installer will give you a warning stating that the installer is going to load the drivers. Once this step is completed, you cannot add any custom drivers. If you are ready to continue, press the Yes button and the drivers will begin to load. When it finishes loading, the installer will say it is 100% completed. Click the Next button to continue the installation.

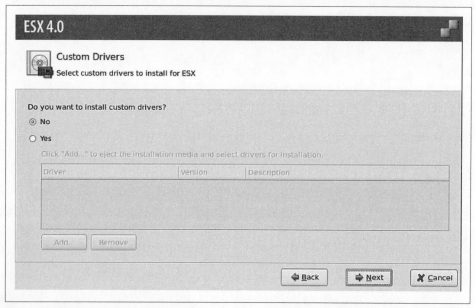

Figure 1-33. ESX4 custom driver options

5. Next, you have the option to enter a license serial number either now or later (Figure 1-34). This is a new screen within the ESX 4.0 installer. If you choose to enter the serial number later, the installer will give you a default 60-day trial license. If you do not have a license, you can use this option to get ESX installed and add your serial number at a later time. Click Next to continue the installation once you have selected an option.

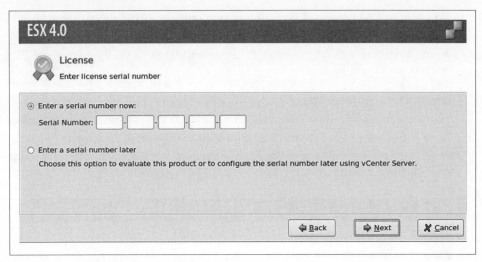

Figure 1-34. Entering the serial number

6. Next, select the network adapter that will be used for system tasks; this is generally called the service console (Figure 1-35). If your network requires VLAN identification, you also have the option to enter that ID here. If you are unsure, leave it blank; you can configure this option later, after you've installed ESX, by using the vCenter client. Once you have selected the network adapter, click the Next button to continue the installation.

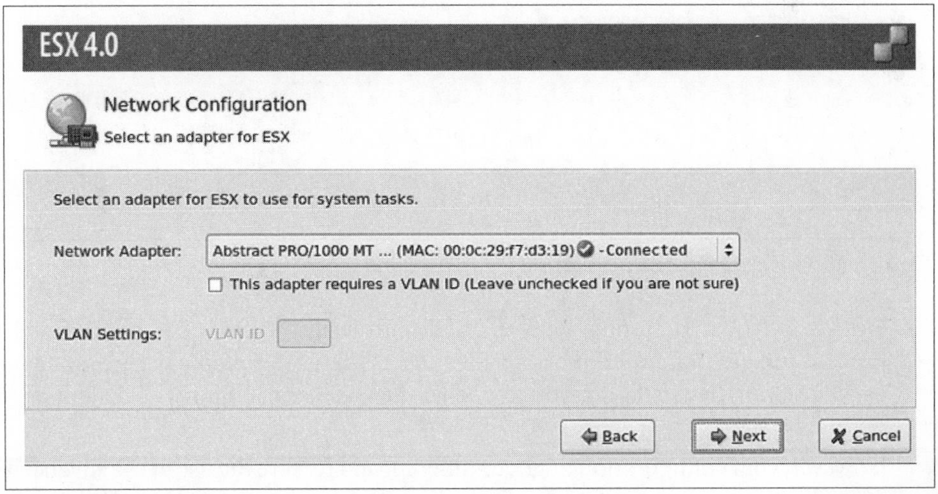

Figure 1-35. Selecting the network adapter

7. Now you will be presented with options to configure networking (Figure 1-36). You have two options here: "Set automatically using DHCP" or "Use the following network settings." Generally, if you are planning on deploying the ESX Server in a production environment, you will want to use the latter option. However, there may be cases where you won't have the necessary IP information; DHCP will work fine, just make sure to change it later.

The network configuration screen in ESX 4.0 also has a "Test these settings" button so you can validate your network settings before continuing the installation.

Once you have entered your network configuration, click the Next button to continue the installation.

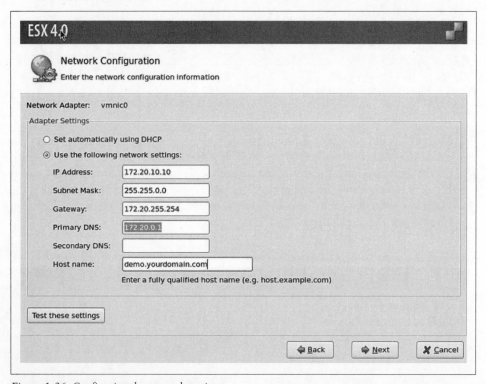

Figure 1-36. Configuring the network settings

8. Next, you will be presented with the option to install with the Standard or Advanced storage configuration options (Figure 1-37). In this recipe we are going to use the Standard installation option and let the installer configure the default partitions for us.

However, your configuration might be different and require the use of the advanced options, where you can manually configure different aspects of the storage partitions. The suggested partition sizes for an advanced disk partitioning installation are listed in Table 1-18.

To avoid possible data loss make sure to remove any attached storage, such as Fibre Channel, DAS, or iSCSI disks, before the initial installation of ESX.

Select the method you wish to use to configure your storage and click the Next button.

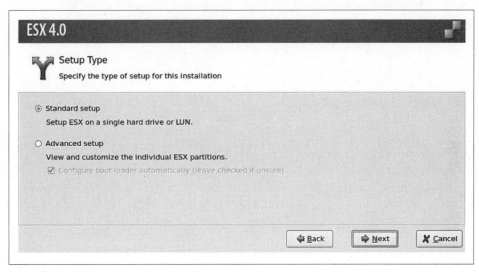

Figure 1-37. ESX4 disk partition method

Table 1-18. Disk partitioning sizes

Mount point	Type	Size	Notes
Swap	Swap	600MB	Allows the service console to use disk-based memory when the physical memory isn't available
/boot	ext3	1.25GB	Holds the ESX Server's kernel bootloader images and *vmkcore* partition
/	ext3	10GB[a]	Holds the operating system, configuration files, and third-party applications
/var	ext3	2GB[b]	Storage for logfiles
/vmfs	vmfs		The remaining portion of the disk should be allocated here[c]

[a] The / partition should be at least 5GB in size. To be on the safe side, we recommend setting this value to 10GB.

[b] The /var partition should be at least 2GB in size.

[c] The /vmfs partition doesn't need to be configured on a local disk, unless you do not have any SAN attached storage. However, it is often convenient to have a local /vmfs file store for testing, generally a local /vmfs partition will use the remainder of space on the local drive.

9. The installer will now present you with the disks available for the ESX installation (Figure 1-38). Select the disk on which you want to install ESX and click the Next button.

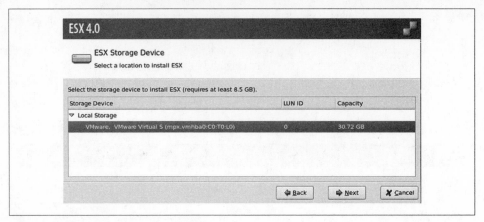

Figure 1-38. *Selecting the installation disk*

10. Once the disks are partitioned, you will need to select the time zone in which your servers are located (Figure 1-39). It's important to ensure that your ESX Servers have the correct time zone set and that all the ESX Servers in your cluster have the same time and time zone configured to ensure compatibility between the nodes.

Once you've selected your time zone, press the Next button to continue the installation.

Figure 1-39. *Selecting the time zone*

11. As mentioned in step 10, it's very important to ensure that your ESX Servers all have the same time and time zone set (Figure 1-40). In this step, you have the option to configure an NTP server or set the time manually. We suggest that if you have an NTP time server, all your ESX hosts point to that.

    Once you've configured the date and time, press the Next button.

12. Next, you need to set the *root* password on the ESX Server (Figure 1-41). The *root* password is what you'll use when initially connecting to the ESX. You also have the option to add other user accounts on this screen if you wish.

    Once you're finished, click the Next button to continue the installation.

13. Finally, you will be shown a summary of the installation, which you should review (Figure 1-42). If any changes need to be made, you can use the Back button to make them. Once you are satisfied, click the Next button and the installation will begin. This process can take between 15 and 20 minutes, depending on the speed of your server.

    When the installation has completed, press the Finish button. Your new ESX4 server will be rebooted, and a screen similar to Figure 1-43 will be shown. At this point, you can now add and configure this server from the vCenter client.

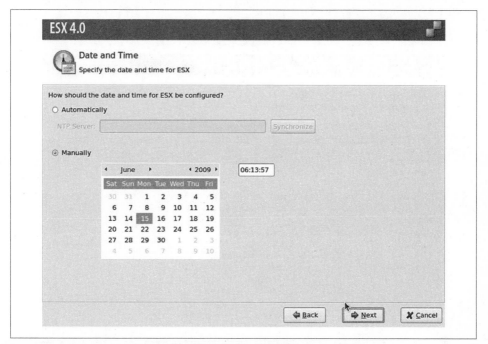

Figure 1-40. Configuring the NTP server and date and time

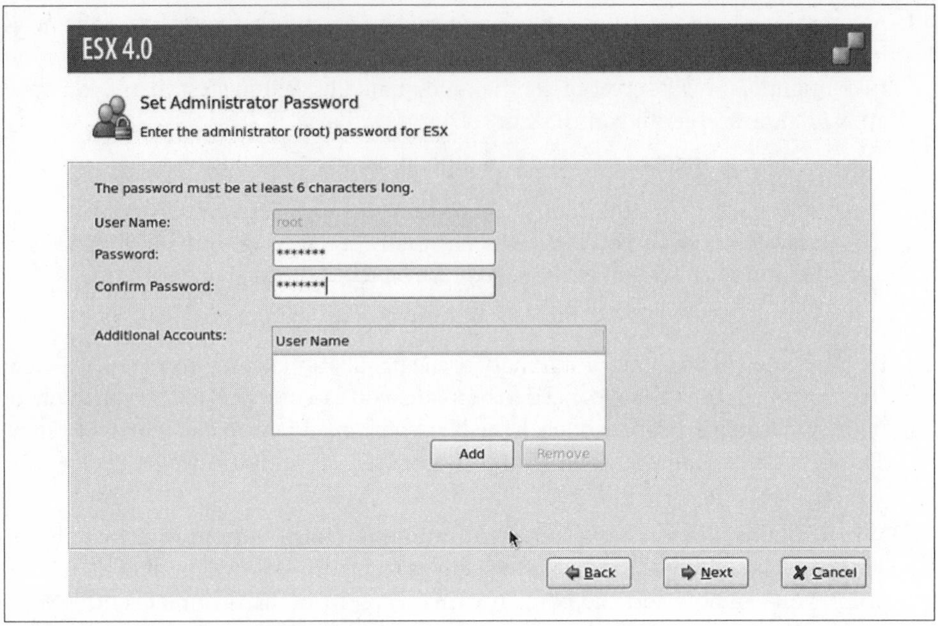

Figure 1-41. Setting the root user password

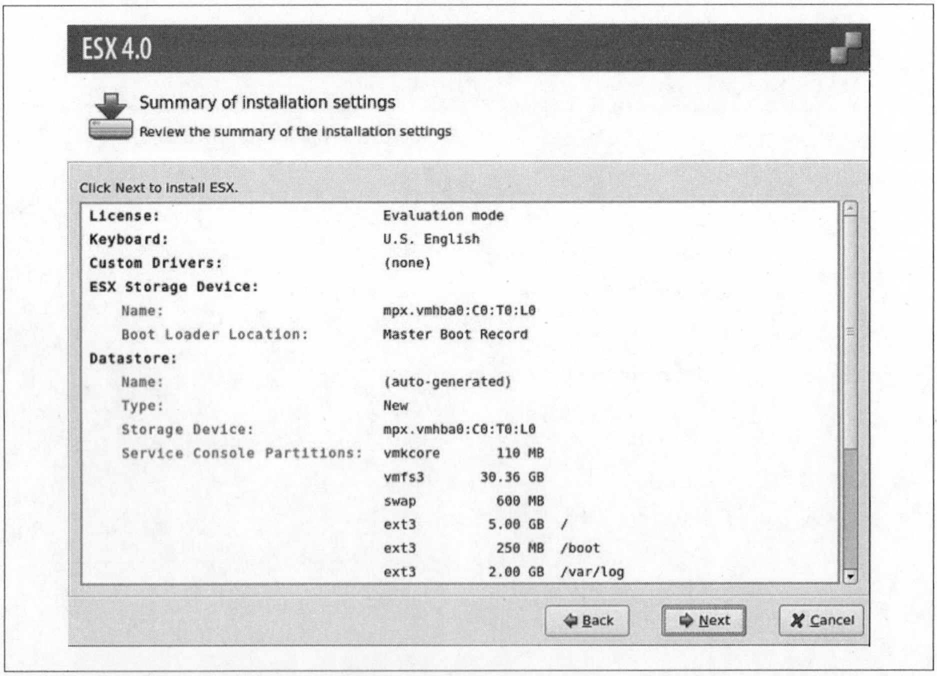

Figure 1-42. ESX4 installation summary

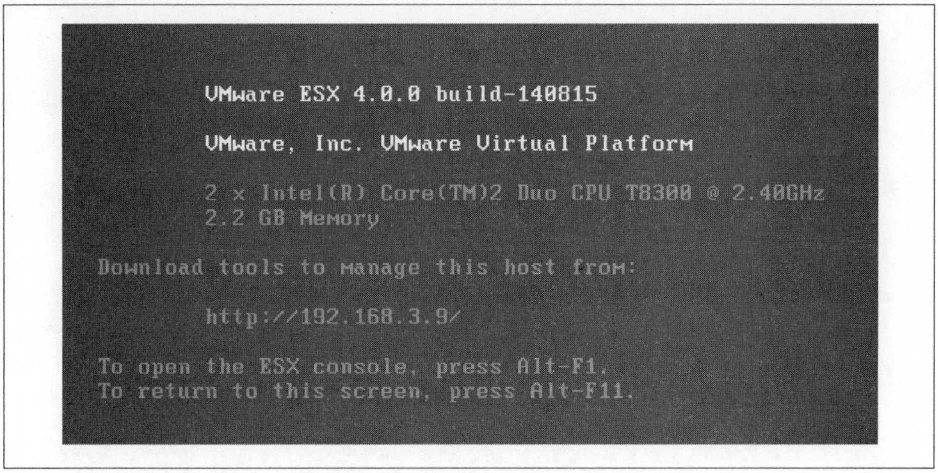

Figure 1-43. Default screen on ESX4 after installation has completed

See Also

Recipes 1.3, 1.5, and 1.7

## CHAPTER 2

Storage

Storage will be one of the key components in your virtualized environment. In this chapter we will look at the different types of storage and ways to successfully configure and use them within the ESX environment.

2.1 Comparing ESX Storage Options

Problem

You want to know which network storage types ESX supports and what each type offers.

Solution

Review the comparison tables in this recipe.

Discussion

Table 2-1 lays out the types of storage ESX supports. Table 2-2 lists the features different storage types can utilize in ESX. It's important to understand the technologies and their capabilities and limitations when setting up your ESX environment.

Table 2-1. Storage options for VMware ESX Servers

Technology	Protocols	Transfer	Interface
Fibre Channel	FC/SCSI	Block access/LUN	FC host bus adapter (HBA)
Local storage	SCSI/SAS	Block access	Local SCSI or SAS controller
iSCSI	IP/SCSI	Block access/LUN	iSCSI HBA for hardware iSCSI Ethernet card for software iSCSI
NAS	IP/NFS	File level	Ethernet card

Table 2-2. Storage features offered by types of storage on VMware ESX Servers

Type	Boot VM	VMotion	RDM	VMCluster	Datastore	HA and DRS
SCSI	Yes	No	No	No	VMFS	No
Fibre Channel	Yes	Yes	Yes	Yes	VMFS	Yes
iSCSI	Yes	Yes	Yes	No	VMFS	Yes
NAS/NFS	Yes	Yes	No	No	NFS	Yes

2.2 Storage Device Naming Scheme

Problem

You wish to understand how ESX names its devices when working with storage in ESX.

Solution

This recipe breaks down the naming scheme so you can understand how it works.

Discussion

The format of a storage device name in ESX consists of three or four numbers separated by colons. As an example, in Figure 2-1, the device name for ELISCSI01 is *vmhba19:0:0:1*. The numbers have the following meanings:

```
HBA:SCSI_target:SCSI_LUN:disk_partition
```

Our ELISCSI01 datastore's HBA has a device ID of 19. The second number, 0, marks it as the first target on the HBA, and the third number indicates that the LUN is number 0. Finally, it is the first partition, as indicated by the 1 in the fourth field.

The second value—the SCSI target number—is incremented for each volume added to the HBA. However, the third and fourth numbers—the SCSI LUN and disk partition—will never change on a particular volume.

The first and second numbers may change for the following reasons (if they are changed, they will still reference the same physical device to which they were originally connected):

- The first number belonging to the HBA can change if an outage occurs on the Fibre Channel or iSCSI network. In this case, ESX will assign a different number to access the storage device. The first number can also change if the card is moved to another PCI slot in the server.

- The second number will change if any modifications are made to the mappings on the Fibre Channel or iSCSI targets that are visible to the ESX Server.

Figure 2-1 shows a typical list of volumes and their device names. In this figure we've listed multiple iSCSI volumes arranged by the identification field, followed by their device names, capacity, free space, and the type of filesystem on the volume.

Configuration	Tasks & Events	Alarms	Permissions	Maps

Storage

Identification	Device	Capacity	Free	Type
ELISCSI01	vmhba19:0:0:1	999.75 GB	173.94 GB	vmfs3
ELISCSI02	vmhba19:1:0:1	999.75 GB	358.02 GB	vmfs3
ELISCSI03	vmhba19:2:0:1	999.75 GB	229.05 GB	vmfs3
ELISCSI04	vmhba19:3:0:1	999.75 GB	195.24 GB	vmfs3
esx1cluster2:stor...	vmhba7:0:0:3	60.00 GB	59.45 GB	vmfs3
ESXCluster2DS	vmhba21:0:2:1	1.09 TB	1,015.41 GB	vmfs3

Figure 2-1. Datastore device names

2.3 Creating a Network for a Software iSCSI Initiator

Problem

You want to create a separate iSCSI network to isolate storage traffic for servers when communicating with the storage device.

Solution

Using vCenter, create a network and VMkernel port for the iSCSI device to communicate on.

Discussion

Before ESX will communicate with an iSCSI device, a VMkernel network port must be created within the network component of vCenter Server.

The VMkernel port can be configured on an existing network, but we strongly advise you to put your iSCSI traffic on its own network and port group, isolated from all other traffic. This ensures maximum performance for your virtual machines. Follow these steps:

1. Log into vCenter Server and select the server from the inventory list.

2. Select the Configuration tab from the right window pane, navigate to *Networking* on the lefthand side, and click the Add Networking link in the upper-right corner.

3. Under Connection Types, select VMkernel and click Next. The VMkernel option allows you set up VMotion, iSCSI, or NAS in your ESX environment.

4. Under Network Access, select an unused network adapter (in Figure 2-2 we've selected *vmnic1* for our VMkernel port) to set up your VMkernel on a separate network (recommended), or select an already existing vSwitch and Ethernet adapter to share iSCSI traffic with other traffic. Your options will be displayed in the lower portion of the screen, in the Preview section (Figure 2-2). Click Next.

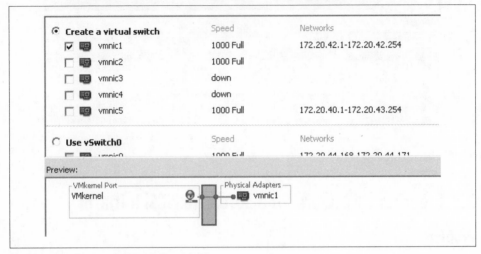

Figure 2-2. Adding an iSCSI VMkernel, selecting vmnic1

5. You will be required to enter some information about the VMkernel port on the Connection Types screen (Figure 2-3).

First, configure the port group properties:

Network Label
> This is the label by which the port group will be recognized within the virtual environment. It's important to give this port group the same name on all physical ESX Servers to ensure that VMotion and other aspects of the ESX environment will work.

VLAN ID (Optional)
> The network VLAN your port group will use to communicate. This should be specified only if you are using VLANs in your network infrastructure.

"Use this port group for VMotion"
> This option should not be selected when configuring a VMkernel for iSCSI or NAS traffic, because this port group will not include VMotion traffic.

Then configure the IP settings:

IP Address
> The IP address of the VMkernel. This is a required field.

Subnet Mask
> The subnet mask of the network. This is also required.

VMkernel Default Gateway

Enter a gateway if your IP address resides on a network other than the one on which you are configuring the port group.

To configure additional options, such as DNS and advanced routing, click the Edit button.

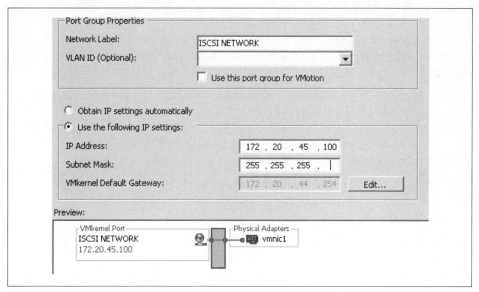

Figure 2-3. Setting information for the iSCSI VMkernel

6. Click Next to view the summary, and then Finish to create the port group.

2.4 Configuring Software iSCSI

Problem

You want to use iSCSI connections to storage area networks on an ESX without an iSCSI host bus adapter.

Solution

Configure the software iSCSI initiator using vCenter.

Discussion

Because SCSI is an efficient, low-cost interface and many systems with network storage use the popular iSCSI protocol to reach this storage over a TCP/IP network, VMware ESX offers iSCSI to connect ESX Servers to SANs. It is strongly recommended that you create a dedicated network for this traffic, as described in Recipe 2.3.

ESX supports two different types of iSCSI out of the box: hardware iSCSI and software iSCSI. Both are very powerful, but they're set up differently and require different components to work. Each uses a different kind of software translation, called an *initiator*, to send traffic from the ESX Server to the network.

Hardware iSCSI uses third-party HBAs to transmit iSCSI traffic over the network. Typically, if you can afford the iSCSI HBA cards, you will benefit from faster data transfers. These cards also offer configuration options for fine tuning and can allow you to boot your ESX Server off the iSCSI SAN. Booting an ESX Server from the iSCSI SAN can be helpful in a situation where you have limited local disk space or are utilizing blade servers.

Software iSCSI uses built-in code in ESX to run the iSCSI protocol over standard Ethernet cards. This eliminates the cost of HBAs, but it puts a significant load on your ESX Server's physical CPUs, which will affect system performance under high I/O loads. However, a lot of enterprise-grade systems will have TCP/IP offload engine–enabled Ethernet ports that can handle this offload and act like HBAs.

This section explains basic configuration for software iSCSI. By default, the iSCSI initiator is disabled, so you must enable it and indicate which SAN volumes you are communicating with:

1. Log into vCenter Server and select the server you are configuring from the inventory list.

2. Select the Configuration tab from the right window pane and click the *Storage Adapters* link on the lefthand side. Select *iSCSI Software Adapter* and then click Properties in the lower window pane (Figure 2-4).

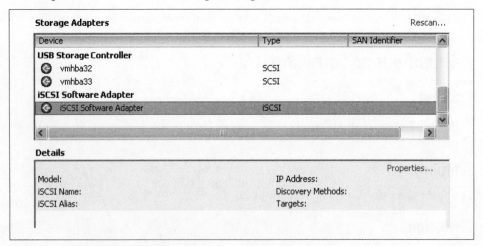

Figure 2-4. Adding software iSCSI support

3. The iSCSI Initiator Properties window will appear (Figure 2-5). Enable software iSCSI by clicking the Configure button, putting a check in the Enabled box under

Status, and clicking OK. A VMkernel port will be required for software-based iSCSI to work within the ESX Server; see Recipe 2.3 for more information.

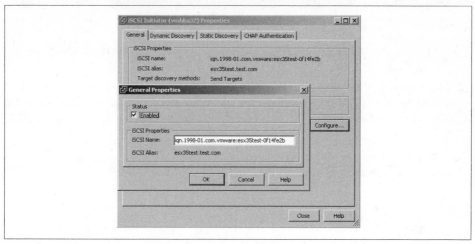

Figure 2-5. Enabling software iSCSI

4. Clicking OK brings you back to the iSCSI Initiator Properties window. From here you can begin to configure the initiator to see the iSCSI SAN volumes. Click the Dynamic Discovery tab, and then the Add button. In the dialog box that appears, enter the IP address and port (the default is 3260) of your iSCSI storage array, then click OK to finish (Figure 2-6).

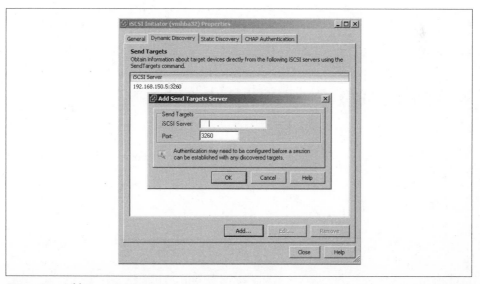

Figure 2-6. Adding an iSCSI target

5. If your iSCSI SAN infrastructure requires use of the Challenge Handshake Authentication Protocol (CHAP), click the CHAP Authentication tab to enable and configure CHAP. Some iSCSI SANs, such as Dell's EqualLogic PS series, will allow you to set three different authentication methods, including IP address matching, iSCSI initiator name matching, and CHAP authentication. It's important to mention that CHAP authentication in ESX 3.5 is one-way, allowing the array to identify the ESX Server.

6. After clicking the Close button, you will be asked if you wish to rescan for new disks. Accept this, and ESX will rescan. Once the scan is complete you will see the new target show up in the iSCSI software initiator's Details window (Figure 2-7).

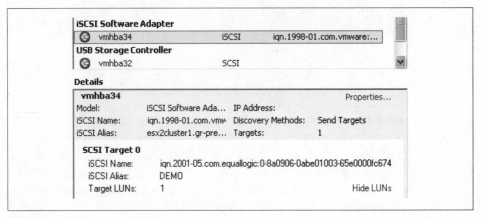

Figure 2-7. Showing the iSCSI target

See Also

Recipes 2.5 and 2.13

2.5 Configuring a Hardware iSCSI Initiator

Problem

You want to use iSCSI connections to storage area networks on an ESX with an iSCSI host bus adapter.

Solution

Use vCenter to configure the iSCSI HBA cards.

Discussion

A hardware-based iSCSI HBA, such as a QLogic HBA, provides a dedicated and specially designed processor to send and receive iSCSI traffic. It requires a hardware iSCSI initiator, which you can set up using the instructions in this section:

1. Log into vCenter Server and select the server from the inventory list.

2. Select the Configuration tab from the right window pane and navigate to the *Storage Adapters* link on the lefthand side. Select the iSCSI HBA and click Properties. A new window will appear.

   Unlike with the software iSCSI initiator, a separate network inside ESX is not required. You will generally create a separate physical network outside your ESX environment and set the IP address and network information directly on the iSCSI HBA.

   The iSCSI HBA we are using for our example is a QLogic QLE4062c, which has dual 1GB interfaces. If your iSCSI HBA has only one port, the model and device name (*vmhbaX*) will differ from those in our screenshot (Figure 2-8).

Storage Adapters

Device	Type	SAN Identifier
⊙ vmhba6	Fibre Channel	21:01:00:1b:32:27:05:6f
QLogic QLE406x		
⊙ vmhba3	iSCSI	iqn.2000-04.com.qlogic:ql...
⊙ vmhba4	iSCSI	iqn.2000-04.com.qlogic:ql...

Figure 2-8. Displaying the QLogic QLE4062c iSCSI HBA

3. Click the Configure button to configure the IP Address, Subnet Mask, Default Gateway, and optional iSCSI Name and iSCSI Alias (Figure 2-9). Once you're finished, click OK to continue.

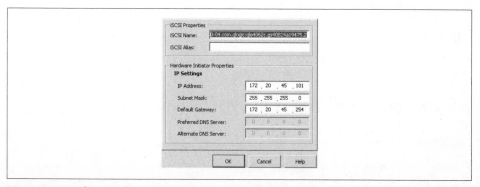

Figure 2-9. Configuring the IP settings for an iSCSI HBA

4. Click the Dynamic Discovery tab, then the Add button. Enter the IP address of the iSCSI server and, if necessary, change the default iSCSI port from 3260 to your customized value. Click OK, then click Close. The ESX Server will begin to scan for new devices.

New LUNs will appear in the Details window of the selected HBA card, as shown in Figure 2-10. The server can have a maximum of 64 LUNs, numbered SCSI Target 0, SCSI Target 1, and so on. In our example, the server has four targets, as identified in the Details window under *vmhba4*.

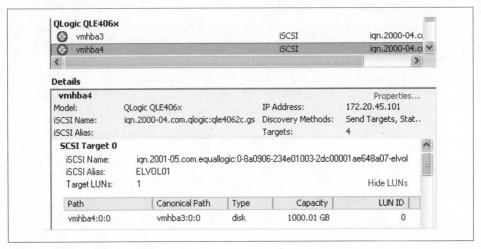

Figure 2-10. Showing the LUN after rescan

On the SCSI Target 0 LUN in Figure 2-10, notice that the Path and the Canonical Path differ. This is because we are looking at the *vmhba4* path view on the second port of the HBA, and the canonical path is set to route all traffic through the first port of the HBA, which is *vmhba3*.

See Also

Recipe 2.4

2.6 Configuring iSCSI in Windows Virtual Machines

Problem

You want a Windows virtual machine to communicate directly with a SAN over your iSCSI connection.

Solution

Using the Microsoft iSCSI Initiator, you can configure your virtual machine to talk to your iSCSI SAN directly.

Discussion

Using Microsoft's iSCSI Initiator, you can directly connect a volume to a virtual machine that is running Windows. This recipe assumes you have set up a separate network for the ESX Server and a virtual machine to use for iSCSI traffic, and that you have assigned a dedicated Ethernet port on the virtual server for ESX traffic. This section explains how to download and install the initiator.

If you are running Windows Vista or Windows 2008, the iSCSI Initiator is already included and no download is necessary. However, if you're using Windows XP, 2000, or 2003, you'll need to download the initiator from Microsoft's website. Microsoft provides both 32-bit and 64-bit versions of the application to ensure both platforms are covered.

Users who are required to download the application can install it by double-clicking the executable and following the on-screen instructions. You will be presented with a new window giving you a set of options that include the following:

Virtual Port Driver
> This is required and cannot be changed after installation.

Initiator Service
> This service handles the work being done.

Software Initiator
> This will handle all the iSCSI traffic.

Microsoft MPIO Multipathing Support for iSCSI
> MPIO increases throughput by utilizing multiple interfaces. If you have a target that supports this, such as a Dell EqualLogic iSCSI SAN, you may wish to utilize this technology if performance becomes an issue for you. This option is not available on Windows XP.

Continue the installation of the initiator by accepting the license agreement. When the installation has completed, you will have a new icon on your desktop called "Microsoft iSCSI Initiator." You'll use this application to manage your iSCSI connections in Windows.

1. When you launch the application, you will be presented with a screen of options to configure the iSCSI connections. On the Discovery tab, click the Add button in the Target Portals section (Figure 2-11).

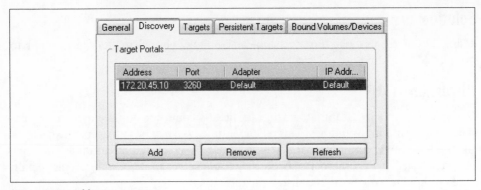

Figure 2-11. Adding a new target

2. The Add Target Portal dialog box allows you to enter the IP address or DNS name of your iSCSI SAN or array. The default port is 3260; you should change this if you're using a different port on the array. If you need to configure CHAP authentication or will be using IPsec for communication between the initiator and the iSCSI array, click the Advanced button and configure the necessary options.

3. Once you are satisfied, click the OK button to make the connection to the iSCSI array. The IP address or DNS name of the target will show up in the Target Portals area of the Discovery tab.

4. After creating the initial connection to the iSCSI array, you need to specify which volume you will connect to and mount on the Windows machine. Click the Targets tab to see the list of targets that are available for you to use (Figure 2-12).

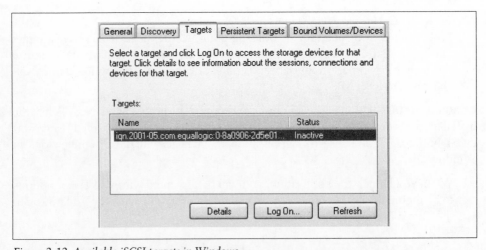

Figure 2-12. Available iSCSI targets in Windows

5. Select the volume to which you will be connecting and click the Log On button. A new window will pop up with the target name and two options (Figure 2-13).

The options are:

"Automatically restore this connection when the system boots"
> Selecting this option will make the system automatically reconnect to the volume each time Windows reboots. Unless you have a very good reason not to, you should always check this box. If this option is not selected, the volume will need to be manually reconnected each time the system boots.

"Enable multi-path"
> This option should be checked only if you plan on using multipathing for better reliability and performance. It requires multiple Ethernet cards dedicated to the iSCSI task.
>
> It can be valuable if you have the necessary hardware, need high availability, and previously configured multipathing when installing the initiator.

Once you are satisfied, click the OK button. The status for the target under the Targets tab will switch to Connected, showing that the volume is connected.

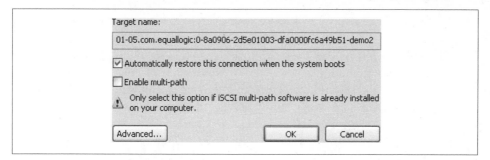

Figure 2-13. iSCSI target options

6. Now that the Windows machine can see the volume, you need to make, configure, and format the volume in Windows. Windows will treat the new iSCSI volume the same as if you'd added a physical hard drive to the server.

Right-click on My Computer and select Manage. Choose the Disk Management option. Since the volume is presumably a new volume with no data, Windows will pop up a new window with the Disk Initialization wizard.

7. Follow the steps presented by this wizard and select from either a basic (recommended) or dynamic disk (this is not recommended for Windows iSCSI). Once the disk has been initialized, you will need to create a partition and format the new volume by right-clicking on the new disk in the Disk Management window.

2.7 Opening Firewall Ports for an ESX iSCSI Software Initiator

Problem

Your firewall is blocking your ESX Server from communicating with storage over its iSCSI connection.

Solution

Use vCenter to open the necessary firewall port.

Discussion

In order for the iSCSI software initiator to communicate with its targets, port 3260 needs to be opened for outbound traffic on the ESX Server's firewall. In ESX 3.5 Update 4, this port will be opened for you automatically when software iSCSI is enabled.

Using vCenter, this task is easy. For each ESX Server that is part of your cluster or will be using the iSCSI software initiator, follow these steps:

1. Log into vCenter Server and select the server from the inventory list.

2. Select the Configuration tab from the right window pane, navigate to the *Security Profile* link on the lefthand side, and click the Properties link in the upper-right corner to display the Firewall Properties window. Look for the Software iSCSI Client service and select the box next to it to open the firewall on the ESX Server (Figure 2-14). Click OK when you're done.

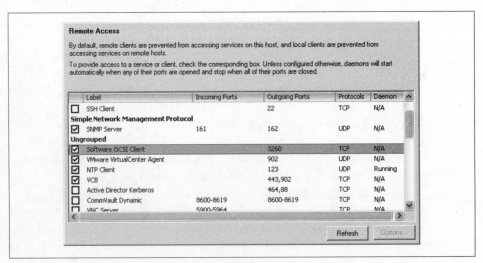

Figure 2-14. Enabling software iSCSI client firewall rules

See Also

Recipe 2.4

2.8 Multipathing with iSCSI

Problem

You want to route iSCSI traffic from an ESX Server over multiple paths for speed or redundancy.

Solution

Use vCenter to view and change multipath settings.

Discussion

One of the nice things about iSCSI is that it is IP-based, so it already has built-in support for multipathing using IP routing if you are using dynamic routing protocols on your network. This configuration of iSCSI represents a simpler alternative to Fibre Channel.

The steps for configuring multipathing are as follows:

1. Log into vCenter Server and select the server from the inventory list.

2. Select the Configuration tab from the right window pane and navigate to *Storage*. Then select the datastore you wish to modify and click Properties.

3. In the Extent Device window, toward the bottom-right corner, Path Selection and Paths will be displayed (Figure 2-15). The Path Selection will be either Fixed or MRU (most recently used).

   The ESX Server will automatically decide the default path depending on the make and model of your SAN. If the array is not an ESX supported device, the default path will be set to active/active and the other options may not be available for you to use. Please refer to the hardware compatibility list found at *http://www.vmware .com/go/hcl* to ensure your hardware is fully supported.

 ESX has built-in support for active/active multipathing, but it's still in the early experimental stages and is not recommended for production environments. At the time of writing, it is recommended that you use one of the more common multipath policies outlined here.

Failover is handled using one of the following policies:

MRU (most recently used)
> Uses the last access path for your storage traffic. For example, if you were using path 1 and it failed over to path 2, the device will continue to use path 2 even after path 1 comes back online.

Fixed
> Tries to use a specific path. For example, if you set your path policy to Fixed on path 1 and it has a failure, the device switches to path 2 until path 1 is restored, then switches all traffic back to path 1. This is the default policy for active/active storage devices such as Dell EqualLogic iSCSI SANs.

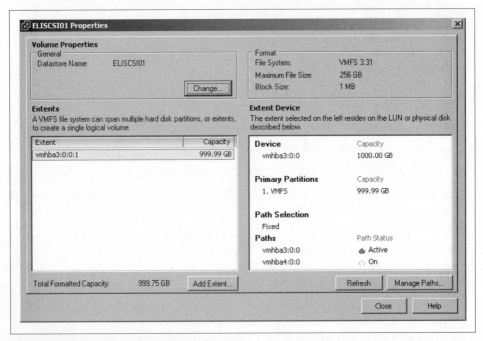

Figure 2-15. Showing hardware iSCSI paths

4. Click the Manage Paths button to configure the path settings as shown in Figure 2-16.

Click the path you wish to modify and then click the Change button, and you will be able to select the Preference and the State of the path, as shown in Figure 2-17. In this figure, we have selected the preferred path (grayed out) and we can enable or disable this path for traffic.

Once you have configured your paths, click the OK button. Then click the Close button to save the configuration.

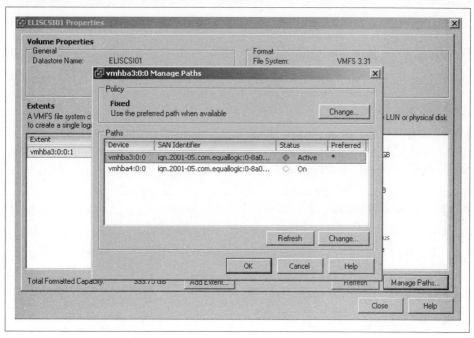

Figure 2-16. Managing paths

Figure 2-17. Enabling or disabling a path

2.9 Adding Fibre Channel Storage in ESX

Problem

You want to give your ESX Servers access to additional storage on a Fibre Channel SAN.

Solution

Use vCenter to configure the new storage and present the LUN to the ESX Servers.

Discussion

Before you can configure the Fibre Channel disk on the ESX side, you must first create the LUN on the disk array and set up specific zoning permissions for the LUN. Normally, this is done in a utility provided by the SAN manufacturer.

When the SAN-side configuration is completed, you can use vCenter to add the new disk to your ESX Servers:

1. Log into vCenter Server and select a server from the inventory list.

2. Select the Configuration tab from the right window pane and navigate to *Storage*. Click the Add Storage link.

3. Select the Disk/LUN storage type and click Next to proceed.

4. Select the Fibre Channel device that will be used for your VMFS datastore. Click Next to continue. If the disk you are formatting is blank, the entire disk space is presented for configuration.

   If the disk is not blank, review the current disk layout in the top panel and select the appropriate configuration method from the bottom panel (this will erase and remove all data from the disk):

   Use the entire device
   Selecting this option will dedicate all the available space to the VMFS datastore. This is the suggested option for VMware access, and selecting this option will remove all data currently on the LUN.

   Use free space
   Selecting this option will use the remaining free space to create the VMFS datastore.

   When you are satisfied with your decision, click Next to continue.

5. In the Disk/LUN properties page, enter the name by which you want to refer to this datastore. Click Next to continue.

6. If you need to adjust the block sizes, do so and click Next to continue.

7. Review the summary and click Finish to add the new datastore.

You do *not* need to add the same datastore to multiple ESX Servers. After it has been added to one, the others will see it if the correct zoning has been configured or if no zoning is present on your fibre switch.

8. After the datastore has been created, you may need to click the "refresh" link to see the new datastore. If multiple ESX Servers connect to the same datastore, you will need to refresh the storage on each one to see the new datastore.

2.10 Raw Device Mapping in Virtual Machines

Problem

You want direct access, without going through the virtual filesystem, from a virtual machine to a disk on your storage network.

Solution

Use vCenter to configure raw device mapping (RDM) for the virtual machine.

Discussion

Raw device mapping allows virtual machines to have direct access to a LUN on a physical storage system without the use of a VMFS datastore.

VMware generally suggests that you store your virtual machine files on a VMFS partition. However, certain situations may require the use of RDM, such as MSCS clustering that spans over physical hosts, or the use of SAN technologies inside your virtual machine. RDM is supported only over Fibre Channel and iSCSI at this time.

RDM has two different modes:

Virtual compatibility mode
   This mode allows the RDM to act like a VMDK (virtual disk file) and allows the use of virtual machine snapshots within ESX. Virtual compatibility mode is also compatible with VMware Consolidated Backup (VCB).

Physical compatibility mode
   This mode allows direct access to the device, but gives you less control within ESX. For example, you will not be able to snapshot the data using ESX. However, if your SAN supports snapshot technology you will be able to use it on this volume.

To add an RDM disk to a virtual machine that has already been created:

1. Log into vCenter Server and select the virtual machine to which you wish to add the RDM.

2. From the Summary tab on the virtual machine, click Edit Settings.

3. When the new window appears, click the Add button.

4. The Add Hardware wizard will open. Select Hard Disk, then click Next.

5. You will be presented with a list of options. Select Raw Device Mapping and click Next.

6. Select the LUN you wish to use for your RDM (Figure 2-18) and click Next.

Adapter:Target:LUN	Capacity
/vmfs/devices/disks/vmhba5:0:0:0	408.697 GB
/vmfs/devices/disks/vmhba5:0:1:0	500.000 GB

Figure 2-18. Selecting the LUN for the RDM

7. From the available list of disks, select the LUN you wish to use for your virtual machine.

8. Select the datastore for your RDM mapping file. You can store the mapping file on the same datastore where the virtual machine files are stored, or on another datastore. If you have N-Port ID Virtualization (NPIV) enabled, ensure that the RDM mapping files are on the same datastore as the virtual machine files. Once selected, click Next to continue.

9. You will be presented with a choice of two compatibility modes, detailed earlier in this recipe. Make your selection and click Next to continue.

10. Select the virtual device node and click Next to continue.

11. If you selected virtual compatibility mode, you will need to choose between the two following modes:

Persistent
Changes are immediately and permanently written to the disk.

Nonpersistent
Changes written to the disk are discarded when the virtual machine is powered off or when the virtual machine is reverted to a previous snapshot image.

Once you have made your selection, click Next to continue and click Finish to add the RDM to the virtual machine.

2.11 Creating a Port to Access NFS Datastores

Problem

You want to hook a Network File System (NFS) file share up to an ESX Server.

Solution

Create a VMkernel port to allow ESX to communicate with NFS.

Discussion

Although a lot of larger ESX environments use Fibre Channel or iSCSI, ESX also supports the use of NFS. As with software-based iSCSI, you will need to create a VMkernel on the ESX Server for NFS traffic to pass over. It is recommended that you configure the VMkernel to use a dedicated network, but you can configure it on an existing network if necessary. Here are the steps:

1. Log into vCenter Server and select the server from the inventory list.

2. Select the Configuration tab from the right window pane and navigate to *Networking* on the lefthand side. Click Add Networking in the upper-right corner.

3. Under Connection Types, select VMkernel and click Next.

4. If you are going to set up your VMkernel on a separate network (recommended), you will want to select an unused network adapter; alternatively, select an already existing vSwitch and Ethernet adapter. The options will appear in the lower portion of the screen, in the Preview section (Figure 2-19). After making your selection, click Next.

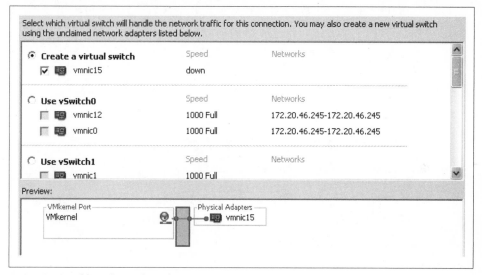

Figure 2-19. Adding the VMkernel port

5. You will be required to enter some information about the VMkernel port on the Connection Types screen (Figure 2-20).

First, set the port group properties:

Network Label
> The label by which the port group will be recognized within the virtual environment. It's important to give the port group the same name on all physical ESX Servers.

VLAN ID (Optional)

> The network VLAN your port group will use to communicate. Specify this if you are using VLANs in your network infrastructure.

"Use this port group for VMotion"

> Because the VMkernel also handles VMotion traffic, this option is available when configuring the NFS VMkernel. However, you should leave it unchecked because it is not recommended to run VMotion traffic over the same network as your storage traffic.

Next, configure the IP settings:

IP Address

> The IP address of the VMkernel. This is a required field.

Subnet Mask

> The subnet mask of the network. This is also required.

VMkernel Default Gateway

> Enter a gateway if your IP address resides on a network other than the one in which you are configuring the port group.

Further options, such as DNS and advanced routing, can be configured by clicking the Edit button.

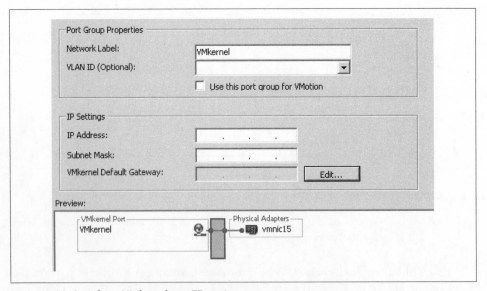

Figure 2-20. Specifying VMkernel port/IP settings

6. Click Next to view the summary, and then click Finish to create the port group.

Before ESX can communicate with the NFS datastore, you have to configure it to use the storage, as described in the next section.

2.12 Configuring ESX to Use NFS

Problem

You wish to add an NFS datastore to your ESX Server.

Solution

Use vCenter to configure the ESX Server so it recognizes the NFS device.

Discussion

Before you run this recipe, set up a VMkernel port to communicate with the NFS datastore, as described in Recipe 2.11. Then configure the ESX Server as follows:

1. Log into vCenter Server and select the server from the inventory list.
2. Select the Configuration tab from the right window pane, navigate to the *Storage* link on the lefthand side, and click Add Storage in the upper-right corner.
3. A new window will appear with two options: Disk/LUN or Network File System (Figure 2-21). Select Network File System and click Next to continue.

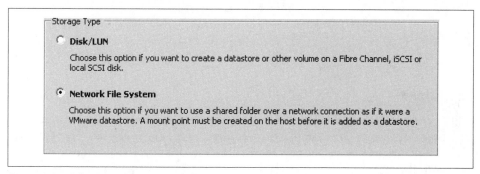

Figure 2-21. Selecting NFS to create a datastore

4. You will now be asked to enter some information about the NFS share (Figure 2-22):

   Server
   The name or IP address of the device that is serving the NFS share

   Folder
   The directory on the NFS device you are going to mount

   Datastore Name
   The name you wish to give the new datastore (for example, *NFS01*)

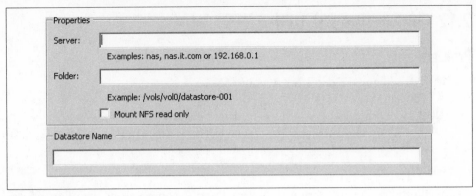

Figure 2-22. Entering NAS device properties

When you're done, click Finish. ESX will proceed to add the new datastore.

2.13 Creating a VMFS Volume in vCenter

Problem

You want to add a new VMFS volume to an ESX Server.

Solution

By using vCenter, you can easily create and attach new VMFS volumes.

Discussion

Adding an additional VMFS volume to your ESX Servers is pretty straightforward for all aspects of storage. For example, once configured on the SAN side, Fibre Channel and iSCSI disks will be visible to your ESX Server, and local disks will be detected automatically.

When adding a new disk to your ESX Servers in a clustered environment, where multiple ESX Servers will be accessing the SAN LUN/datastore, you only need to add it to one ESX Server. After the datastore is created, you can rescan or refresh the existing servers and the datastore will appear.

 If you try to add the same datastore to each individual ESX Server, you will get data corruption and configuration problems.

Follow these steps to create the VMFS volume:

1. Log into vCenter Server and select the server from the inventory list.
2. Select the Configuration tab from the right window pane, navigate to *Storage*, and click the Add Storage link.
3. Select the Disk/LUN storage type and click Next to proceed.
4. Select the device to use for your VMFS datastore. The device may be a local, iSCSI, or Fibre Channel disk. Click Next to continue. If the disk you are formatting is blank, the entire disk space is presented for configuration.

   If the disk is not blank, review the current disk layout in the top panel and select the appropriate configuration method from the bottom panel:

   "Use the entire device"
   > Selecting this option will dedicate all the available space to the VMFS datastore. This is the suggested option for VMware servers, and selecting this option will remove all data currently on the LUN.

   "Use free space"
   > Selecting this option will use the remaining free space to create the VMFS datastore.

   After making your choice, click Next to continue.

5. On the Disk/LUN properties page, enter the name you want to give this datastore. Click Next to continue.
6. If you need to adjust the block sizes, do so. Click Next to continue.
7. Review the summary and click Finish to add the new datastore.
8. After the datastore has been created, you may need to click "refresh" to see the new datastore. If multiple ESX Servers connect to the same datastore, you will need to refresh the storage on each one to see the new datastore.

See Also

Recipe 2.15

2.14 Performing a Storage Rescan

Problem

You need to rescan your storage adapters.

Solution

Use the rescan feature in vCenter.

Discussion

There may be times when it is necessary to rescan your ESX Server's storage devices. These situations include:

- When changes are made to the disks or LUNS available to the ESX Server.
- When changes are made to the storage adapters in the ESX Server.
- When a new datastore is created or removed.
- When an existing datastore is reconfigured, for example by adding an extent to increase storage.

To rescan a server's storage adapters:

1. Log into vCenter Server and select the server from the inventory list.
2. Select the Configuration tab from the right window pane, navigate to *Storage Adapters* on the lefthand side, and click Rescan.

    Alternatively, to rescan a specific adapter, you can right-click on that adapter and select Rescan.

3. If you wish to rescan for new disks or LUNs, select Rescan in the upper-right corner and then choose the "Scan for New Storage Devices" option. If new LUNs are discovered, they will appear in the disk/LUN view.

4. To discover new datastores or update existing datastores after a configuration change, select the "Scan for New VMFS Volumes" option. If a new datastore is found, it will be displayed in the datastore view.

2.15 Creating a VMFS Volume via the Command Line

Problem

You must create a new VMFS volume but do not have access to vCenter, or you want to create an automation script.

Solution

Using the vmkfstools command on your ESX Server allows you to create new volumes.

Discussion

The vmkfstools command creates a new VMFS volume. It also assigns it a unique UUID, which is a hexadecimal value that incorporates the SCSI ID and label name into the volume's metadata. Run the command as follows on the ESX host's service console:

```
vmkfstools -C vmfs3 -S volume_name vmhbaX:hba:scsi_target:scsi_lun:disk_partition
```

The -C option tells the command which type of VMFS volume to create. In our case, we created a VMFS3 volume. The -S option allows you to specify a label for your volume, which should be a simple name.

See Also

Recipe 2.13

2.16 Viewing the Files That Define a VMFS Volume

Problem

You need to find information about a VMFS volume, but this information is contained in files on that volume rather than in vCenter.

Solution

Each virtual machine has a directory with files that define and control the virtual machine. You can view the contents of this directory and read the files themselves, as they're text-based.

Discussion

Many files make up a virtual machine. Understanding the purpose of each one helps you keep your virtual machine environment running at top performance:

.vmx
Holds the configuration for the virtual machine.

.vmss
This file is present when the virtual machine is suspended.

.vmdk
Holds the operating system and data for the virtual machine. This file is based on the *.vmx* file.

.vmem
Virtual machine memory is mapped to this file.

.vmsd
The dictionary file for snapshots and associated disks. If you have snapshots or multiple disks, this file keeps track of them.

.nvram
Holds the BIOS for the virtual machine.

.vmx.lck
A lock file is created when the virtual machine is powered on.

-flat.vmdk
> A single preallocated disk that contains data.

f001.vmdk.filepart
> The first extent of a preallocated disk that has been split into 2GB files.

s001.vmdk
> The first extent of a growable disk that has been split into 2GB files.

-delta.vmdk
> Holds the differences between the actual virtual machine and snapshot differences. This allows you to roll back your virtual machine to a previous state or merge the current state with the old state.

-Snapshot#.vmsn
> The configuration of a snapshot.

These files are located within the virtual machine's directory on the storage volume, which is typically */vmfs/volumes/DATASTORE/VIRTUALMACHINE*. For example, our server, which is named *W2KStandardBase*, is on the *ELISCSI01* database store, and its path is */vmfs/volumes/ELISCSI01/W2K3StandardBase*.

2.17 Extending a VMFS Volume

Problem

One of the datastores on your ESX Server is running out of space.

Solution

Using vCenter, you can add an extent to your existing datastore to add more space.

Discussion

An extent is a physical hard drive partition on a physical storage device, such as a Fibre Channel, iSCSI SAN, or local disk. These partitions can be dynamically added to an existing VMFS-based datastore, allowing you to grow it above the 2TB limit. Datastores can span multiple extents and will be presented to ESX as a single volume.

Adding new extents can be done while the existing VMFS datastore is online. This makes adding new space really easy.

Adding more extents to an existing VMFS datastore can also improve performance. By having multiple VMkernel queues, you can disperse I/O traffic over multiple paths, distributing the load.

It should be noted that the first VMFS datastore (disk) in the extent holds the metadata for the entire datastore, including all new extents. If the first extent is corrupted or damaged, you are at risk of losing all the data on the entire extent set.

Add an extent as follows:

1. Log into vCenter Server and select the server from the inventory list.
2. Select the Configuration tab from the righthand window pane, navigate to *Storage* on the lefthand side, and select the datastore to which you wish to add the extent.
3. Once the datastore is highlighted, click the Properties link (Figure 2-23).

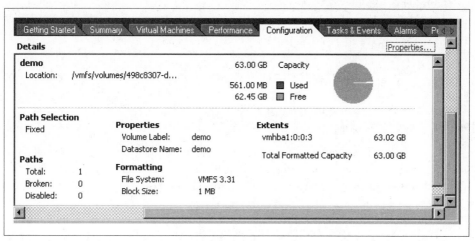

Figure 2-23. Showing the storage volume that will get an extent

4. A new window will appear with information regarding the datastore. Click the Add Extent button in the lower-left corner to launch the wizard that will guide you through the process.

Once the extent has been added to the datastore, you can click on the datastore to view the new extent in the lower Details window.

You cannot remove individual extents after they have been added to a datastore; you can only remove the entire VMFS datastore, which will result in losing all its data.

See Also

Recipes 2.4, 2.5, and 2.15

2.18 Reading VMFS Metadata

Problem

You wish to view the metadata for a specific VMFS volume.

Solution

Use the `vmkfstools` command.

Discussion

The metadata in a VMFS volume is made up of six parts:

- Block size
- Number of extents
- Volume capacity
- VMFS version
- Label
- VMFS UUID

The `vmkfstools` command lets you view the metadata in a specific VMFS volume:

    vmkfstools -P -h *pathname*

The `-P` option allows you to read the metadata, while the `-h` option tells the `vmkfstools` command to display amounts in MB, KB, or GB instead of the default bytes. The *pathname* is the pathname of your VMFS filesystem. For example:

```
bash#: vmkfstools -P -h /vmfs/volume/ESXCluster2DS

VMFS-3.31 file system spanning 1 partitions.
File system label (if any): ESXCluster2DS
Mode: public
Capacity 1.1T, 1015G available, file block size 1.0M
UUID: 47cd6dd2-31a2a254-a6a1-001e4f1e7171
Partitions spanned (on "lvm"):
    vmhba5:0:2:1
```

2.19 Renaming a VMFS Volume Label from the Command Line

Problem

You need to rename a volume from the command line when vCenter isn't available.

Solution

You can accomplish this using some Linux (Bash shell) or VMware-specific commands. Renaming a volume in vCenter is much easier, however.

Discussion

First, you need to find the UUID that is mapped to the VMFS volume you wish to rename. This can be accomplished by running one of the following commands:

```
vmkfstools -P datastorename
vdf
ls -al /vmfs/volumes
```

If you decided to use one of the latter two commands, look for the pathname of the VMFS filesystem in the output. The pathname is linked to a UUID that represents the volume.

Using the following Linux commands, you can rename a VMFS volume. The ln command creates a link. The -s option makes it a symbolic link, while the -f option forces the command to overwrite what is already stored in the link:

```
ln -sf /vmfs/volume/UUID /vmfs/volumes/new_volume_name
```

If this change is being made on a set of ESX Servers that all access the same VMFS volume, repeat this command on each one. Once complete, run the following command to restart the VMware-hosted process:

```
service mgmt-vmware restart
```

2.20 Manually Creating and Aligning a VMFS Partition

Problem

You want to use the command line to create a VMFS partition.

Solution

A combination of standard Linux (Bash shell) tools can accomplish this.

Discussion

VMware suggests that partitions be aligned to 64K track boundaries. This improves throughput by an average of 12% and reduces latency by an average of 10%. If you create a new partition inside vCenter, it will automatically align it for you. However, if you want to create the partition manually using the command line, this recipe will walk you through the steps.

If you already have an active partition, you can verify its alignment by issuing the fdisk -lu command. If you are unsure of the actual path of the disk, use the esxcfg-mpath -l command to get a listing. The output will be similar to this:

```
bash#: fdisk -lu /dev/sdg

Disk /dev/sdg: 1197.8 GB, 1197851279360 bytes
255 heads, 63 sectors/track, 145630 cylinders, total 2339553280 sectors
Units = sectors of 1 * 512 = 512 bytes

   Device Boot    Start      End     Blocks   Id System
/dev/sdg1           128 -1955421347 1169772911  fb Unknown
```

Aligned partitions start at position 128. If the start value is 63, which is the default, the partition is not aligned and you should follow the steps outlined here.

 This process will delete all the data and partitions on your entire disk.

To create and align a partition:

1. Run the `fdisk` command on the disk where you wish to create the partition (disk names are *sda*, *sdb*, etc.):

   ```
   fdisk /dev/sdX
   ```

2. Determine whether any partitions exist by using the **p** command. If partitions exist, delete them using the **d** command and enter the number of the partition.

3. Type **n** to create a new partition.

4. Type **p** to set the new partition as the primary partition.

5. When prompted, type **1** (the number one). This will set the new partition to number 1.

6. Select the defaults to use the complete disk. These will vary depending on your disk size.

7. Type **t** to configure the partition's system ID. VMware uses the ID of *fb* to identify VMFS partitions.

8. Enter expert mode by typing **x**, and then type **b** to adjust the starting block number.

9. Select the first partition by typing **1** (the number one).

10. Type **128** to set the partition position using a 64K boundary.

11. Finally, type **r** to return to the main menu, and **w** to write the label and partition information to the disk. Exit *fdisk*.

Once complete, you will be able to run the `fdisk -lu` command to see the start point set to 128.

2.21 Creating a Diagnostic Partition

Problem

Your ESX Server is missing a diagnostic partition.

Solution

Use vCenter to create a diagnostic partition.

Discussion

ESX Servers need to have a diagnostic or dump partition in order to run. These partitions store core dumps for debugging and are used by the VMware technical support team. Diagnostic partitions can be created on a local disk, on a shared LUN on a Fibre Channel device, or on a device accessed by a hardware-based iSCSI initiator connection. Diagnostic partitions are not supported on software-based iSCSI initiators.

The diagnostic partition must be at least 100MB in size. If you use a shared storage device, each ESX Server must have its own separate diagnostic partition.

If you choose the "Recommended Partitioning" scheme when installing your ESX Server, the installer automatically creates the diagnostic partition for you. The following steps create a diagnostic partition if your ESX installation is missing it:

1. Log into vCenter Server and select the server from the inventory list.
2. Select the Configuration tab from the right window pane, navigate to *Storage*, and click Add Storage.
3. A new window will appear allowing you to select the storage type. Select the Diagnostic option and click Next to continue. If you do not see the Diagnostic option, your ESX Server already has a diagnostic partition. If your ESX Server already has a diagnostic partition, you can access it by issuing the `esxcfg-dumppart -l` command at the command line.
4. Select the type of diagnostic partition you wish to create. You have three options:

   Private Local
   > Create the diagnostic partition on a local disk.

   Private SAN Storage
   > Create the partition on a nonshared storage LUN using Fibre Channel or hardware-based iSCSI.

   Shared SAN Storage
   > Create the diagnostic partition on a shared LUN that is accessible by multiple ESX Servers and may store information for more than one ESX Server.

   After making your selection, click Next.
5. Select the device on which to create the partition and click Next.
6. Finally, review the partition configuration and then click Finish to create the diagnostic partition.

2.22 Removing Storage Volumes from ESX

Problem

You wish to remove an old datastore from your ESX Server.

Solution

Use vCenter to remove a volume from ESX.

Discussion

The steps to remove a volume follow:

1. Log into vCenter Server and select the server from the inventory list.
2. Select the Configuration tab from the right window pane and navigate to *Storage*. Right-click on the datastore you wish to remove, and choose Remove.
3. A pop-up window will appear asking you to confirm the removal of the datastore. It's very important to make sure you know which datastore you want to remove, as this window provides no details on the datastores.
4. Click Yes if you are positive the correct datastore has been selected. Once you've done this, the datastore will be removed and the data will be deleted.

2.23 Determining Whether a VMFS Datastore Is on a Local or SAN Disk

Problem

Using vCenter, it's hard to tell whether a VMFS datastore is on a local or SAN disk.

Solution

Through a combination of vCenter and the command line, you can determine the physical location of a VMFS datastore.

Discussion

To find out where your VMFS datastore is located:

1. Log into vCenter Server and select the server from the inventory list.
2. Select the Configuration tab from the right window pane and navigate to *Storage*.
3. Look at the device for the VMFS datastore you want to locate. The name will be similar to *vmhba7:0:0:1*.
4. Open an SSH or Telnet session on the ESX Server.
5. Enter `grep vmhbaN /proc/vmware/pci`, replacing *N* with the number of your adapter. For example, in step 3 our adapter was *vmhba7*.
6. The fourth field in the output gives you a clue about the physical storage. For instance, the following output from a local SCSI disk controller says `RAID`:

```
$ grep vmhba7 /proc/vmware/pci
033:00.0 1000:0060 1028:1f0c RAID Symbios  10/ 17/0x71 A V megaraid_sas vmhba7
```

The next example shows the output for a Fibre Channel controller (the fourth entry from the left says FC for Fibre Channel):

```
$ grep vmhba5 /proc/vmware/pci
022:00.0 1077:2432 1077:0138 FC QLogic  10/ 26/0x69 A V qla2300_707_vmw vmhba5fro
```

Finally, here's the output for our iSCSI storage controller. Notice the difference from the first example—instead of RAID, it lists a hexadecimal value:

```
$ grep vmhba3 /proc/vmware/pci
020:01.1 1077:4032 1077:0158 0x280 QLogic   6/ 23/0x89 B V qla4022   vmhba3
```

Thus, on our system, all devices that are using *vmhba7* are on a local storage controller, devices using *vmhba5* are on a Fibre Channel controller, and devices using *vmhba3* are located on an iSCSI controller.

2.24 Adjusting Timeouts When Adding Storage in vCenter

Problem

When you try to add new storage in vCenter, you receive timeout errors.

Solution

Adjust the timeout value in vCenter.

Discussion

Timeouts can occur for various reasons when adding new storage via vCenter. It may be simply that the timeout values are just too short, but be aware that lengthening these values is not a fix-all solution; there may be a larger underlying problem in networking or I/O that you should investigate.

To lengthen the timeout in the vCenter client, navigate to Edit→Client Settings→Remote Command Timeout→Use a custom value. The value is shown in seconds. Adjust it to a higher number (perhaps two times what is already set).

2.25 Setting Disk Timeouts in Windows

Problem

A Windows guest operating system will sometimes time out when a SAN is rebooted or goes through a failure and recovery.

Solution

You can adjust the disk timeout value in the Windows registry.

Discussion

Default timeouts on Windows servers may be too short for a SAN recovery. During the time your SAN is down and Windows is trying to write data, it is possible for data to be lost or corrupted if your timeout values are not high enough. You can change the timeouts on both Windows Server 2000 and 2003 by editing the system registry:

1. Click Start→Run, type **regedit**, and click OK.
2. In the left panel view, double-click the first `HKEY_LOCAL_MACHINE\SYSTEM\CurrentControlSet`, then click Services, and finally Disk.
3. Select the `TimeOutValue` and set the data value to **3c** (hexadecimal) or **60** (decimal).
4. Save the changes and exit the registry.

Once these changes have been made, Windows will wait 60 seconds before generating disk errors. If 60 seconds isn't long enough, you can adjust the value to suit your specific needs.

## CHAPTER 3

Networking

Networking is a crucial aspect of the ESX virtual environment. It's important to understand the technology, including the different pieces that make it up and how they work together. In this chapter we will look at different networking elements inside the ESX platform and how to configure and build those different pieces.

3.1 Understanding Differences Between ESX 3.5 and ESXi 3.5 in Network Support

Problem

Limitations on networking can be confusing because ESXi does not support everything in ESX.

Solution

This recipe summarizes the differences between the two versions.

Discussion

ESX 3.5 and ESXi 3.5 share a common set of features, but they differ in significant ways. VMware has published a Knowledge Base article (1003345) describing some of the differences in the networking portions of the two products, and we'll discuss those differences briefly in this recipe. It's important to understand the differences in order to avoid conflicts when configuring your environment. Here are the key points:

- ESX 3.5 and ESXi 3.5 both support the Cisco Discovery Protocol (CDP) by default. However, only in ESX 3.5 can you configure the CDP so that information about the physical NIC, or *vmnic* in VMware terms, is passed to upstream switches. ESXi 3.5 doesn't currently support that feature.

- In ESX 3.5, jumbo frames are supported in the guest (virtual machine) and in the ESX kernel's TCP/IP stack. However, in ESXi, jumbo frame support is currently available only in the guest (virtual machine) environment.

- NetQueue, a technology that allows the use of 10 Gigabit Ethernet within virtual environments, is supported only in the ESX 3.5 version of ESX. It is not supported in ESXi 3.5.

As the technologies evolve, these limitations will most likely be removed from the ESXi version.

3.2 Configuring ESX Network Ports and Firewall

Problem

You need to identify the ports used by ESX services and ensure they are open for traffic to pass.

Solution

Review and discuss the ports and their functions within the environment.

Discussion

Connections to the ESX Server through vCenter, SSH, or the Web must use specific ports. ESX handles most communication through the following ports; they cannot currently be changed, so make sure they are open on your firewall:

Port 902
> vCenter Server uses this port to send data to the ESX Servers it manages. The listening process (*vmware-authd*) on the ESX Server handles the flow of traffic.

Port 903
> Both the vCenter client and the web client use this port to provide mouse-keyboard-screen (MKS) service from the virtual machine to the end user over TCP/IP. This port also handles all interaction with the virtual machine when it is accessed via the console in the vCenter client or via the Web.

Port 443
> vCenter clients, web clients, and the SDK all use this port to send data to an ESX Server managed by vCenter Server. This port is also used if you directly connect to the ESX Server, bypassing the vCenter server. The clients will connect to the ESX Server via the Tomcat or SDK instance, and the running process on the ESX Server (*vmware-hostd*) will handle the traffic.

When communications regarding VMware HA (high availability), migrations, cloning, or VMotion take place between multiple ESX Servers, it's important to have the following firewall ports open to ensure all the traffic gets from the source to the destination without any problems:

- Port 443 for server migrations and provisioning traffic
- Ports 2050–2250 and 8042–8045 for high availability traffic
- Port 8000 for VMotion traffic

By default, to ensure you don't unintentionally leave open services that could be a security risk, ESX is installed with no firewall ports open. You have to configure it to open the ports just mentioned, along with any needed for the actual services you run on your guests, such as Web Services, DNS, etc.

In Chapter 6, we will discuss how to manage the ESX firewall via the command line and how to enumerate the ports that are available using the `esxcfg-firewall` command. Here, we'll take a look at some of the firewall features, using the vCenter client. It provides some useful additional features—notably, the ability to tie the starting and stopping of services to the opening and closing of ports. Any changes made via the command line will not take advantage of these settings.

Configure the firewall and services as follows:

1. Log into vCenter Server and select the server from the inventory list.
2. Select the Configuration tab from the right window pane and navigate to *Security Profile*. A list of services and ports will appear in the righthand window (Figure 3-1).

Security Profile		
Firewall	Refresh	Properties...
Incoming Connections		
CIM SLP	427 (UDP,TCP)	
SNMP Server	161 (UDP)	
aam	2050-2250,8042-8045 (TCP,UDP)	
SSH Server	22 (TCP)	
CIM Secure Server	5989 (TCP)	
Outgoing Connections		
NTP Client	123 (UDP)	
VMware License Client	27000,27010 (TCP)	
NFS Client	111,2049 (UDP,TCP)	
CIM SLP	427 (UDP,TCP)	
VMware VirtualCenter Agent	902 (UDP)	
VCB	443,902 (TCP)	
SNMP Server	162 (UDP)	
aam	2050-2250,8042-8045 (TCP,UDP)	
updateManager	80,9000-9100 (TCP)	
Software iSCSI Client	3260 (TCP)	
SSH Server	22 (TCP)	

Figure 3-1. Displaying firewall services and ports

3. Click the Properties link in the upper-right corner to open the Firewall Properties window. From here, you can open the port on the firewall by putting a check in the box next to the service (Figure 3-2).

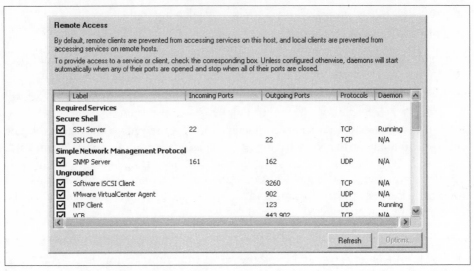

Figure 3-2. The services/firewall ports configuration screen

4. You can enable automatic starting and stopping by selecting a service and clicking the Options button (in the bottom-right corner of Figure 3-2). This button will be displayed for certain services that support options, such as SSH or NTP. Figure 3-3, for instance, shows the options available for SSH. Not all services offer these three options, and ESXi offers them for fewer services than ESX.

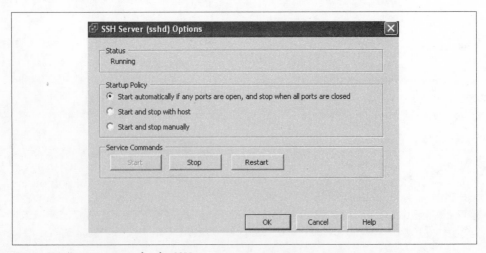

Figure 3-3. Service options for the SSH service

The configurable options for SSH running under ESX are:

"Start automatically if any ports are open, and stop when all ports are closed"
This is the default setting for many services, such as NTP and SSH. VMware recommends keeping this option checked.

"Start and stop with host"
The service will start shortly after the host startup scripts have been run and will stay up until the host shutdown scripts run, even if you close their ports on the firewall. Using this option might lead to a small delay in a service used for routine background traffic, such as NTP, if its port is opened after the host starts. However, once the port is opened, the connection will begin transmitting data.

"Start and stop manually"
The ESX host will not attempt to start or stop services automatically. For example, NTP may not be started on a reboot, but if you start it manually and the necessary firewall port is specified in the Remote Access area, the firewall will automatically open the port.

3.3 Creating a vSwitch for Virtual Machines

Problem

A vSwitch is needed for your virtual machines to interact with the physical network.

Solution

Use vCenter to build a complex or simple network for your virtual machines.

Discussion

A vSwitch, or virtual switch, behaves much like a physical switch. A vSwitch will automatically detect which virtual machines are connected and route the traffic either to other virtual machines using the VMkernel, or to the physical network using a physical Ethernet port (sometimes referred to as an "uplink port"). Each uplink or physical adapter will use a port on the vSwitch. By using vSwitches you can combine multiple network adapters, balance traffic, facilitate network port failover, and isolate network traffic.

A single ESX Server can have a maximum of 127 vSwitches. A single vSwitch has a default of 56 logical ports. However, a vSwitch can be configured with up to 1,016 ports. A single virtual machine will use one port on the vSwitch. A logical port on the vSwitch is also a member of a port group, which we'll discuss later in this chapter. If you choose the standard defaults during the installation of ESX, your initial vSwitch and *vswif* interfaces will already have been created for you.

Create a vSwitch and assign it key configuration properties as follows:

1. Log into vCenter Server and select the server from the inventory list.

2. Select the Configuration tab from the right window pane and navigate to *Networking*. Any current network configurations will be displayed. Click the Add Networking link to create a new virtual switch.

3. Three options will be presented. Choose the default option, "Virtual Machine," which allows you to add a labeled network for virtual machine traffic (Figure 3-4). Click Next to continue.

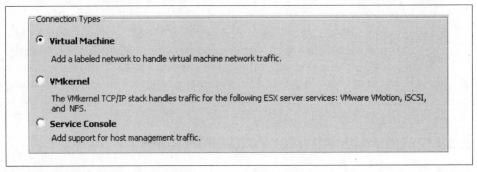

┌─ Connection Types ──┐

  ⊙ **Virtual Machine**

     Add a labeled network to handle virtual machine network traffic.

  ○ **VMkernel**

     The VMkernel TCP/IP stack handles traffic for the following ESX server services: VMware VMotion, iSCSI, and NFS.

  ○ **Service Console**

     Add support for host management traffic.

└──┘

Figure 3-4. Selecting the network type

4. Select "Create a virtual switch" (Figure 3-5). A new vSwitch can be created with or without Ethernet adapters assigned to it.

   If the vSwitch is configured without network adapters, all traffic will be confined to that vSwitch itself. Traffic on each of the virtual machines on the same switch will be isolated from other virtual machines and vSwitches.

   A vSwitch that is configured with an Ethernet adapter will communicate with other physical hosts or virtual machines on its network. However, it can be isolated from other networks by using VLAN tagging.

   Click Next to continue.

5. The Port Group Properties section allows you to configure the network label (Figure 3-6). This is used to identify the network and will be used by the virtual machine to associate itself with that specific network. Optionally, if you are using VLANs in the physical network, you can specify a VLAN ID of between 1 and 4094. This can generally be left blank, but check with your network administrator.

   Click Next to continue.

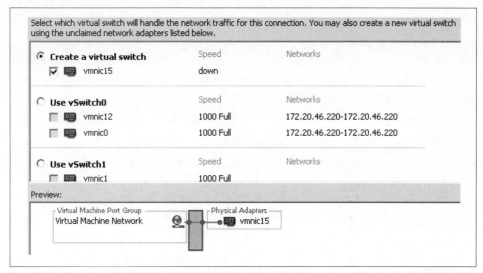

Figure 3-5. Creating a new vSwitch for vmnic15

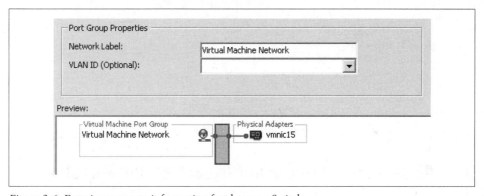

Figure 3-6. Entering property information for the new vSwitch

6. Once you're done configuring the vSwitch, click Finish to create it. The new vSwitch will now be available for use.

3.4 Removing a Virtual Switch

Problem

You need to remove a previously configured vSwitch.

Solution

Use vCenter to remove the vSwitch.

Discussion

Removing a vSwitch is simple with vCenter. However, it may disrupt your network, so you should take precautions before removing a vSwitch that has virtual machines attached to it. Those virtual machines will need to be moved to another vSwitch in order to maintain their connectivity on the physical network.

Follow these steps to remove a vSwitch using vCenter:

1. Log into vCenter Server and select the server from the inventory list.
2. Select the Configuration tab from the right window pane and navigate to *Networking*.
3. All configured virtual switches will be displayed in the Network window. Identify the vSwitch to be removed and click the Remove link above it (Figure 3-7).

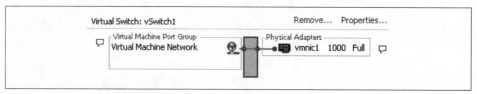

Figure 3-7. A vSwitch with the Remove link

4. A confirmation dialog will appear asking if you want to remove the vSwitch. Select Yes. As mentioned earlier, be aware that any virtual machines connected to this vSwitch might lose their connections to the physical LAN.

3.5 Adding VMotion to Enable Virtual Machine Migration

Problem

You want to enable VMotion so virtual machines can be migrated to another ESX Server.

Solution

Use vCenter to create a vSwitch attached to a VMkernel port and to enable VMotion.

Discussion

VMotion allows you to migrate virtual machines between ESX hosts without taking down the virtual machines or ESX hosts. This is called *migrating*. The migration uses a VMkernel port.

We looked briefly at VMkernel ports in Chapter 2, during our discussion of the configuration and setup of such ports for iSCSI and NFS traffic. ESX3 uses a VMkernel port to handle all network-based traffic for software iSCSI, VMotion, and NFS, because these technologies are network-based and can use the same VMkernel.

However, you can also configure a VMkernel port with support for VMotion. Some architectural restrictions should be observed to make VMotion work, though:

- VMotion is designed to allow migration between similarly configured ESX hosts. CPU types must be compatible, and migration doesn't work between AMD and Intel processors.

- Typically, the VMkernel port that has VMotion configured will be on an isolated network away from all other traffic. This ensures that the complete network is available while the migration is taking place.

VMkernel ports can be configured in vCenter or via the command line. We will show you only how to use vCenter. If you read the recipes in Chapter 2 on configuring NFS and iSCSI, you will notice that the following steps are similar, but add the use of VMotion:

1. Log into vCenter Server and select the server from the inventory list.

2. Select the Configuration tab from the right window pane and navigate to *Networking*. Any current network configurations will be displayed. Click the Add Networking link to create a new virtual switch.

3. Three options will be presented. Choose the VMkernel option, which allows you to add a VMkernel port to handle TCP/IP traffic for VMotion, NFS, or iSCSI (Figure 3-8). Click Next to continue.

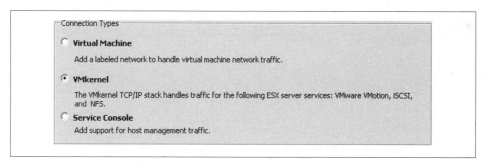

Figure 3-8. Creating a new VMkernel port

4. Select "Create a virtual switch" and select the *vmnic* that will be used to handle the VMotion traffic. Details about the configuration will be presented in the Preview window (Figure 3-9). Click Next to continue.

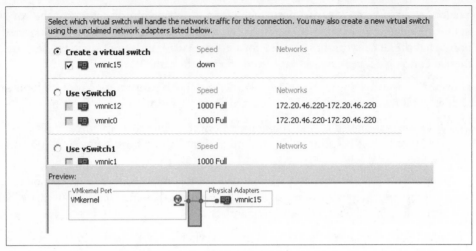

Figure 3-9. Creating a new VMkernel vSwitch for vmnic15

5. The Port Group Properties section allows you to configure the network label, which is used to identify the network. It's extremely important to use the exact same naming scheme on all your ESX Servers to ensure that VMotion will initiate smoothly, remembering that network labels are case sensitive. If VLANs are utilized on your network, enter the relevant information in the VLAN ID field. The step that configures a VMkernel for VMotion is also done here: "Use this port group for VMotion" must be checked and enabled. This allows the port group to advertise that it is going to handle VMotion traffic (Figure 3-10).

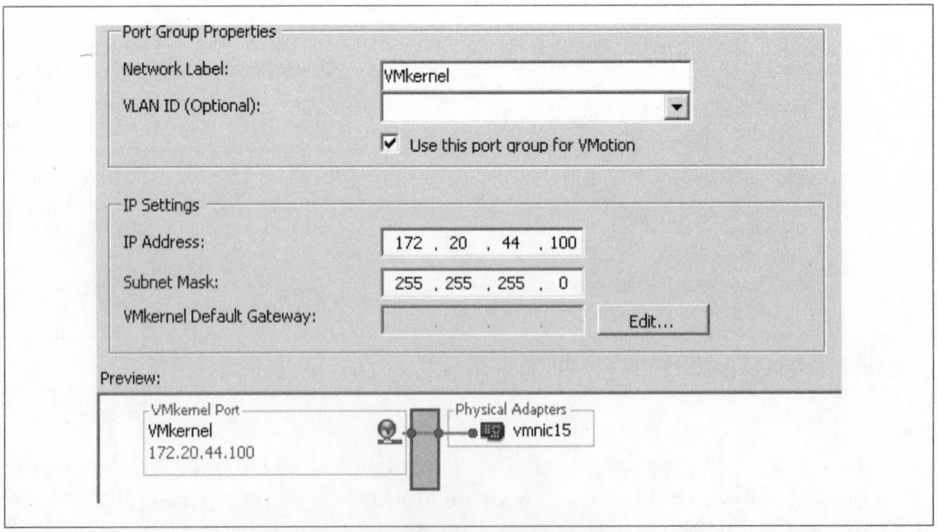

Figure 3-10. Adding new VMkernel properties information

6. Fill in the IP Address and Subnet Mask fields. If there are more detailed network settings that need to be configured, such as gateways, routing, and DNS servers, click the Edit button to configure them. Save your changes by clicking OK, and click Next to continue.

7. View the summary on the "Read to Complete" screen and click Finish to finalize the configuration.

See Also

Recipe 2.11

3.6 Creating a Service Console Network via the CLI

Problem

You need to create a service console network on your ESX 3.5 server without using vCenter.

Solution

Using the command line, add a new vSwitch and associate it with a service console network.

Discussion

The service console handles all traffic to the ESX Server, such as management, authentication, and the heartbeat services that run when high availability is enabled on your ESX Server.

ESXi 3.5 doesn't have an option for a service console network, so this recipe does not apply to ESXi.

Creating a service console from the ESX 3.5 server's command line is a little more complex than using vCenter. However, once you become familiar with the commands, it's pretty easy. Bear in mind that the server must already be on a network. Here are the steps:

1. Log into the ESX Server's console and become the *root* user.

2. Find out what network adapters are available to use for a new vSwitch:

```
$ esxcfg-nics -l

Name     PCI       Driver    Link Speed      Duplex MTU  Description
vmnic47 1a:00.01 e1000      Down 0Mbps      Half   1500 Intel Corpor
vmnic0   05:00.00 bnx2      Up   1000Mbps Full   1500 Broadcom Cor
vmnic44 19:00.00 e1000      Up   1000Mbps Full   1500 Intel Corpor
vmnic1   07:00.00 bnx2      Up   1000Mbps Full   1500 Broadcom Cor
vmnic49 1f:00.01 e1000      Down 0Mbps      Half   1500 Intel Corpor
```

```
vmnic45 19:00.01 e1000        Up   1000Mbps Full   1500   Intel Corpor
vmnic48 1f:00.00 e1000        Up   100Mbps  Full   1500   Intel Corpor
vmnic46 1a:00.00 e1000        Up   1000Mbps Full   1500   Intel Corpor
vmnic50 20:00.00 e1000        Up   100Mbps  Full   1500   Intel Corpor
vmnic2  09:00.00 bnx2         Up   1000Mbps Full   1500   Broadcom Cor
vmnic51 20:00.01 e1000        Up   1000Mbps Full   1500   Intel Corpor
vmnic3  0b:00.00 bnx2         Up   1000Mbps Full   1500   Broadcom Cor
```

3. Get a list of the current vSwitches on the ESX Server, if any exist:

```
$ esxcfg-vswitch -l
Switch Name    Num Ports    Used Ports   Configured Ports  MTU    Uplinks
vSwitch0       64           6            64                1500   vmnic12,vmnic0

   PortGroup Name     VLAN ID   Used Ports   Uplinks
   Internal ESX       0         0            vmnic0,vmnic12
   NFS                0         1            vmnic0,vmnic12


Switch Name    Num Ports    Used Ports   Configured Ports  MTU    Uplinks
vSwitch1       64           4            64                1500   vmnic1

   PortGroup Name     VLAN ID   Used Ports   Uplinks
   vMotion            0         1            vmnic1
```

Notice that we have two separate vSwitches with different port groups.

4. Create a new vSwitch. Depending on how many vSwitches your current ESX Server has, the number in this example may vary. In our case, because step 3 showed us that we already had a *vSwitch0* and a *vSwitch1*, we'll create a third vSwitch named *vSwitch2*:

```
$ esxcfg-vswitch -a vSwitch2
```

5. Once you've created the new vSwitch, you'll need to add a port group with the label "Service Console". Make sure you execute the command with the quotation marks around the label:

```
$ esxcfg-vswitch -A "Service Console" vSwitch2
```

6. Attach a *vmnic* from step 1 to the new vSwitch to create an uplink. In this example we choose to use *vmnic49* because it was not already in use:

```
$ esxcfg-vswitch -L vmnic49 vSwitch2
```

7. Create the *vswif* (service console) interface on the newly created vSwitch. The -i option allows us to specify the ESX Server's IP address, -p allows us to provide a label, and the -n option specifies the network mask:

```
$ esxcfg-vswif -a vswif0 -i 172.10.45.11 -n 255.255.255.0 -p "Service Console"
```

3.7 Checking Connectivity Using vmkping

Problem

Your ESX Servers are having connectivity problems, and you want to know whether their network connection is functional.

Solution

Use the vmkping command to verify connectivity.

Discussion

The vmkping command works much like the standard Linux ping command, but it talks to the VMkernel ports on other ESX Servers.

 If you encounter timeouts or network problems when running the vmkping command, they could be the result of an incompatible NIC teaming configuration on VMotion. According to VMware, you can resolve this by setting one of the NICs to standby.

When you are logged into the ESX Server's console as the *root* user, you can run vmkping with any other server as the destination. For instance, the following command will output three pings to esx2cluster2, then stop and show the results:

```
$ vmkping -v esx2cluster2
PING esx2cluster2 (172.20.46.2): 56 data bytes
64 bytes from 172.20.46.2: icmp_seq=0 ttl=64 time=0.503 ms
64 bytes from 172.20.46.2: icmp_seq=1 ttl=64 time=0.295 ms
64 bytes from 172.20.46.2: icmp_seq=2 ttl=64 time=0.314 ms

--- esx2cluster2 ping statistics ---
3 packets transmitted, 3 packets received, 0% packet loss
round-trip min/avg/max = 0.295/0.371/0.503 ms
```

The vmkping command can be controlled through a few options, as the following help output shows:

```
$ vmkping -h
vmkping [args] [host]
   args:
      -D             vmkernel TCP stack debug mode
      -c <count>     set packet count
      -i <interval>  set interval
      -s <size>      set send size
      -v             verbose

   NOTE: In vmkernel TCP debug mode, vmkping traverses
         VSI and pings various configured addresses.
```

3.8 Modifying the Speed of a Network Adapter

Problem

You need to make changes to the network speed on a physical network adapter.

Solution

Modify the network adapter's properties in vCenter.

Discussion

vCenter offers control over a much smaller set of features on the physical adapter than you can control using command-line tools. However, vCenter does let you change the port speed of specific network adapters.

To configure your network adapter's speed:

1. Log into vCenter Server and select the server from the inventory list.
2. Select the Configuration tab from the right window pane and navigate to *Networking*. The current network configurations will be displayed.
3. Click the Properties link of the vSwitch you wish to modify (Figure 3-11).

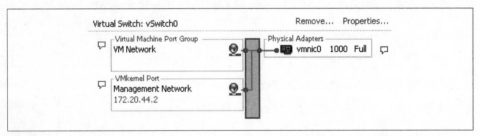

Figure 3-11. vSwitch Properties link

4. A new window will appear. Click the Network Adapters tab. From here, select the network adapter you wish to modify and click the Edit button.
5. A dialog box pops up allowing you to change the speed (Figure 3-12). Make your choice and click OK.

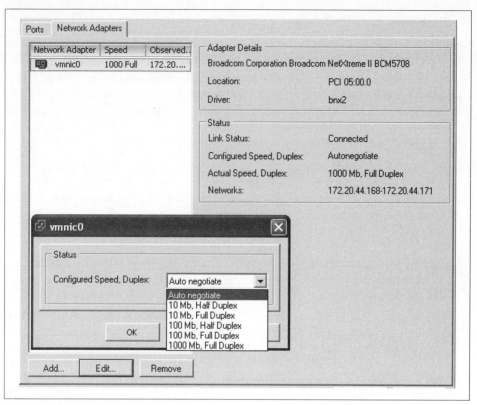

Figure 3-12. Network adapter properties

3.9 Choosing Network Elements That Protect Security

Problem

You want to make sure that the network tying your ESX and virtual servers reflects your site's needs and matches up with the security on your physical networks.

Solution

Examine the different security measures available in the ESX network and create the appropriate architecture or firewalls.

Discussion

Securing your virtual network is just as important as securing the physical network to which your ESX Servers are connected. A virtual network may be subjected to the same attacks as a physical network. Virtual machines that are isolated from a physical network could even be targets of attacks from other virtual machines within the same ESX network, so it's important to take these things into consideration when planning your ESX network configuration. In general, the security measures you use on your physical network should be replicated on your virtual network.

Within the ESX network, virtual machines that are connected on separate network segments are isolated from each other, so they cannot read from, write to, or communicate with virtual machines on a separate network unless the ESX network specifically enables such communication through vSwitches.

Some ways to add additional security are:

- Keep virtual machines isolated by using separate physical network adapters for each internal ESX network. This setup is the most secure one, because you are not sharing virtual machine traffic over the same physical network adapter.

   For example, your physical network might have an external DMZ and an internal network. By connecting those separate physical networks to separate network adapters in ESX, you physically separate the traffic. In contrast, putting those networks on a single network adapter would lead to routing of internal and external traffic over the same network adapter inside ESX, which could make the entire internal network just as vulnerable as your DMZ. Minimizing the potential attack locations will help you more easily defend your entire infrastructure.

- Use software-based firewalls inside the ESX Server's virtual network. Software-based firewalls can use Windows, Linux, or a virtual server appliance provided by a third-party vendor (*http://www.vmware.com/appliances/*) that sits between virtual machines.

- Create virtual LANs (VLANs). ESX fully supports VLAN tagging to isolate your network segments. Using VLANs allows you to route traffic from multiple networks on the same network, while keeping traffic separated by VLAN ID.

3.10 Setting the Basic Level 2 Security Policy

Problem

Establish security on your network interfaces.

Solution

Use vCenter to select the layer 2 security model that fits your environment.

Discussion

Port groups and vSwitches in ESX have a layer 2 security policy with three different parameters you can control:

Promiscuous mode
> This option gives you access to the standard operating system feature of the same name. Promiscuous mode allows the virtual machine to receive all traffic that passes by on the network.

> Although this mode can be beneficial for an administrator tracking network activities, it's a very insecure operation mode because users can see packets on the network that are designated for other systems. In other words, if enabled it would be possible for virtual machines to see other virtual machines' traffic on the same network.

> Therefore, by default, this option is set to Reject. Each virtual machine on the ESX Server receives only traffic directed to it.

Forged transmits
> This option is set to Accept by default, meaning that the ESX Server does not compare source IP addresses and MAC addresses. However, setting this to Reject causes the ESX Server to compare the source MAC address being transmitted by the operating system with the effective MAC address for its adapter.

MAC address changes
> This option is set to Accept by default, meaning that the ESX Server accepts requests to change the MAC address associated with the sender. This affects traffic that the virtual machine receives.

> If you are worried about MAC address impersonations, this can be set to Reject. However, ESX will not honor requests to change the effective MAC address to anything other than the original MAC address. More information on this setting can be found in the ESX documentation.

You can change these three settings using vCenter as follows:

1. Log into vCenter Server and select the server from the inventory list.
2. Select the Configuration tab from the right window pane and navigate to *Networking*. Any current network configurations will be displayed.
3. Click the properties link of the vSwitch you wish to modify (Figure 3-13).

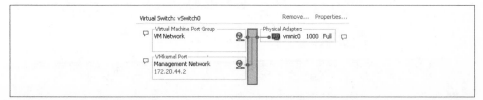

Figure 3-13. vSwitch Properties link

4. Select the vSwitch or port group you wish to modify and click the Edit button (Figure 3-14).

5. A new pop-up window will appear. Click the Security tab to change the security policy settings (Figure 3-15).

From here, you can change the options to fit your needs.

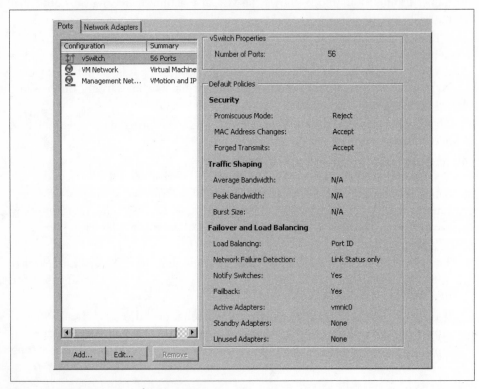

Figure 3-14. Viewing vSwitch properties

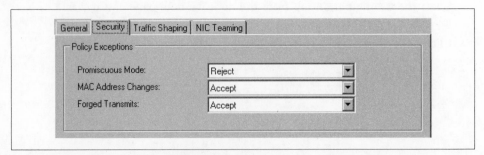

Figure 3-15. Changing security policy exceptions

3.11 Ethernet Traffic Shaping

Problem

You want to make sure that a server does not overload or hog your network.

Solution

ESX Server offers traffic shaping under the administrator's control.

Discussion

ESX Server can throttle and shape network traffic by adjusting three outbound characteristics:

Average bandwidth
> The number of bits per second to allow across the vSwitch, averaged over time.

Peak bandwidth
> The maximum amount of bandwidth in kilobits per second (kbps) the vSwitch or port group can handle. If the traffic exceeds the peak bandwidth specified, the packets will be queued for later transmission. If the queue is full, the packets will be discarded and dropped.

Burst size
> The maximum number of bytes that the port is allowed to burst. If the packet exceeds the burst size parameter, the remaining packets will be queued for later transmission. If the queue is full, the packets will be discarded and dropped. If you set the average and the peak, then this is a multiplicative factor of how long the bandwidth can exceed the average at any rate before it must come back down to the average. The higher it goes, the less time it can stay there with any particular burst size.

These values can be configured using the vCenter client on a specific port group within the vSwitch. Bandwidth shaping in ESX is currently supported only on outbound traffic; these characteristics are ignored for inbound traffic.

To make changes to the traffic shaping policy:

1. Log into vCenter Server and select the server from the inventory list.
2. Select the Configuration tab from the right window pane and navigate to *Networking*. Any current network configurations will be displayed.
3. Click the properties link of the vSwitch you wish to modify (Figure 3-16).

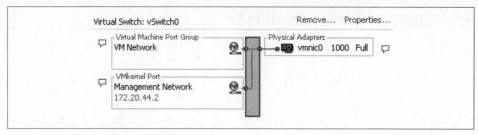

Figure 3-16. vSwitch Properties link

4. Select the vSwitch or port group you wish to modify and click the Edit button (Figure 3-17).

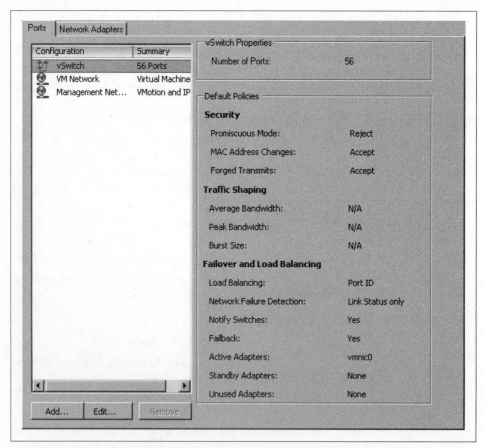

Figure 3-17. Viewing vSwitch properties

5. A new pop-up window will appear. Click the Traffic Shaping tab to change the policy exceptions (Figure 3-18).

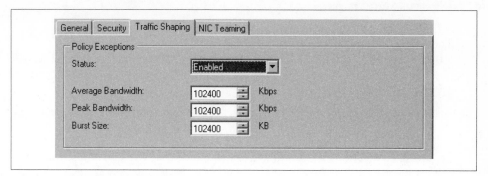

Figure 3-18. Traffic shaping enabled

6. Notice that the traffic shaping status is disabled by default. When this is disabled, you will not be able to make any changes to the various settings. To enable it, select Enabled from the status drop-down box, and the three configurable options will become available for you to modify to suit your needs.

The traffic shaping policy is then applied to each individual virtual adapter that is attached to the port group (not to the entire vSwitch).

3.12 Using Multiple Gateways

Problem

Your network has separate subnets and you need to configure multiple routes for them.

Solution

Edit the ESX 3.5 network scripts to add multiple gateways.

Discussion

Depending on the network setup for your ESX Servers, it may be necessary to add multiple gateways for different subnet masks:

1. Log into the physical console of the ESX Server and gain *root* privileges.
2. Edit or add a file named */etc/sysconfig/network-scripts/route-vswif*N (where the final N is the adapter number), where you can specify different gateways.
3. Add information like the following, altering the numbers as necessary for your network:

```
GATEWAY0=172.20.10.254
NETMASK0=255.255.255.0
```

```
ADDRESS0=10.10.10.254

GATEWAY1=172.20.20.254
NETMASK1=255.255.255.0
ADDRESS1=10.20.20.254
```

The GATEWAY variable should specify the IP address of the gateway, while the ADDRESS variable specifies the IP address of the virtual machine on the subnet. Additional entries can be created by incrementing the numbers in each GATEWAY, NETMASK, and ADDRESS variable.

4. When you are satisfied with the changes, save the file and restart networking:

```
$ /etc/init.d/network restart
```

Ensure all connections are working as intended. If not, you can adjust the file to correct the values.

3.13 Load Balancing and Failover

Problem

You want to set up multiple network adapters on a vSwitch to perform load balancing and support failover.

Solution

Set up load balancing and failure detection policies within your ESX network.

Discussion

Load balancing helps you distribute traffic evenly among network adapters, whereas failover protects you in case adapters or upstream network elements stop working. This can be particularly useful when setting up a service console network, to appease ESX's redundancy requirements for the service console.

When determining the policies that will be applied to your vSwitch, you need to consider three things:

Load-balancing policy
    Determines how outbound traffic will be distributed between the network adapters assigned to the vSwitch. It's important to understand that inbound traffic is not affected by this setting.

Network failover detection policy
    Determines how aggressively the server monitors links for failures.

Network adapter order
    Indicates which adapters are active and which are standby.

---

vCenter allows you to configure these options and a few related ones. By doing so, you can set up a load-balanced and failover-ready network within your ESX environment:

1. Log into vCenter Server and select the server from the inventory list.

2. Select the Configuration tab from the right window pane and navigate to *Networking*. Any current network configurations will be displayed.

3. Click the Properties link of the vSwitch you wish to modify (Figure 3-19).

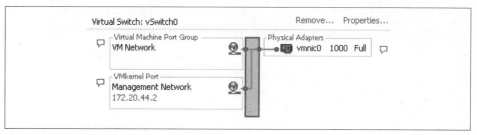

Figure 3-19. vSwitch Properties link

4. Select the vSwitch or port group you wish to modify and click the Edit button (Figure 3-20).

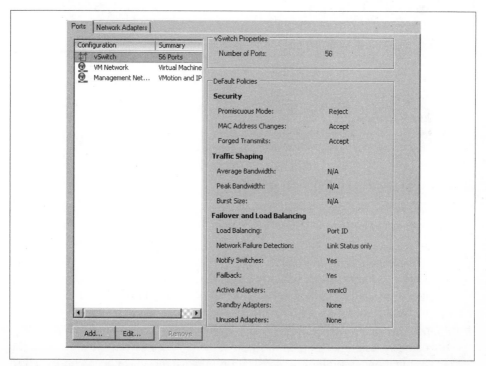

Figure 3-20. Viewing vSwitch properties

5. A new pop-up window will appear. Click the NIC Teaming tab to change the policy exceptions (Figure 3-21).

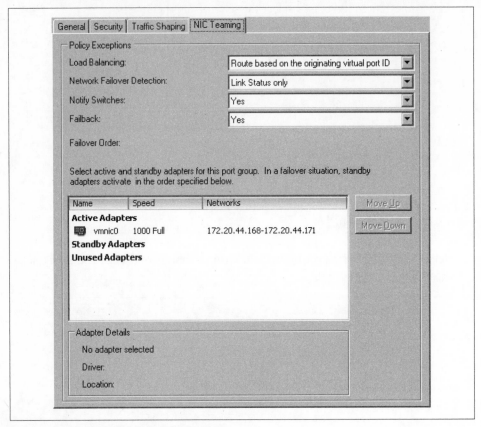

Figure 3-21. Showing the NIC teaming options

From here, the configurable options include:

Load Balancing

Allows you to choose one of four load-balancing methods:

Route based on the originating virtual port ID

Choose an uplink based on where the virtual port's traffic entered the switch. This is useful because each virtual machine has a vSwitch port ID assigned to it and the load is balanced based on that port ID. It also encompasses all protocols, including TCP and UDP.

Route based on IP hash

Choose an uplink based on the hash of the IP address from the source and the destination, assuming the physical uplink switches have been configured to use 802.3ad/LACP. This method will have some additional overhead as the packets are handled not on the virtual machine layer, but instead on the physical network.

Route based on source MAC hash

Choose an uplink based on a hash of the source MAC address. This option uses the virtual machine's MAC address for the basis of its load balancing. This can cause problems if you change your virtual machine's MAC address often or during a stream.

Use explicit failover order

Always use the first available uplink chosen in order from the list of active adapters. Using this option will not give you any load balancing, but will give you failover capabilities.

Network Failover Detection

Allows you to choose the method to be used for failover detection:

Link Status only

This method relies solely on the link status from the network adapter. It will detect an external networking error such as a bad cable or upstream switch failure, but not physical switch configuration errors.

Beacon Probing

This method sends out and listens for a beacon probe on all the NICs in the team. It will then use that information to determine whether there is a network failure. This option offers more end-to-end error checking.

Notify Switches

If this is set to Yes, in the event of a failure the server will send out a notice to the upstream switches to update their lookup tables. This is desirable, but it should not be used in conjunction with Microsoft Load Balancing in unicast mode.

Failback

Allows the originating physical adapter to fail back and take over the workload after a failure.

Failover Order

Here you can specify which physical adapters will handle the load and in which order they will do it. There are three different modes:

Active Adapters

These are used as the primary network connections, so long as the adapters are working.

Standby Adapters

These are not used until an active adapter fails, whereupon one of these takes its place.

Unused Adapters

These adapters will not be used under any circumstances.

3.14 Creating a Jumbo Frame VMkernel Interface for iSCSI

Problem

You want to improve performance through the use of jumbo frames on your software iSCSI network.

Solution

Using the console on the physical ESX Server, you can enable jumbo frames support.

Discussion

The jumbo frames feature increases the maximum frame size beyond the traditional 1,500 bytes, thus potentially reducing overhead and speeding up traffic on the link. ESX supports jumbo frames as of version 3.5. Before enabling this feature, please check with your hardware vendor to ensure it is supported.

As of ESX 3.5, the following operating systems support jumbo frames and have the enhanced *vmxnet* driver that supports the feature:

- Microsoft Windows 2003 Server with Service Pack 2
- Red Hat Enterprise Linux 5
- SuSE Enterprise Linux 10

To get jumbo frames working, you have to configure the VMkernel, the vSwitch, and each virtual machine on your server. This recipe and the next two cover these tasks.

Enable jumbo frames on a VMkernel port as follows:

1. Log into the ESX Server's console and become the *root* user.
2. Enter an `esxcfg-vmknic` command to create a VMkernel interface:

        esxcfg-vmknic -a -i *ip address* -n *netmask* -m *mtu_size port_group_name*

   The arguments you need to supply are:

   `-a`
   : Adds the VMkernel interface.

   `-i`
   : The IP address of the VMkernel interface.

   `-n`
   : The netmask of the VMkernel interface.

   `-m`
   : The MTU, which should be 9000 for jumbo frames. The default is typically 1500.

Following these options is the *port_group_name*, which is the same as the label in the vCenter client interface.

To verify that the change took place, you can enter:

```
$ esxcfg-vmknic -l
```

See Also

Recipes 3.15 and 3.16

3.15 Enabling Jumbo Frames on a vSwitch

Problem

You want to continue the task of enabling the use of jumbo frames by setting them up on your vSwitch.

Solution

Using the command line on the ESX Server, you can enable jumbo frames on the vSwitch.

Discussion

Enabling jumbo frames on a vSwitch is very similar to enabling the feature on a VMkernel port:

1. Log into the ESX Server's console and become the *root* user.
2. Enter the `esxcfg-vswitch` command to enable jumbo frames on a specific vSwitch:

   ```
   esxcfg-vswitch -m mtu_size vSwitch
   ```

   For instance, to set the MTU to the standard 9,000-byte jumbo frames size on *vswitch1*, enter:

   ```
   $ esxcfg-vswitch -m 9000 vswitch1
   ```

   This will enable the MTU of 9,000 on all uplinks for the vSwitch. To verify that the change has taken place, you can enter:

   ```
   $ esxcfg-vswitch -l
   Switch Name    Num Ports   Used Ports   Configured Ports   MTU    Uplinks
   vSwitch1       64          6            64                 9000   vmnic44
   ```

See Also

Recipes 3.14 and 3.16

3.16 Enabling Jumbo Frames on a Virtual Machine

Problem

You wish to enable jumbo frames on your virtual machines.

Solution

Using vCenter, you can enable jumbo frames on one or more virtual machines.

Discussion

To complete the configuration of jumbo frames, log into vCenter Server and perform the following steps for each virtual machine on which you wish them to be supported:

1. Select the virtual machine from the list presented to you and shut it down. Select the Summary tab, then select Edit Settings. You can also right-click on the virtual machine and select Edit Settings.

2. Select the network adapter from the hardware list and copy the MAC address that is displayed.

3. Now you must re-create the network adapter. Click the Add button and select Ethernet Adapter. Click Next. In the Adapter Type drop-down menu, select "Enhanced vmxnet." Click Next and then Finish.

4. Now that the network adapter has been re-created using the enhanced *vmxnet* driver, you need to add the old MAC address. The new NIC is still highlighted at this point. Select the network adapter from the hardware list, change the MAC address radio button to Manual, and enter the old MAC address (if you did a Ctrl-C to copy it previously you can do a Ctrl-V to paste it). Click OK to continue.

5. It's important also to enable jumbo frames on the operating system running on the virtual machine. Power on the operating system and configure jumbo frames per the instructions for that OS.

See Also

Recipes 3.14 and 3.15

3.17 Changing the Service Console IP Address

Problem

You need to change the network IP address for host management, which uses the service console.

Solution

Use the console at the physical server to change the IP address.

Discussion

In some situations you may be required to change the IP address of your service console network.

VMware has a set of tools that can be run from the physical host's console that can do the job safely, but avoid making these changes over SSH, Telnet, or vCenter unless you have multiple service consoles configured, as it will result in a disconnection of the session. Follow these steps to change the IP address:

1. Log into vCenter Server. Right-click the server whose IP address you want to change and select the option to put it into maintenance mode. The virtual machines will migrate off the ESX Server if you are in a DRS/cluster scenario. Once the server is in maintenance mode, right-click it and select Disconnect. When the disconnection is complete, select Remove to remove the server from vCenter.

2. Log into the physical console of the ESX Server and gain *root* privileges.

3. Determine which service consoles are already configured by running the following command:

   ```
   $ esxcfg-vswif -l
   Name    Port Group IP Address   Netmask       Broadcast    Enabled  DHCP
   vswif0  ServiceCon 10.10.10.10  255.255.255.0 10.10.10.255 true     false
   ```

   In our example, the service console is using the interface *vswif0*. Make a note of this parameter, along with the IP address, netmask, and broadcast address. You will need to respecify all four parameters later.

4. Remove the service console interface by running the following command, replacing *vswif0* with the interface you want to remove:

   ```
   $ esxcfg-vswif -d vswif0
   ```

5. With the service console removed, you now need to create a new one with the IP address you wish to use. Again, this can be accomplished using the esxcfg-vswif command:

   ```
   $ esxcfg-vswif -a vswif0 -p "Service Console" -i 10.10.10.20 -n 255.255.255.0
   -b 10.10.10.255
   ```

   The options have the following meanings:

   -a

   Use the interface from the original service console.

   -b

   Use the broadcast address from the original service console.

-i

Use the IP address from the original service console.

-n

Use the netmask from the original service console.

-p

Specify "Service Console".

6. If the new IP address is on another network, you will need to change the default gateway by editing the */etc/sysconfig/network* file using a text editor. If the network is the same, you can simply ignore this step and continue.

7. To ensure the new settings have taken effect, try disabling (stopping) and then re-enabling the *vswif* interface. This can be done using the `esxcfg-vswif` command, again replacing *vswif0* with the interface you previously configured.

   To disable the interface:

   ```
   $ esxcfg-vswif -s vswif0
   ```

   To enable the interface:

   ```
   $ esxcfg-vswif -e vswif0
   ```

8. You should now be able to add the ESX host back into vCenter and migrate your virtual machines to it.

3.18 Using the Command Line to Locate Physical Ethernet Adapters

Problem

You have to map the physical Ethernet adapters to the appropriate *vmnic* without using vCenter.

Solution

Use command-line commands to identify the physical Ethernet adapters.

Discussion

There may be a time when you need to identify the physical Ethernet adapters that exist in your ESX host. This can also be accomplished in vCenter by clicking on the ESX host, clicking the Configuration tab, and then clicking Networking.

To do so, log into the physical console of the ESX Server and gain *root* privileges. Then run the `esxcfg-nics` command, which displays all the physical Ethernet adapters along with their speeds, drivers, MTUs, PCI devices, *vmnics*, link status, and descriptions.

The following is an example of output on a server with 12 physical Ethernet adapters:

```
$ esxcfg-nics -l
```

```
Name     PCI       Driver    Link  Speed      Duplex  MTU    Description
vmnic47  1a:00.01  e1000     Down  0Mbps      Half    1500   Intel Corpor
vmnic0   05:00.00  bnx2      Up    1000Mbps   Full    1500   Broadcom Cor
vmnic44  19:00.00  e1000     Up    1000Mbps   Full    1500   Intel Corpor
vmnic1   07:00.00  bnx2      Up    1000Mbps   Full    1500   Broadcom Cor
vmnic49  1f:00.01  e1000     Down  0Mbps      Half    1500   Intel Corpor
vmnic45  19:00.01  e1000     Up    1000Mbps   Full    1500   Intel Corpor
vmnic48  1f:00.00  e1000     Up    100Mbps    Full    1500   Intel Corpor
vmnic46  1a:00.00  e1000     Up    1000Mbps   Full    1500   Intel Corpor
vmnic50  20:00.00  e1000     Up    100Mbps    Full    1500   Intel Corpor
vmnic2   09:00.00  bnx2      Up    1000Mbps   Full    1500   Broadcom Cor
vmnic51  20:00.01  e1000     Up    1000Mbps   Full    1500   Intel Corpor
vmnic3   0b:00.00  bnx2      Up    1000Mbps   Full    1500   Broadcom Cor
```

(The description field is cut off in this example in order to fit the output on the page.) You can then use the esxcfg-vswitch command to see which vSwitches the Ethernet adapters are assigned to:

```
$ esxcfg-vswitch -l
Switch Name     Num Ports    Used Ports   Configured Ports   MTU    Uplinks
vSwitch0        64           6            64                 1500   vmnic44,vmnic0

   PortGroup Name     VLAN ID   Used Ports   Uplinks
   Internal ESX       0         0            vmnic0,vmnic44
   Service Console    0         1            vmnic0,vmnic44
   NFS                0         1            vmnic0,vmnic44
```

See Also

Recipe 3.19

3.19 Changing the Ethernet Port Speed via the Command Line

Problem

You want to change the speed on an Ethernet port using the command line.

Solution

Use the esxcfg-nics command on the desired physical adapter.

Discussion

Although the port speed on a physical adapter is easily changed within vCenter, it's almost as important to understand how to change it using the command line, in the event that vCenter isn't available. Here's how:

1. Log into the physical console of the ESX Server and gain *root* privileges.

2. List the available adapters by following the steps in the previous recipe, and make a note of the names of the adapters you wish to change.

3. Run the `esxcfg-nics` command on each desired adapter to change the speed. For instance, the following command changes the *vmnic1* port speed to 100Mbps with the duplex set to full (you can instead set the duplex to half by specifying the `-d half` option):

   ```
   $ esxcfg-nics -s 100 -d full vmnic1
   ```

4. To verify the changes, you can run the `esxcfg-nics -l` command as outlined in the previous recipe:

   ```
   $ esxcfg-nics -l vmnic1
   ```

See Also

Recipe 3.18

3.20 Restoring a Service Console via the CLI

Problem

You need to re-create a service console network without using vCenter.

Solution

Use the command line to remove and re-create the service console network.

Discussion

There are several reasons why you might need to re-create the service console network, including changes to physical Ethernet adapters, changes to other network components inside ESX, or configuration problems.

In this situation, you need to re-create the service console network from the command line of the ESX 3.5 server. You can't use SSH or Telnet because they rely on the presence of a service console and therefore can't operate once you remove it.

Follow these steps to restore your service console via the command-line interface:

1. Log into the physical console of the ESX Server and gain *root* privileges.

2. List the current service consoles or *vswif* interfaces. The output in the following example wraps around on new lines to fit onto the page:

   ```
   $ esxcfg-vswif -l
   Name     Port Group       IP Address      Netmask
            Broadcast        Enabled   DHCP
   ```

```
vswif0    Service Console    172.20.46.1       255.255.255.0
    172.20.46.255    true      false
```

3. Delete the *vswif* interface of the service console that you want to re-create. You may have more than one *vswif* interface, so double-check that you are about to remove the correct one before you enter this command to remove it:

    ```
    $ esxcfg-vswif --del vswif0
    ```

4. You also need to delete the vSwitch, so that it can be re-created. Running the following command lists all the currently configured vSwitches so you can choose the one you wish to delete:

    ```
    $ esxcfg-vswitch -l
    Switch Name    Num Ports    Used Ports    Configured Ports    MTU      Uplinks
    vSwitch0       64           6             64                  1500     vmnic44,vmnic0

        PortGroup Name      VLAN ID    Used Ports    Uplinks
        Service Console     0          1             vmnic0,vmnic44
    ```

5. Remove the vSwitch, specifying the correct name for your system:

    ```
    $ esxcfg-vswitch -d vSwitch0
    ```

6. Once the vSwitch has been removed, you can re-create it using the -a option. Typically, you will want to re-create a vSwitch with the same name as the one you deleted in the previous steps. We deleted the vSwitch numbered *0*, so we'll re-create it here:

    ```
    $ esxcfg-vswitch -a vSwitch0
    ```

7. Next, the port group must be created on the vSwitch created in step 6. Notice the uppercase -A and the quotation marks around "Service Console", which need to be present in order for the command to run correctly:

    ```
    $ esxcfg-vswitch -A "Service Console" vSwitch0
    ```

8. Create the *vswif* adapter for the service console using the following command as an example (replace the IP address and subnet mask with your network's information):

    ```
    $ esxcfg-vswif -a vswif0 -i 172.10.45.11 -n 255.255.255.0 -p "Service Console"
    ```

9. Verify that the following file has the correct network information:

    ```
    $ cat /etc/sysconfig/network
    ```

Now, ensure that you can ping the newly created interface. If not, review the previous steps, and remember that you can always use the -h switch on any VMware command-line tool to get more options to help you troubleshoot.

## CHAPTER 4

Resource and vCenter Management

Resource management is key in any virtualized environment. In the context of VMware ESX and vSphere, resource management includes clustering, high availability (HA), and the distributed resource scheduler (DRS). This chapter takes a look at the available technologies and how they work together to help you manage your environment effectively. We'll explore:

VMware clusters

> Clusters within the ESX environment allow you to pool multiple physical ESX hosts to create a virtual pool of resources from the combined resources of all of the ESX hosts. The three main elements of VMware clustering are the DRS, fault tolerance (FT, available in ESX 4.x), and HA pieces.

VMware HA

> This provides you with a cost-effective and intelligent engine that can provide high availability within your ESX cluster. For example, if you have a four-node cluster and one node in the cluster goes down, you can configure HA to automatically start up the virtual machines from the failed node on any remaining node that has available resources.

VMware DRS

> The distributed resource scheduler actively monitors all virtual machines in a cluster and manages their resources. DRS can be configured to provide you, the administrator, with guidelines on which virtual machines can benefit from being moved to another host. You can also configure DRS to automatically take care of the migration through VMotion.

In this chapter we will discuss various aspects of these technologies and how to configure, set up, and maintain resources in vCenter.

4.1 Understanding Virtual Machine Memory Use Through Reservations, Shares, and Limits

Problem

You want to apportion memory among your virtual machines to meet specific application needs.

Solution

Specify the minimum and maximum amounts of RAM that should be available to your virtual machines.

Discussion

Much like CPU resource management, which we'll discuss later in this chapter, memory management involves configuring reservations, shares, and limits. In this recipe, we will look at each resource setting and discuss their differences:

Available memory
: Allocates a particular amount of RAM on the ESX Server to the virtual machine when it is created. This amount reflects the initial amount of memory available for the virtual machine, but the value can grow or shrink as the virtual machine takes on work and contends with other virtual machines for memory.

Memory reservations
: Set a minimum amount of memory, measured in megabytes, that will always be available for a virtual machine.

Memory shares
: Work the same as CPU shares (described in Recipe 4.3) and are specified in increments of Low (500 shares), Normal (1,000 shares), High (2,000 shares), or Custom, which allows you to enter a custom value.

Memory limits
: Allow you to set a limit on the maximum amount of RAM that the virtual machine can consume. Memory limits are measured in megabytes (MB). The memory limit on the virtual machine should be enough to satisfy the requirements of the operating system inside the virtual machine. The initial available memory limit is specified when creating the virtual machine, but it can rise in accordance with the options discussed in this chapter.

You'll start to see the benefits of using limits when you build your first virtualization cluster with a small number of virtual machines. This will allow you to manage user expectations and monitor your servers for actual usage so you can make adjustments later. However, you may notice performance degrade as you add more virtual machines to the cluster.

VMware also controls memory through the *vmmemctl* driver, which runs on a virtual machine and works with the server to reclaim unused memory and reassign it back to the resource pool for other virtual machines to utilize. This is called *ballooning* and kicks in when memory resources may be low or running out on the cluster.

Reservations help virtual machines to meet response time and workload requirements, but they can also lead to wasted idle resources. For example, if you give your virtual machine 1GB of memory but it's only using 256MB, the remaining memory will not be available to the other virtual machines to use.

A server can allocate more memory than the amount specified in a reservation, but it will never allocate more than the limit. When you use reservations and limits together, you should set the reservation for each machine to 50% of its limit and make sure it's set high enough for the operating system and applications to avoid surrender requests from the memory ballooning driver.

We recommend that you use limits only to satisfy specific needs. For other purposes, use shares instead. As with CPU shares, you can also leave the memory shares set to Normal as a base to start. However, if you have a mission-critical application that might have higher resource requirements, you can give it a High or Custom share value to ensure that the virtual machine will win the resources it needs when contention occurs.

You can set any of these memory measurements for a virtual machine as follows:

1. Load the vCenter client and log into your vCenter server.
2. Right-click on the virtual machine and select Edit Settings from the menu. This will bring up another window where you can configure the virtual machine's memory resources (see Figure 4-1).
3. Click on the Resources tab. Here you can set specific memory, CPU, advanced CPU, and disk variables. We will specifically look at the memory options, so click Memory in the lefthand menu.
4. In the righthand pane, you can specify Shares, Reservation, and Limit values for memory resources, as seen in Figure 4-1. When you've completed your configurations, click the OK button to save the changes and have them applied to the virtual machine.

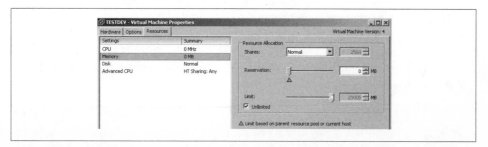

Figure 4-1. Memory resource configuration

4.2 Configuring Virtual Machine CPU Limits

Problem

You need to understand CPU limits and how to use them effectively.

Solution

Apply CPU limits using vCenter.

Discussion

CPU limiting within the ESX environment is a way to restrict the CPU consumption, measured in megahertz (MHz), for specific virtual machines. Setting a limit on a virtual machine's CPU consumption allows better management of contention issues within your environment. It also allows you to know what the CPU on that virtual machine is capable of achieving when operating at full strength.

However, setting the CPU limit too high or too low can cause performance issues on the virtual machine. The limit should be balanced such that there is enough CPU power at the machine's disposal to handle load spikes and high application usage, but not so high that CPU cycles are being wasted.

It's important to observe your virtual machines and adjust their CPU limits accordingly. For example, if you set a virtual machine's CPU limit at 1,000MHz but notice that its usage never exceeds 700MHz, you might consider adjusting the CPU limit on that virtual machine to 800MHz. By doing this, you are effectively freeing up 200MHz for other virtual machines and not wasting the cycles. That said, virtual machines' CPU usage is generally low, and the DRS will do a good job of managing those resources; if you set your virtual machine's limit to 1,000MHz the unused cycles will be put back into the pool of resources.

Adding a CPU limit to a virtual machine is simple using the vCenter client:

1. Load the vCenter client and log into your vCenter server.

2. Right-click on the virtual machine on which you wish to adjust the CPU limit and select Edit Settings from the menu. This will bring up another window in which you can configure the virtual machine's CPU limit.

3. Click on the Resources tab. From here you can set specific values for memory, CPU, advanced CPU, and disk variables. We will specifically look at the CPU limit variable in this recipe. Click the CPU option in the left window pane to configure this setting (Figure 4-2).

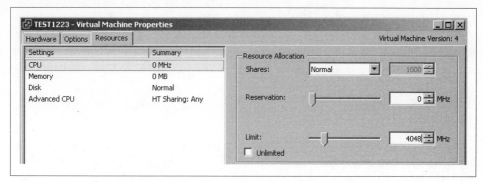

Figure 4-2. Setting a CPU limit

4. A slider bar next to the Limit label allows you to configure a CPU limit by dragging the bar; alternatively, you can enter an amount in the box or click the up and down arrows. As you can see in this example, we have given virtual machine *TEST1223* a CPU limit of 4,048MHz—all of the CPU resources available in the DRS cluster. We could achieve the same effect by checking the Unlimited box. Keeping the Unlimited box checked will allow you to also use the other variables that we will discuss later in this chapter.

Once you are satisfied, click the OK button to make the change.

See Also

Recipes 4.3 and 4.4

4.3 Configuring Virtual Machine CPU Shares

Problem

You want to apportion CPU, memory, or disk resources among machines unequally, while remaining flexible in case resources change.

Solution

Configure CPU shares using the vCenter client.

Discussion

CPU shares allow you to regulate how many competitions a virtual machine will "win" when trying to access resources within the pool. For example, when contention occurs within the ESX host or cluster, a virtual machine with 2,000 shares will receive more CPU resources than a virtual machine with, say, 1,000 shares. Shares are configured relative to the other shares; thus, only the proportion of shares matters, not the values of the shares. Three virtual machines with share values of (1,000, 2,000, 3,000) will act exactly the same as three virtual machines with share values of (1, 2, 3). You may choose to use any number scheme you prefer, although we suggest leaving ample space between the numbers to make future additions to your resource pool easier to configure within your existing scheme (this way, you won't have to renumber the share values of all or many of your existing virtual machines).

When there is no contention for resources, shares mean very little to the operations of the virtual machines.

One benefit of using shares rather than limits or reservations is that when you upgrade the ESX host's memory or CPU, you will not have to adjust the resources used by each virtual machine: because each virtual machine keeps the same number of shares, new resources will automatically be apportioned in the same ratios as the old ones.

Using shares really comes in handy when planning your environment to ensure your resource pool is balanced. Of course, you can change a virtual machine's settings at any time if you specifically have to allocate it X amount of resources, and at that point shares may not be useful.

Typically, VMware recommends that you use shares instead of setting reservations, although we will discuss setting fixed reservations in the next recipe just in case you find yourself in a situation that requires it.

Let's take a look at configuring shares on a virtual machine using the vCenter client:

1. Load the vCenter client and log into your vCenter server.
2. Right-click on the virtual machine to which you wish to assign the shares and select Edit Settings from the menu. This will bring up another window in which you can configure the virtual machine's CPU share values.
3. Click on the Resources tab. From here, you can set specific values for memory, CPU, advanced CPU, and disk variables. We will look at the CPU Shares variable in this recipe. To configure it, click the CPU option in the left window pane (Figure 4-3).

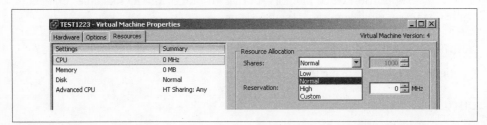

Figure 4-3. Setting CPU shares

4. In the drop-down box next to the Shares label you can choose between Low (500 shares), Normal (1,000 shares), High (2,000 shares), and Custom. Giving a virtual machine more shares increases its chances of "winning" when virtual machines compete for more CPU cycles.

   Generally, you can start with the Normal share selection until you reach a point of contention, at which point you can go back and adjust your virtual machines based on their usage and requirements.

   Once you have selected the appropriate level for your virtual machine, click the OK button to save this change.

See Also

Recipes 4.2 and 4.4

4.4 Configuring Virtual Machine CPU Reservations

Problem

You want to reserve some percentage of the CPU on the ESX Server for particular virtual machines.

Solution

Configure CPU reservations on the virtual machines using the vCenter client.

Discussion

In addition to shares and limits, you can also set *reservations* on your virtual machines. A reservation is a set number in MHz that you allocate to a particular virtual machine. Typically, this is between 5% and 10% of the processor's capacity, but it will vary based on your environment.

Setting a reservation guarantees that a certain minimum amount of resources will be available to the virtual machine, so that it can power on (if these resources do not exist or are not available, the virtual machine will not power on). Once the virtual machine is started, the reservation amount is taken away from the pool of resources over which other virtual machines compete. In other words, each of the virtual machines will take its individual reservation first, and then compete with the other virtual machines for the remainder of the (unreserved) resources.

You can add a reservation to a virtual machine through the vCenter client:

1. Load the vCenter client and log into your vCenter server.
2. Right-click the virtual machine you wish to modify and select Edit Settings from the menu. This will bring up another window, which you will use to configure the virtual machine's CPU reservation.
3. Click on the Resources tab. From here you can set specific values for memory, CPU, advanced CPU, and disk variables. We will look at the CPU Reservation variable in this recipe; to configure it, click the CPU option in the left window pane (Figure 4-4).
4. CPU reservations are the second available option. Notice there is a slider bar as well as a box in which you can specify how much CPU to allocate to the virtual machine: you can either drag the bar to the desired amount, type a value in the box, or click the up and down arrows (also shown in Figure 4-4).

   Once you have selected the appropriate level for your virtual machine, click the OK button to save this change.

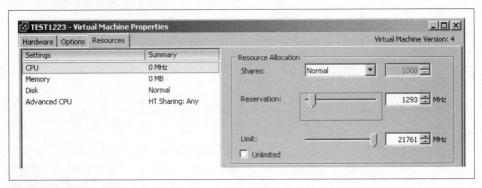

Figure 4-4. Setting CPU reservations

See Also

Recipes 4.2 and 4.3

4.5 Setting Up Resource Pools

Problem

You want to group virtual machines and manage the allocation of resources to various groups.

Solution

Create resource pools and assign resources to them.

Discussion

Resource pools are a great way to manage and divide resources among groups or departments within your organization.

Before resource pools can be enabled on a cluster you will need to ensure DRS is enabled (see Recipe 4.10).

To enable a resource pool on a cluster, log into your vCenter server and follow these steps:

1. Right-click on the cluster in which you wish to create the resource pool and choose "New Resource Pool" (Figure 4-5).

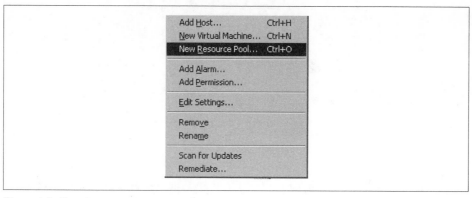

Figure 4-5. Creating a new resource pool

2. You will now be presented with a new window from which you can configure the resource pool (Figure 4-6).

    The CPU and memory resource allocations for the resource pool work similarly to the way they work for virtual machines. For example, we have given this resource pool a reservation of 12,066MB of memory and 12,066MHz of CPU. Because we left the Expandable option checked, the pool can burst above the 12,066MHz reservation if required and if the resources are available in the cluster. Refer to Recipes 4.6 and 4.7 for more detailed information.

    You can adjust these values to suit your needs and divide your resource pools between production, development, etc.

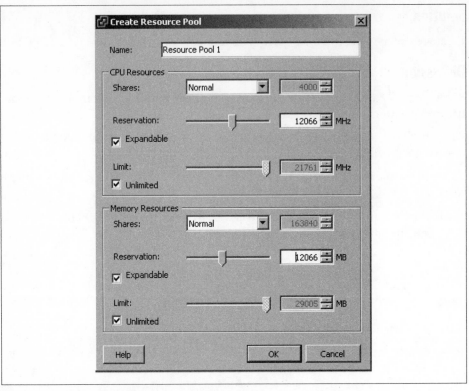

Figure 4-6. Setting values on the new resource pool

3. When you're finished, click the OK button and the resource pool will be added.

Adding new virtual machines to the resource pool can be done in two ways:

- By dragging the virtual machine into the resource pool in the vCenter client
- By placing a new virtual machine into an existing resource pool when you create the virtual machine

See Also

Recipe 4.6

4.6 Understanding Resource Pools

Problem

You want to understand how resource pools work and what capabilities they offer.

Solution

Investigate the various resource pool options and how to utilize them.

Discussion

Resource pools can be used to create partitions of available CPU and memory. By using resource pools, you can better manage and utilize resources across different departments or within a group of servers.

For example, perhaps you want to give your production team 20GHz of CPU and 20GB of memory, and your development team 10GHz of CPU and 10GB of memory. You can accomplish this by creating resource pools and assigning the virtual machines for the given departments to their respective pools (Figure 4-7).

Figure 4-7. Example resource pool layout

Notice that in Figure 4-7 we have a master resource pool called *General* and two sub-resource pools called *Development* and *Production*. In this configuration, the subresource pools are assigned resources from the master (General) resource pool. In this example, the Development and Production subresource pools have been assigned the amounts shown in Figure 4-8.

CPU Reservation:	0 MHz	Memory Reservation:	0 MB
CPU Reservation Used:	17667 MHz	Memory Reservation Used:	20964 MB
CPU Unreserved:	4094 MHz	Memory Unreserved:	8041 MB
CPU Reservation Type:	Expandable	Memory Reservation Type:	Expandable

View: CPU Memory

Name	Reservation - MHz	Limit - MHz	Shares	Shares Value	% Shares	Type	App Owner
Development	12496	Unlimited	Normal	4000	50	Expandable	
Production	5171	Unlimited	Normal	4000	50	Expandable	

Figure 4-8. Example resource pool reservations

Let's take a closer look at the reservations we've given each resource pool:

General resource pool
> The General resource pool has 4,094MHz and 8,041MB of unreserved resources available for the development and production subpools to use. It is not handed out all at once at the start, but rather is made available as needed (see the next recipe for details).

Development subresource pool
> We have given the Development resource pool a total of 12,496MHz of reserved CPU.

Production subresource pool
> The Production resource pool has only 5,171MHz of reserved CPU.

In this example, if the resources required by the Production pool exceed 5,171MHz of CPU, it will borrow resources from the master resource pool, which has 4,094MHz available.

See Also

Recipes 4.5, 4.7, and 4.10

4.7 Expandable Reservations in Resource Pools

Problem

You want to understand expandable reservations.

Solution

Investigate expandable reservations and when and how they should be used.

Discussion

Expandable reservations give extra flexibility when you allocate resources to a specific resource pool. You can assign a minimum set of resources to each subresource pool and allow it, by defining the reservation as Expandable, to get more resources from the ESX Server as needed. Thus, on a day when the development team is racing to do a lot of bug fixing to meet a deadline, its subresource pool may expand beyond the normal limits. On another day, the production subresource pool may get more resources.

However, be aware that once a reservation has been exceeded/expanded, those additional resources will not be freed up again until the virtual machine is shut down and you explicitly reduce its reservation. You should also be careful when using expandable resource pools to ensure that your virtual machines do not become dependent on extra resources being available. If a subresource pool routinely expands far beyond its original allocation, you should increase the original allocation and add more hardware resources if necessary.

Notice that in Figure 4-9 we have two resource pools, Development and Production, which are each set to Expandable. Examining this figure further, you'll see that we have 4,094MHz of CPU and 8041MB of memory unreserved at the top level of our resource pool. Since both of our subresource pools are set to Expandable, when they use the reservations we have set for them they can borrow from the unreserved values available in the top-level resource pool.

CPU Reservation:		0 MHz	Memory Reservation:				0 MB
CPU Reservation Used:		17667 MHz	Memory Reservation Used:				20964 MB
CPU Unreserved:		4094 MHz	Memory Unreserved:				8041 MB
CPU Reservation Type:		Expandable	Memory Reservation Type:				Expandable

View: CPU Memory

Name	Reservation - MHz	Limit - MHz	Shares	Shares Value	% Shares	Type	App Owner
Development	12496	Unlimited	Normal	4000	50	Expandable	
Production	5171	Unlimited	Normal	4000	50	Expandable	

Figure 4-9. Expandable resource pools

Expandable reservations also come in handy when a resource pool has used all its resources and a virtual machine needs to be powered on: if the resource pool has no available resources left, it can borrow resources from the top-level pool to ensure that the virtual machine can be powered on.

Let's look at how to configure expandable reservations on a resource pool:

1. Load the vCenter client and log into your vCenter server.

2. Right-click on the resource pool you wish to edit and select Edit Settings (Figure 4-10).

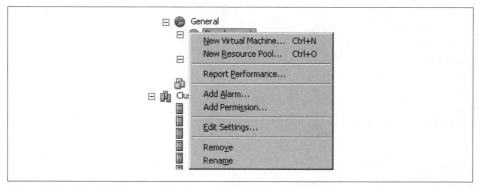

Figure 4-10. Editing a resource pool

3. The Edit Settings screen (Figure 4-11) lets you adjust the memory and CPU resources reserved for the selected resource pool. Notice that you can set expandable reservations on both CPU and memory resources, independently. To enable expandable resources, put a check in the Expandable box.

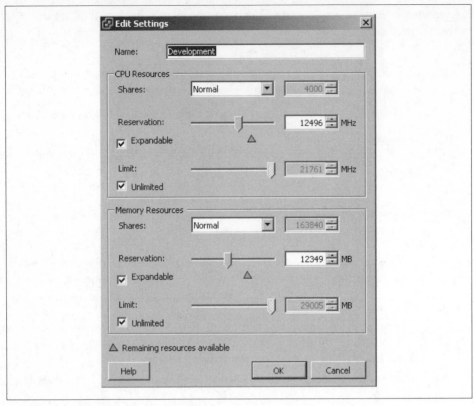

Figure 4-11. Editing expandable reservations

Once you're finished, click OK to have the changes applied.

See Also

Recipe 4.5

4.8 Creating a Cluster

Problem

You want to create a cluster to manage the resources offered by multiple ESX Servers together.

Solution

Use the vCenter client to create a VMware cluster.

Discussion

Creating a cluster inside vCenter allows you to combine multiple ESX hosts in a centralized group, placing all of their CPU and memory resources into a general pool for use by virtual machines. When you add an ESX host to a cluster, the resources will automatically become available for use by the virtual machines.

For example, Figure 4-12 shows six ESX hosts, each of which has 64GB of memory and two quad-core CPUs (i.e., eight CPUs per ESX host, for a total of 48). Because clustering pools the resources, you effectively have an enormous unified pool of CPUs and memory for the virtual machines to run. Combining a cluster with HA and DRS will further enhance your environment.

General	
VMware DRS:	**Enabled**
VMware HA:	**Enabled**
VMware EVC mode:	**Disabled**
Total CPU Resources:	**114 GHz**
Total Memory:	**384 GB**
Number of Hosts:	**6**
Total Processors:	**48**
Number of Virtual Machines:	**100**
Total Migrations:	**1707**

Figure 4-12. VMware cluster overview

 You do not need a license to create ESX clusters. However, to take advantage of HA and DRS you will need to obtain a license key from VMware.

VMware allows for a maximum of 16 ESX hosts in a vCenter 2.5x cluster. In vCenter 4.x you can have up to 32 ESX hosts in a cluster.

VMware has done a really nice job of making it simple to add a new cluster in vCenter:

1. Load the vCenter client and log into your vCenter server.
2. Right-click on the datacenter name and select New Cluster, as shown in Figure 4-13.

   The New Cluster wizard will launch to guide you through the process of creating the new cluster. The first screen in the wizard will ask you to enter a name for the cluster and indicate whether or not to enable two features:

VMware HA

This feature is available only to users who have a license for the HA product extension. When you enable VMware HA, it will detect and provide rapid recovery of virtual machines if an ESX host fails. This is an optional feature and doesn't need to be enabled to create a basic cluster.

VMware DRS

This feature also requires a license. DRS allows vCenter server to manage hosts as an aggregate pool of resources. Clusters can be broken down into smaller groups by using resource pools. VMware DRS also allows vCenter to manage resources on virtual machines, even placing them on different hosts if used in conjunction with VMotion. This is an optional feature that is not required to create a cluster.

When you've made your selections, press the Next button to continue. Additional cluster features (including DRS and HA) can be enabled or disabled at a later time using processes described elsewhere in this chapter.

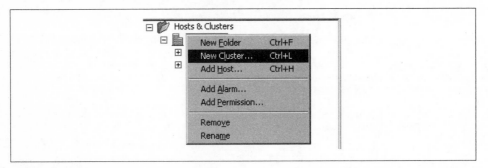

Figure 4-13. Adding a new cluster to a datacenter

3. Next, you will be asked where to store the swapfiles for the virtual machines. VMware gives you two options here:

   • Store the swapfile in the same directory as the virtual machine. (Recommended.)

   • Store the swapfile in the datastore specified by the host. (This option is not recommended because you could experience degraded performance.)

   Make your selection, then press the Next button to continue.

4. Finally, review the summary and click Finish to initiate the build of the cluster.

You can now add ESX hosts to the cluster (see Recipe 4.9).

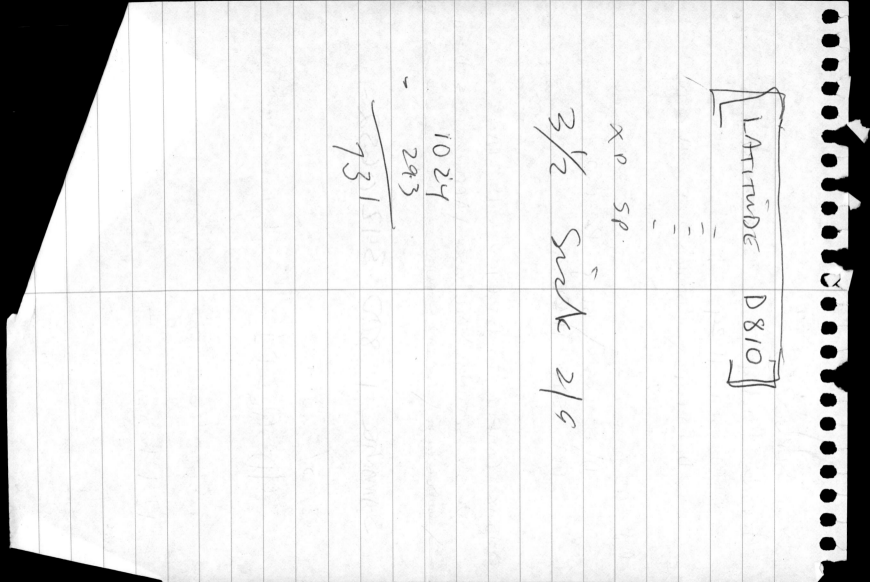

LATITUDE D810

3½ Smile 2/5

x° 50

1024
- 293
73 | 15 | 2

WEB SERVER -

Acronis Backup   Network aware

Every Sat. 11:29

D: Backups / SW00016 / SFTP server Tob

My SQL Backup -   Network aware

D/ Backups / Blog Backup

Fri Sat 11:00

Sysax Config To Back up is in

Docs & Settings / All users / Applications Data

/ Code origin / sysax server

Symantec | 800 342 0652 -

7/6/2010

9DSQ7DJ   Lee Stewart

866-461-3355

- 124 165 818 -

See Also

Recipes 4.9 and 4.10

4.9 Adding Hosts to a Cluster

Problem

You wish to add more hosts to your ESX cluster.

Solution

Use the vCenter client to add new hosts to an existing ESX cluster.

Discussion

Adding additional ESX Servers to an already established cluster is easy in vCenter:

1. Load the vCenter client and log into your vCenter server.

2. Right-click on the datacenter name and select Add Host. This launches the Add Host wizard in a new window (Figure 4-14).

   The first screen in the Add Host wizard will ask you for some basic information:

   Hostname
   > Enter the hostname of the server, such as *esx01.yourdomain.com*. Although ESX allows you to use an IP address, you should *always* use a fully qualified domain name as the hostname to ensure maximum compatibility, as ESX relies heavily on DNS.

   Username
   > Enter the username of the user who has administrative privileges. Typically this is the *root* user, although this can be changed if required.

   Password
   > Enter the password for the username just entered.

   When you are satisfied with your entries, click the Next button.

3. Next, you will be presented with an informational summary showing you the name, model, version, and vendor of the host that is being added and listing any virtual machines on that host. Click Next to continue.

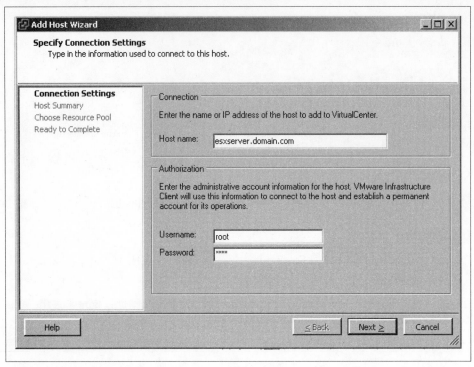

Figure 4-14. Adding your IP address and login information in the Add Host wizard

4. If you are adding an ESX host, skip to step 5. If you are adding an ESXi host, at
   this point you will be asked whether you want to enable lockdown mode (Figure 4-15).

   Lockdown mode, when enabled, prevents remote users from logging into the ESXi
   host using administrative accounts such as *root* or *admin*. If this mode is enabled
   and no other accounts exist, the ESXi host can be managed only from vCenter.
   However, the administrative accounts will be able to log into the console on the
   ESXi host. This feature can be changed at a later time, so if you are unsure you can
   leave it unchecked and enable lockdown mode later, if security becomes a concern.

   Click Next to continue the installation.

5. The next screen in the wizard is the resource pool configuration screen. You will
   be presented with two options, as shown in Figure 4-16. These options are pretty
   self-explanatory, but we'll take a quick look at them anyway:

   *"Put all of this host's virtual machines into the cluster's root resource pool. Resource
   pools currently present on the host will be deleted."*

   Assuming you have a resource pool set up in your cluster, this option will take
   all the virtual machines from the single ESX resource pool and move them into
   the cluster's pool. Once that operation is completed, it will remove the

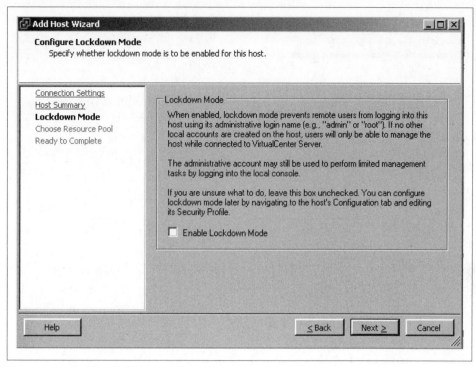

Figure 4-15. Enabling lockdown mode on ESXi

resource pools from the single ESX Server. Be careful here—remember that the virtual machines currently in the pool are getting their resources based on their pool's settings, and adding virtual machines to the pool could take resources away from the existing virtual machines.

"Create a new resource pool for this host's virtual machines and resource pools. This preserves the host's current resource pool hierarchy."

This option allows you to keep the resource pools you have already set up on your single ESX host. It will create new resource pools within the cluster that match those currently available on the ESX host.

Once you have selected which resource pool option you want to use, click the Next button to continue.

6. You will now be presented with a summary. Use the Back button if you need to make any changes, and when you're satisfied click the Finish button to add the ESX host to the cluster.

If HA is enabled on the cluster in which the host is being added, the host will automatically be configured for HA. If you are not adding the host to an HA cluster, the host will run standalone.

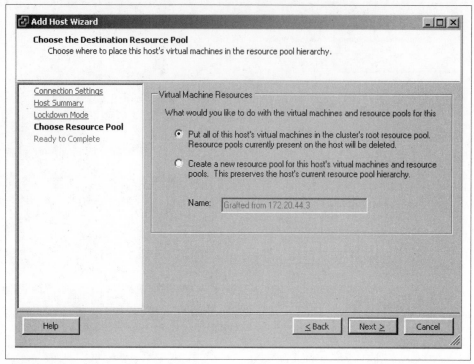

Figure 4-16. Resource pool settings

See Also

Recipe 4.8

4.10 Enabling DRS in a Cluster

Problem

You wish to enable DRS in your current cluster.

Solution

Use the vCenter client tool to enable DRS.

Discussion

Enabling DRS inside an already created cluster is easy using the vCenter client. If you have VMware Infrastructure 3 Enterprise, DRS is integrated already. With the standard version of VMware Infrastructure, DRS is an optional add-on. Regardless of which version you have, we'll walk you through the steps of enabling DRS and explain the different settings along the way:

1. Load the vCenter client and log into your vCenter server.

2. Right-click on your cluster and select Edit Settings from the menu. This will bring up another window with configuration options for the cluster. We are going to be looking at the General area as well as the VMware DRS area and its subsections.

3. Click the General label in the lefthand window. You will now be able to rename your cluster and enable or disable HA and DRS on the cluster (Figure 4-17). Put a check next to "Enable VMware DRS."

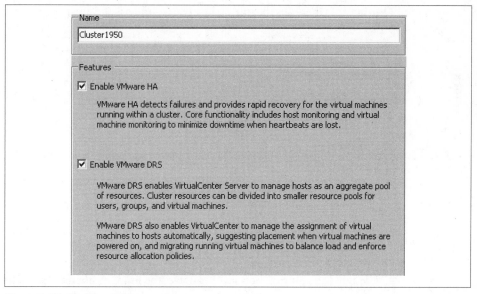

Figure 4-17. Enabling DRS on a cluster

4. Click the General label in the lefthand window. You will now be able to rename your cluster and enable or disable HA and DRS on the cluster (Figure 4-17). Put a check next to "Enable VMware DRS."

5. Click on the VMware DRS item in the menu tree on the left and you will be presented with a choice between three different automation levels (Figure 4-18).

   The choices are:

   Manual
   When you power on a virtual machine, DRS will display a list of suggested hosts for placement. Also, if it determines that there is a better host for a virtual machine, DRS will suggest migration through a manual migration.

Partially automated

> When you power on a virtual machine, DRS will automatically put it on the host it feels is the best. As with the manual level of automation, when a cluster node becomes unbalanced DRS will give you a list of suggested hosts for placement of the virtual machine(s).

Fully automated

> When you power on a virtual machine, DRS will automatically place it on the most suitable host. When a cluster becomes unbalanced, DRS will automatically start the VMotion process and automatically move the virtual machine(s) without involving the system administrator.

The migration threshold, shown below the automation options, is based on a star system of 1 through 5, where 1 is the most conservative and 5 is the most aggressive:

Level 1

> This is the most conservative level of automation and applies only to 5-star recommendations.

Level 2

> This level of automation applies to recommendations with 4 or more stars and aims to improve the cluster's load balance.

Level 3

> This is the default level of automation and applies to recommendations with 3 or more stars.

Level 4

> This level of automation applies to 2 or more stars.

Level 5

> This is the most aggressive method of automation and applies to recommendations with any number of stars.

Essentially, the higher the automation level you use, the more minor and frequent migrations you will see if DRS deems improvements can be made. A less aggressive selection will result in changes only when DRS deems that they will make a large improvement to the cluster's load balance.

Within the DRS environment you can also set a *per-virtual-machine automation level*, which will override the automation level set on the entire cluster. By setting the automation levels on this more granular basis, you can fine-tune your cluster for your specific needs (Figure 4-19).

Another important feature of DRS is the ability to set rules and guidelines for virtual machines within the cluster. Along with the star system, these affect the choices made by DRS. You can specify two kinds of rules for your virtual machines:

- *Affinity rules* allow you to specify certain virtual machines that should be run on the same host and in multi-virtual-machine environments when better performance can be achieved by such a configuration. For example, machines that communicate frequently may perform better when run on the same host.

- *Anti-affinity rules* allow you to force virtual machines to run on separate hosts. This can be important when you have two servers that are in a failover or load-balancing environment and you want them to *always* run on separate ESX nodes in the cluster.

In Figure 4-20, we have set an anti-affinity rule telling DRS that we want the virtual machines *TESTDEV* and *TEST1223* to run on separate physical ESX nodes. DRS will always ensure that those virtual machines are separate from one another.

Some tips about using DRS follow:

- When removing a host from a cluster, always put that host in maintenance mode.
- When you have your automation level set to Manual and DRS makes strong recommendations (typically level 4 or 5), follow them. Otherwise, balance and fairness within the cluster will deteriorate.
- Let DRS automatically handle most virtual machines, and set the override on virtual machines you do not want DRS to automatically handle.

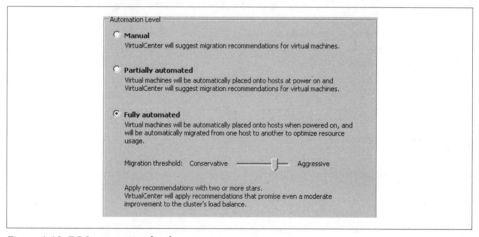

Figure 4-18. DRS automation levels

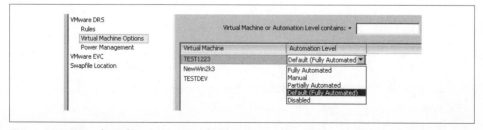

Figure 4-19. Virtual machine automation levels

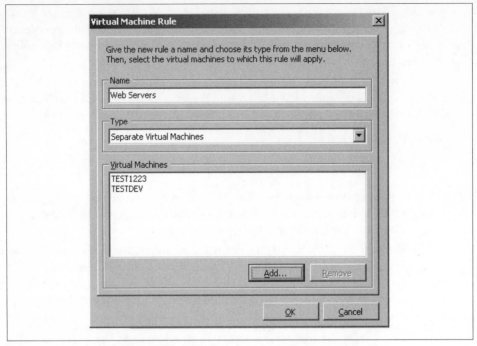

Figure 4-20. Virtual machine DRS rules

4.11 Understanding Cluster States and Warnings

Problem

You need to know the different states and warnings possible within a cluster.

Solution

Familiarize yourself with the various states in vCenter and what they mean.

Discussion

VMware has three separate warnings that give the administrator basic information about the state of the cluster, virtual machine, or ESX host.

For example, if there is no network redundancy on the service console port, you will see a yellow triangle on your cluster. The detailed configuration issues will then be listed on the Summary tab of the cluster, telling you what configuration warnings exist.

Let's take a look at the three different statuses that VMware provides for clusters:

Green (valid)

Clusters are considered valid as long as they have no configuration issues, resource overcommitments, or failed ESX hosts. A valid cluster will have a working configuration and all resources will be available for use by the virtual machines. In addition to all the resources being available, a valid cluster will also have one host available for standby in case an ESX host fails.

A cluster can become invalid or overcommitted if a single or multiple hosts fail. A cluster can also become invalid if vCenter is unable to power on a virtual machine, if an HA cluster's capacity is lower than the configured failover, or if the primary hosts in the cluster do not respond in a timely fashion to HA heartbeat checks.

Yellow (overcommitted)

This warning shows a potential risk of resources. For example, removing a host from the cluster might cause the reserve of available resources to fall below the level needed by the virtual machines. Minor configuration issues, such as no network redundancy on the service port network group, may also trigger this status.

Red (invalid)

A cluster can become invalid when there are not enough resources available to handle all the virtual machines in the cluster. Clusters can also become invalid because of configuration issues such as HA becoming disabled on an ESX host or one of the ESX hosts in the cluster going down without being properly taken offline in vCenter (and thereby taking away necessary resources).

Depending on the type of failure that causes the cluster to become invalid, you may attempt to resolve the issue by adding more resources, reconfiguring HA on the ESX host, or powering off unneeded virtual machines so that the resource requirements of the other virtual machines can be satisfied.

It's very important to remedy an invalid cluster as soon as possible to avoid the cluster becoming imbalanced.

4.12 Reconfiguring HA on a Host

Problem

You want to reconfigure VMware HA on a single host.

Solution

Use vCenter to reconfigure HA on the desired host.

Discussion

At times, such as after an upgrade or change to the cluster, HA may become unavailable or just stop working on your ESX host.

Using the vCenter client, you can easily repair the host by following these few steps:

1. Log into vCenter server and select the server from the inventory list.
2. Right-click on the server on which you wish to reconfigure HA and select "Reconfigure for VMware HA" from the menu (Figure 4-21). This will initiate a reinstallation of the HA scripts on the ESX host.

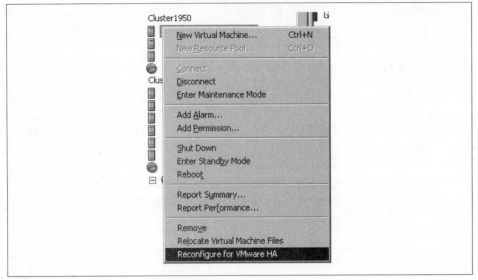

Figure 4-21. Reconfiguring VMware HA

The reconfiguration process typically takes one to two minutes, depending on how busy the server is and the quality of the network connections. When the process starts you will see an item in the Recent Tasks area at the bottom of the vCenter client window, showing you the status of the reconfiguration (Figure 4-22).

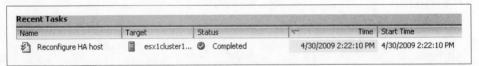

Figure 4-22. Showing reconfiguration of HA in the Recent Tasks list

Reconfiguration processes sometimes fail. If this is the case, the status field will display "An error occurred during configuration of the HA Agent on the host." If this happens, simply reinitiate the reconfiguration using the steps outlined in this section to solve the problem.

4.13 Using ESX 4.x CPU/RAM Hot Add/Hotplug Support

Problem

You want to add more CPUs or memory to a virtual machine.

Solution

Utilizing technology within VMware ESX 4.x, you can add CPUs, memory, and devices to a virtual machine while it is running.

Discussion

vSphere 4.x Enterprise, Enterprise Plus, and Advanced customers have the ability to hotplug or hot add CPUs, memory, and devices to their virtual machines without powering them off. These new technologies illustrate the improvements VMware is making in its products in an effort to reduce downtime on mission-critical applications and servers.

Hot add support in ESX 4.x is limited to a specific set of guest operating systems: Windows Server 2003; Windows Vista; Windows Server 2008; Windows 7; Red Hat Linux 4.x and 5.x; SLED 9, 10, and 11; and Ubuntu 6.x, 7.x, and 8.x. For complete details on the OSs supported, please refer to the Guest Operating System Installation Guide found on VMware's website (*http://vmware.com/pdf/GuestOS_guide.pdf*).

To enable hot add support on a virtual machine:

1. Log into your vCenter server, right-click on the virtual machine on which you wish to enable support, and select Edit Settings.
2. Click Advanced and select Memory/CPU Hotplug.
3. Select "Enable memory hot add" for the virtual machine, and then select "Hot add CPU support" for the virtual machine.
4. Click OK when you're finished to finalize the changes.

 VMware Tools must be installed on the guest OS for this procedure to work correctly.

4.14 Surviving a vCenter Server Failure or Outage

Problem

Your vCenter server has gone down or refuses to start, and you want to continue operations until the problem can be fixed.

Solution

This recipe discusses what pieces of ESX will continue to run when your vCenter server is down or offline.

Discussion

When your vCenter server needs an upgrade or maintenance, or when it suffers a crash, it's important to know what pieces of the environment can and will function without the benefit of a vCenter server orchestrating and managing the various resources within the environment.

When the vCenter server is offline, your virtual machines will continue to function, along with HA. However, other key pieces will be unavailable or will work in a degraded mode. Tables 4-1 through 4-8 list the impacts that a vCenter server outage can have on an environment.

Table 4-1. vCenter server outage effects on VMware HA

VI function	Available	Comment
Restart virtual machine	Yes	No impact
Admission control	No	vCenter is required as the source of the load information
Add new host to cluster	No	vCenter is required to resolve IP addresses of cluster members
Allow hosts to rejoin the cluster	Yes	Resolved host information is stored on the ESX host itself in */etc/FT_HOST*

Table 4-2. vCenter server outage effects on VMware DRS

VI function	Available	Comment
Manual	No	Requires vCenter to manage
Automatic	No	Requires vCenter to manage
Affinity rules	No	Requires vCenter to manage

Table 4-3. vCenter server outage effects on resource pools

VI function	Available	Comment
Create	No	Requires vCenter to manage
Add VM	No	Requires vCenter to manage
Remove VM	No	Requires vCenter to manage

Table 4-4. vCenter server outage effects on VMotion

VI function	Available	Comment
VMotion	No	Requires vCenter to manage

Table 4-5. vCenter server outage effects on ESX host

VI function	Available	Comment
Shutdown	Degraded	Through a direct connection to the ESX host server only
Startup	Yes	Expires within 14 days
Maintenance mode	Degraded	Requires vCenter to manage
Deregister	No	Requires vCenter to manage
Register	No	Requires vCenter to manage

Table 4-6. vCenter server outage effects on virtual machine

VI function	Available	Comment
Power on	Degraded	Expires in 14 days; direct connection to ESX host server only
Power off	Degraded	Direct connection to ESX host server only
Register	No	Requires vCenter to manage
Deregister	No	Requires vCenter to manage
Hot migration	No	Requires vCenter (VMotion)
Cold migration	Degraded	Within the same ESX host only

Table 4-7. vCenter server outage effects on templates

VI function	Available	Comment
Convert from virtual machine	Degraded	Direct connection to host only; requires vCenter to manage
Convert to virtual machine	Degraded	Direct connection to host only; requires vCenter to manage
Deploy virtual machine	No	Requires vCenter to manage

Table 4-8. vCenter server outage effects on virtual machine (guest)

VI function	Available	Comment
Guest OS (virtual machine)	Yes	No impact, will run without vCenter

## CHAPTER 5

Useful Command-Line Tools

Many important VMware-related tips will take you from vCenter to the console. Along with other things in this chapter, we'll examine some important command-line utilities that will aid you in monitoring and configuring your ESX Server, and we'll take a look at general best practices for setting up services that will be crucial to your ESX Server.

5.1 Entering Maintenance Mode via the Command Line

Problem

You are unable to access your vCenter GUI and you want to put your ESX Server into maintenance mode.

Solution

Log into your ESX host via SSH or directly from the console.

Discussion

To enter maintenance mode, use this command:

```
vimsh -n -e /hostsvc/maintenance_mode_enter
```

To exit maintenance mode, enter:

```
vimsh -n -e /hostsvc/maintenance_mode_exit
```

These commands are undocumented and unsupported by VMware. However, they work correctly in ESX 3.x. Alternatively, you can use the VI Perl ToolKit to initiate maintenance mode via the API provided by VMware.

5.2 Displaying Server Information

Problem

You want to display current information about your ESX Server.

Solution

Run the `esxcfg-info` command on the ESX Server.

Discussion

This command-line tool is a powerful yet simple way to find out about your ESX Server and its environment. By using the `esxcfg-info` command, you can get detailed information about your configuration and server hardware:

```
$ esxcfg-info -h
Usage: esxcfg-info mode
  -a, --all         Print all information
  -w, --hardware    Print hardware information
  -r, --resource    Print resource information
  -s, --storage     Print storage information
  -n, --network     Print network information
  -y, --system      Print system information
  -o, --advopt      Print advanced options
  -u, --hwuuid      Print hardware uuid
  -b, --bootuuid    Print boot partition uuid
  -e, --boottype    Print boot type
  -c, --cmdline     Print vmkernel command line
  -F, --format      Print the information in the given format
                    Valid values are "xml" and "perl"
  -h, --help        Print this message.
```

The options can be entered in any combination to display the specified information. If you run the `esxcfg-info` command alone or with the `-a` switch, it will dump all values. The following example displays the first few lines of output on one of our systems:

```
$ esxcfg-info | more
+Host :
  \==+Hardware Info :
     |----BIOS UUID...............................................0x44 0x45 0x4c
0x4c 0x34 0x0 0x10 0x38 0x80 0x56 0xb6 0xc0 0x4f 0x4b 0x46 0x31
     |----Product Name............................................PowerEdge R900
     |----Vendor Name.............................................Dell Inc.
     |----Serial Number...........................................XXXXXXXX
     |----Hardware Uptime.........................................1762529093951
..............
```

The information you can gather about your system from this command is so comprehensive that you may wish to export it to a text file, like this:

```
esxcfg-info > esxcfginfo12102008.txt
```

The -F option will also let you export the data in XML or Perl. This can be useful if you wish to parse the output and store it in a proprietary or third-party application.

An example of exporting network and storage information in XML format follows (we've truncated the output in this example to save space):

```
$ esxcfg-info -s -n -F xml | more

<network-info>
    <value name="current-max-virtual-switches" type="uint32"
        format="dec">128</value>
    <value name="next-reboot-max-virtual-switches" type="uint32"
        format="dec">128</value>
    <console-nic-info>
        <console-nics>
            <vswif>
                <value name="name" type="string">vswif0</value>
                <value name="port-group" type="string">Service Console</value>
                <value name="port-id" type="uint32" format="dec">16777221</value>
                <value name="enabled" type="bool">true</value>
                <value name="exists" type="bool">true</value>
                <value name="mac-address" type="string">00:50:56:41:a6:93</value>
                <value name="mtu" type="uint32" format="dec">1500</value>
                <configured-ip-settings>
                    <value name="type" type="string">Static</value>
                    <value name="ipv4-address" type="string">172.20.46.2</value>
                    <value name="ipv4-netmask" type="string">255.255.255.0</value>
                    <value name="ipv4-broadcast" type="string">172.20.46.255</value>
                    <value name="valid-config" type="bool">true</value>
                </configured-ip-settings>
                <actual-ip-settings>
                    <value name="type" type="string">Static</value>
                    <value name="ipv4-address" type="string">172.20.46.2</value>
                    <value name="ipv4-netmask" type="string">255.255.255.0</value>
                    <value name="ipv4-broadcast" type="string">172.20.46.255</value>
                    <value name="valid-config" type="bool">true</value>
                </actual-ip-settings>
            </vswif>
        </console-nics>
    </console-nic-info>
```

5.3 Viewing the ESX Version

Problem

You want to find the version of ESX you are running. This may be needed for a variety of reasons, such as upgrading or support issues.

Solution

There are multiple ways to find the version of ESX you are running. Two easy ways we'll cover are:

- Displaying it within vCenter
- Creating a report

Discussion

To find the version of ESX that you are running within vCenter, click on your ESX host. The version will be displayed to the right of the hostname. For instance, Figure 5-1 shows we are running ESX 3.5.0 build 123630.

Figure 5-1. Displaying the ESX version in vCenter

If you need to store the version, you can generate a report within vCenter. Choose File→Report→Host Summary and save the file. The results include version information.

5.4 Changing the Virtual Disk from BusLogic to LSI Logic

Problem

You need to change the virtual disk SCSI driver after a physical-to-virtual conversion.

Solution

Use vCenter to make the change.

Discussion

After using VMware's Converter application, you may notice that your virtual machine's SCSI controller has switched from LSI Logic to BusLogic. This is because on some OSs—notably, Windows 2003—the VMware Converter automatically uses the BusLogic driver, unlike when you create a new virtual machine using the vCenter client, which uses an LSI Logic driver. The LSI Logic driver offers better performance, so it's a good idea to switch back:

1. Log into your vCenter server, navigate to the virtual machine whose bus/controller you wish to change, and power it off.

2. Once the virtual machine is powered off, click the tab labeled Summary, then click Edit Settings.

3. A new window will appear (Figure 5-2). Click on the "SCSI Controller 0" option listed under the Hardware tab.

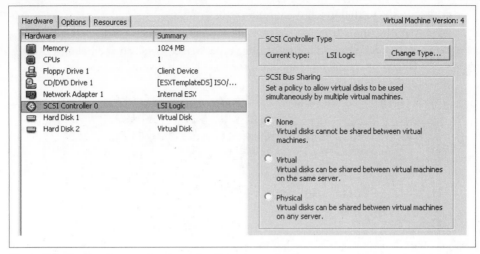

Figure 5-2. Configuring your hardware in vCenter

4. Click the Change Type button on the right side of the screen. A new window will appear, in which you can change your SCSI controller type (Figure 5-3). Choose the type you wish to switch to (in this case, LSI Logic). A warning will pop up saying that changing the controller may have unexpected results when the virtual machine boots.

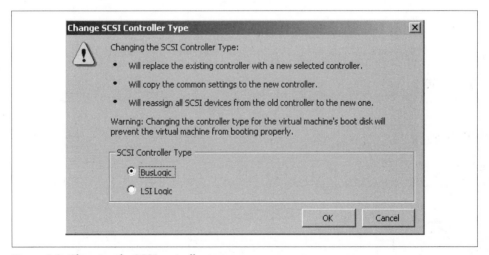

Figure 5-3. Changing the SCSI controller type

5. To complete the process, press the OK button. Then, on the Settings screen, press the OK button again. VMware will make the changes needed and convert the virtual machine to the new SCSI controller type.

6. Power on the virtual machine to finalize the changes.

7. A Virtual Machine Question screen will pop up, warning you that you should be cautious when changing the controller type. Select Yes, and then click OK (Figure 5-4). If your virtual machine has problems booting with the new driver, switch back to the old one and reboot again.

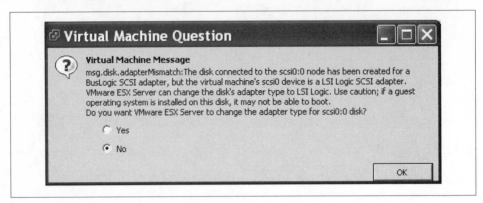

Figure 5-4. Warning when virtual machine boots

5.5 Hiding the VMware Tools Icon

Problem

Many VMware users would like to hide or remove the VMware tools icon, and are frustrated because the VMware tools configuration offers no way to do it.

Solution

You can hide the tools icon by editing the Windows registry.

Discussion

Open the registry and navigate to the following key:

```
HKEY_CURRENT_USER\Software\VMware, Inc.\VMware Tools\ShowTray
```

 Do this with caution and back up your registry first!

Set the ShowTray variable to 0 (zero) and save it. Reboot your virtual machine, and the settings will be reflected: the tools icon will now be hidden.

5.6 Emptying a Large Virtual Machine Logfile

Problem

A virtual machine's logfile has become too large.

Solution

From the command line, you can empty the logfile.

Discussion

To remove all the contents, while leaving the logfile in place to accept new log messages, log into your ESX Server's console and navigate to the virtual machine's directory (e.g., */vmfs/volumes/storage1/TESTVM01*). Run the following command:

```
cat /dev/null > vmware.log
```

You can, of course, back up this file if you need to preserve information for legal, forensic, or analytical purposes.

This command lets you free space held by the logfile without rebooting your virtual machine. If you are able to turn off the virtual machine, you can implement a more sophisticated means of controlling your logfiles.

5.7 Viewing Disk Partitions via the Console

Problem

You want to view information on the current mounts and disks attached to your ESX Server.

Solution

Use the vdf -h command to view this information.

Discussion

VMware has a command similar to the df command in Linux, called vdf. Just as df shows information on filesystems from a Linux point of view, vdf adds in your VMFS filesystem mounts. Typical output looks like this:

```
$ vdf -h
Filesystem        Size  Used Avail Use% Mounted on
/dev/sda2         4.9G  1.4G  3.2G  31% /
/dev/sda1          99M   28M   67M  30% /boot
none              132M     0  132M   0% /dev/shm
/dev/sda6         2.0G  107M  1.8G   6% /var/log
/vmfs/devices      67G     0   67G   0% /vmfs/devices
```

```
/vmfs/volumes/475eb4d4-9b600ac2-1a89-0015c5f2406a
                   60G   560M   59G   0%  /vmfs/volumes/esx2:storage1
/vmfs/volumes/47668165-05f97e46-5570-001b210cb31c
                   408G   34G  373G   8%  /vmfs/volumes/ESXClusterDS
/vmfs/volumes/4766e976-80ec4aa8-0ade-001b210caf2e
                   499G  178G  321G  35%  /vmfs/volumes/ESXTemplateDS
/vmfs/volumes/47cd6dd2-31a2a254-a6a1-001e4f1e7171
                   1.1T   3.2G  1.1T   0%  /vmfs/volumes/ESXCluster2DS
```

This example shows our local OS-level disks and partitions along with the VMFS filesystems that are recognized only by the ESX Server.

For comparison, here is the output from a normal `df` command on the same server:

```
$ df -h
Filesystem       Size  Used Avail Use% Mounted on
/dev/sda2        4.9G  1.4G  3.2G  31% /
/dev/sda1         99M   28M   67M  30% /boot
none             132M     0  132M   0% /dev/shm
/dev/sda6        2.0G  107M  1.8G   6% /var/log
```

Notice that all the VMFS disk volumes are missing.

5.8 Monitoring CPU Usage

Problem

You want to monitor your ESX Server's CPU usage.

Solution

Use the *esxtop* utility.

Discussion

From the command line on your ESX Server, run the following:

```
esxtop
```

If you are familiar with the Unix *top* utility, *esxtop* will feel similar. Once *esxtop* is running, press **c** to switch to CPU mode. This will display your server's current CPU usage statistics (Figure 5-5).

Figure 5-5. esxtop default CPU display

The first line displayed tells you:

- The current time (8:56:45 a.m., in our example)
- The time elapsed since the last reboot
- The number of currently running worlds (VMware virtual machines)
- CPU averages over 1, 5, and 15 minutes

The PCPU(%) line displays the percentage of CPU utilization per physical CPU and the total average across all the physical CPUs.

The CCPU(%) line shows the CPU time as reported by the ESX Server or console. This is a user time variable, as opposed to the PCPU, which measures time from the CPU's point of view.

Below the PCPU and CCPU lines, the following attributes are available:

ID
> The number of the processor

GID
> The ID of the running world's resource pool

NAME
> The name of the currently running process

NWLD
> The number of worlds in the group

%USED
> The percentage of physical CPU used by the resource pool, virtual machine, or world

%RUN
> The percentage of total time scheduled (not taking into account hyper-threading and system time)

%SYS
> System time: the time that elapses while kernel code is running

%WAIT
> The total percentage of time the resource pool or world has spent in a wait state

%RDY
> The percentage of time the resource pool, virtual machine, or world has spent ready to run but waiting to get a CPU

%IDLE
> The percentage of time the VCPU world has spent in an idle loop (this applies only to the VCPU world; for other worlds, this field will be zero)

%OVRLP
> The percentage of time spent by system services working on behalf of other worlds

%CSTP

The percentage of time the world has spent in a ready, co-descheduled state (this state applies only to SMP VMs)

%MLMTD

The percentage of time the world spent ready to run but deliberately wasn't scheduled to avoid violating the CPU limit settings

You can find additional information regarding performance monitoring at *http://communities.vmware.com/servlet/JiveServlet/download/2380-17272/technote_Performance Counters-11-03-08.pdf*.

See Also

Recipes 5.9, 5.10, and 5.11

5.9 Monitoring Memory

Problem

You want to monitor your ESX Server's memory using the command line.

Solution

Use the *esxtop* utility.

Discussion

From the command line on your ESX Server, run the following command:

```
esxtop
```

Once *esxtop* is running, press the m key to switch to memory mode. This will display your server's current memory usage statistics. Your output will be similar to that in Figure 5-6. Note that here we have two virtual machines running, *TEST01* and *TEST02*.

```
6:27:47am up  1:03, 53 worlds; MEM overcommit avg: 0.27, 0.25, 0.14
PMEM  /MB:  1047  total:   272    cos,   135 vmk,     55 other,    585 free
VMKMEM/MB:   731 managed:   43 minfree,  222 rsvd,  417 ursvd,  high state
COSMEM/MB:    30    free:  543  swap_t:   543 swap_f:  0.00 r/s,   0.00 w/s
PSHARE/MB:    12  shared,    4 common,    8 saving
SWAP  /MB:     0    curr,    0 target:           0.00 r/s,   0.00 w/s
MEMCTL/MB:     0    curr,    0 target,    0 max

 GID NAME              NWLD    MEMSZ    SZTGT    TCHD %ACTV %ACTVS %ACTVF %ACTVN   OVHDUW    OVHD  OVHDMAX
  15 vmware-vmkauthd      1     5.48     5.48    1.59     0      0      0      0     0.00    0.00     0.00
  16 TEST01               5   512.00   320.54   30.72     0      2      0      0    15.38   26.81    78.32
  17 TEST02               5   256.00   253.68   30.72     0      3      0      0    13.12   24.79    94.65
```

Figure 5-6. esxtop default memory view

---

esxtop has a similar feel to the standard Unix *top*, but it provides added information specific to your ESX Server. The first line displayed tells you:

- The current time (6:27:47 a.m., in our example)
- The time since the last reboot
- The number of currently running worlds
- Memory overcommitment averages over 1, 5, and 15 minutes

The next line, `PMEM`, break downs the total physical memory. In this example, the ESX Server has 1GB (1047MB) of memory. Let's take a look at the variables:

`total`
> The total amount of memory in the ESX Server

`cos`
> How much memory is allocated to the ESX Server console

`vmk`
> The amount of memory being used by the ESX Server VMkernel

`other`
> The amount of memory being used by everything but the VMkernel and the console

`free`
> The amount of memory that is free on the server

The `VMKMEM` line displays the memory statistics for the VMkernel, including these variables:

`managed`
> The total amount of machine memory being managed by the ESX Server's VMkernel

`minfree`
> The minimum amount of virtual memory that the ESX tries to keep free

`rsvd`
> The amount of memory reserved by resource pools

`ursvd`
> The total amount of unreserved machine memory

`state`
> The current state of machine memory—this will have one of the four values outlined in this excerpt from the official VMware document (DOC-9279[*]):
>
> The memory "state" is "high", if the free memory is greater than or equal to 6% of "total" – "cos". [It] is "soft" at 4%, "hard" at 2%, and "low" at 1%. So, high implies that the machine memory is not under any pressure and low implies that the machine memory is under pressure.

---

[*] *http://communities.vmware.com/docs/DOC-9279*

While the host's memory state is not used to determine whether memory should be reclaimed from VMs (that decision is made at the resource pool level), it can affect what mechanisms are used to reclaim memory if necessary. In the high and soft states, ballooning is favored over swapping. In the hard and low states, swapping is favored over ballooning.

Please note that "minfree" is part of "free" memory; while "rsvd" and "ursvd" memory may or may not be part of "free" memory. "reservation" is different from memory allocation.

COSMEM displays memory statistics that are being reported by the ESX Server console. All values are specified in megabytes. The values present here are:

free
> The amount of idle memory your ESX Server has

swap_t
> The total swap space configured on your ESX Server

swap_f
> The amount of free swap space your ESX Server has

r/s
> The rate at which memory is being swapped from the disk

w/s
> The rate at which memory is being swapped to the disk

PSHARE tells you the current page-sharing status, in the following categories. All values are specified in megabytes:

shared
> The amount of physical memory being shared

common
> The amount of physical memory that is being shared among worlds

saving
> The amount of physical memory that is saved because of page sharing

SWAP tells you about the swap usage on the ESX Server. Again, all values are in megabytes:

curr
> The current amount of swap memory being used by the ESX Server

target
> The disk location where the ESX Server expects the swap memory file to be

r/s
> The rate at which the ESX Server is swapping memory in from the disk

w/s
> The rate at which the ESX Server is swapping memory out to the disk

MEMCTL displays the memory ballooning statistics. All stats are measured in megabytes:

curr
> The amount of memory that has been reclaimed using the vmmemctl module

target
> The total amount of memory the ESX Server hopes to reclaim using the vmmemctl module

max
> The maximum physical memory that the ESX Server can reclaim using the vmmemctl module

After the general status lines, the output shows the memory usage of each virtual machine. The line with a white background contains a header.

Additional variables can be configured by pressing the **F** key while in *esxtop* memory mode.

The variables reported for each virtual machine are:

%ACTV
> The percentage of guest physical memory that is being referenced by the guest

MEMSZ
> The amount of physical memory allocated to a resource pool or virtual machine

MCTLSZ
> The amount of memory that has been reclaimed from the resource pool by ballooning

SWCUR
> The current amount of swap memory in (MB) being used by the virtual machine or resource pool

SWR/s
> The rate at which the ESX Server is swapping memory from the disk for the virtual machine or resource pool

SWW/s
> The rate at which the ESX Server is swapping memory to the disk for the virtual machine or resource pool

OVHD
> The current overhead for the resource pool, in megabytes

For additional details, please refer to the VMware documentation located at *http://communities.vmware.com/servlet/JiveServlet/download/2380-17273/VI+3.5+Memory+Statistic+Definitions.pdf*.

See Also

Recipes 5.8, 5.10, and 5.11

5.10 Monitoring Storage Performance

Problem

You want to find out how well your storage system is working with ESX Server.

Solution

Using *esxtop*, you can also monitor your disk statistics and troubleshoot your storage infrastructure.

Discussion

From the command line on your ESX Server, run the following:

```
esxtop
```

If you are familiar with the Unix *top* command *esxtop* will feel similar. Once *esxtop* is running, press the **d** key to switch to storage mode. This will display statistics for your server's SCSI adapters, including host bus adapters (HBAs) attached through iSCSI and Fibre NAS. Figure 5-7 shows multiple adapters, including local SCSI, Fibre, and iSCSI HBAs, but there is no indication on this screen as to which adapter belongs to which storage type.

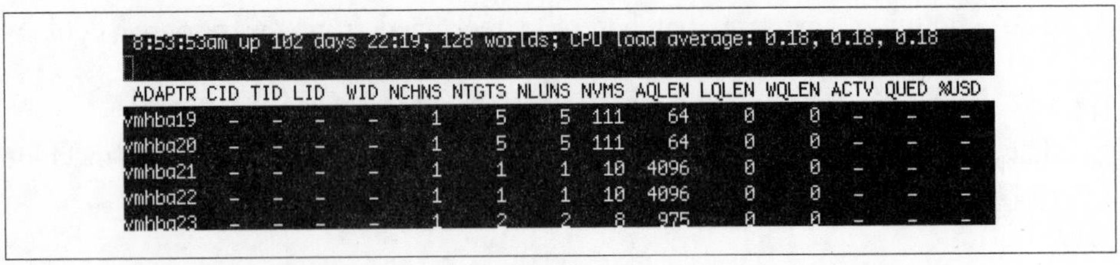

ADAPTR	CID	TID	LID	WID	NCHNS	NTGTS	NLUNS	NVMS	AQLEN	LQLEN	WQLEN	ACTV	QUED	%USD
vmhba19	-	-	-	-	1	5	5	111	64	0	0	-	-	-
vmhba20	-	-	-	-	1	5	5	111	64	0	0	-	-	-
vmhba21	-	-	-	-	1	1	1	10	4096	0	0	-	-	-
vmhba22	-	-	-	-	1	1	1	10	4096	0	0	-	-	-
vmhba23	-	-	-	-	1	2	2	8	975	0	0	-	-	-

8:53:53am up 102 days 22:19, 128 worlds; CPU load average: 0.18, 0.18, 0.18

Figure 5-7. esxtop default storage view (truncated)

The first line displayed tells you the following information:

- The current time (8:53:53 a.m., in our example)
- The time since the last reboot
- The number of currently running worlds
- The CPU load averages for the system

The header that follows lists columns that will describe each disk. To view additional variables while in *esxtop*, you can press the **f** key to toggle them:

ADAPTR
: The adapter for which statistics are being shown.

AQLEN

> The storage adapter queue depth. This is the maximum number of ESX Server VMkernel active commands that the adapter driver is configured to support.

LQLEN

> The number of active commands the LUN is allowed to have.

QUED

> The commands that the system is currently queuing. This applies to worlds/LUNs only.

READS/s

> The number of commands being read per second. Multiple paths will be shown separately.

WRITES/s

> The number of writes issued per second. Multiple paths will be shown separately.

MBREAD/s

> The number of megabytes read per second. Multiple paths will be shown separately.

MBWRTN/s

> The number of megabytes written per second. Multiple paths will be shown separately.

DAVG/cmd

> The device latency per command between the storage and the adapter.

KAVG/cmd

> The VMkernel latency per command.

GAVG/cmd

> The average guest OS latency per command.

Other useful tools to monitor disk usage, such as *perfmon* and *iostat*, can also be launched from the ESX Server's command line. These are useful tools that are native to Linux and that can help you troubleshoot alongside *esxtop*.

See Also

Recipes 5.8, 5.9, and 5.11

5.11 Monitoring Network Usage

Problem

You want to monitor your network adapters via the command line.

Solution

Use the *esxtop* utility to monitor network usage.

Discussion

From the command line on your ESX Server, run the following:

    esxtop

Once *esxtop* is running, press the **n** key to switch to network mode. This will display your server's current network statistics (Figure 5-8).

```
9:25:20am up 20 days 23:58, 162 worlds; CPU load average: 0.31, 0.30, 0.26

  PORT ID UPLINK           USED BY DTYP           DNAME  PKTTX/s   MbTX/s  PKTRX/s   MbRX/s %DRPTX %DRPRX
  16777217    Y             vmnic0    H          vSwitch0    10.84     0.02    12.05     0.01   0.00   0.00
  16777218    N              0:NCP    H          vSwitch0     0.00     0.00     0.00     0.00   0.00   0.00
  16777219    Y            vmnic44    H          vSwitch0     0.20     0.00     1.61     0.00   0.00   0.00
  16777220    N              0:CDP    H          vSwitch0     0.00     0.00     0.00     0.00   0.00   0.00
  16777221    N           0:vswif0    H          vSwitch0    10.84     0.02    10.64     0.01   0.00   0.00
  16777222    N        1116:VDI01    H          vSwitch0     0.20     0.00     0.00     0.00   0.00   0.00
  33554433    Y             vmnic1    H          vSwitch1     0.00     0.00     0.60     0.00   0.00   0.00
  33554434    N              0:NCP    H          vSwitch1     0.00     0.00     0.00     0.00   0.00   0.00
  33554435    N              0:CDP    H          vSwitch1     0.00     0.00     0.00     0.00   0.00   0.00
  33554436    N 0:vmk-tcpip-172.20.4  H          vSwitch1     0.00     0.00     0.00     0.00   0.00   0.00
  50331649    Y            vmnic49    H          vSwitch2     0.00     0.00     0.00     0.00   0.00   0.00
  50331650    N              0:NCP    H          vSwitch2     0.00     0.00     0.00     0.00   0.00   0.00
  50331651    Y            vmnic45    H          vSwitch2   472.42     0.33  1171.51    11.72   0.00   0.00
  50331652    N              0:CDP    H          vSwitch2     0.00     0.00     0.00     0.00   0.00   0.00
```

Figure 5-8. esxtop default network view

If you are familiar with the Unix *top* command, *esxtop* will feel similar. Let's take a look at some of the values displayed in Figure 5-8:

PORT ID
> The virtual network device port ID

UPLINK
> Whether or not the network port is an uplink (Y = yes, N = no)

USED BY
> The virtual network device user

DTYP
> The virtual network device type (H = hub, S = switch)

DNAME
> The virtual network device name

PKTTX/s
> The number of packets transmitted per second

MbTX/s
> The number of megabits transmitted per second

PKTRX/s
> The number of packets received per second

MbRX/s

The number of megabits received per second

%DRPTX

The percentage of transmitted packets that were dropped

%DRPRX

The percentage of received packets that were dropped

See Also

Recipes 5.8, 5.9, and 5.10

5.12 Managing Virtual Switches

Problem

You want to manage internal virtual switch (vSwitch) entities within your ESX environment.

Solution

Run the `esxcfg-vswitch` command on the ESX Server.

Discussion

You'll find this one of the most useful commands to use from your ESX Server's console. It allows you to list, add, modify, or delete virtual Ethernet switches on your server:

```
$ esxcfg-vswitch -h
esxcfg-vswitch [options] [vswitch[:ports]]
 -a|--add             Add a new virtual switch.
 -d|--delete          Delete the virtual switch.
 -l|--list            List all the virtual switches.
 -L|--link=pnic       Set pnic as an uplink for the vswitch.
 -U|--unlink=pnic     Remove pnic from the uplinks for the vswitch.
 -M|--add-pg-uplink   Add an uplink to the list of uplinks for a portgroup
 -N|--del-pg-uplink   Delete an uplink from the list of uplinks for a portgroup
 -p|--pg=portgroup    Specify a portgroup for operation
                      Use ALL to set VLAN IDs on all portgroups
 -v|--vlan=id         Set vlan id for portgroup specified by -p
                      0 would disable the vlan
 -c|--check           Check to see if a virtual switch exists.
                      Program outputs a 1 if it exists, 0 otherwise.
 -A|--add-pg=name     Add a new portgroup to the virtual switch.
 -D|--del-pg=name     Delete the portgroup from the virtual switch.
 -C|--check-pg=name   Check to see if a portgroup exists.  Program
                      outputs a 1 if it exists, 0 otherwise.
 -B|--set-cdp         Set the CDP status for a given virtual switch.
                      To set pass one of "down", "listen", "advertise", "both".
 -b|--get-cdp         Print the current CDP setting for this switch.
 -m|--mtu=MTU         Set MTU for the vswitch. This affects all
```

```
    the nics attached on the vswitch.
  -r|--restore          Restore all virtual switches from the configuration file
                        (FOR INTERNAL USE ONLY).
  -h|--help             Show this message.
```

The -l option lists the virtual switches and portgroups that are configured on your ESX Server. Its output will look something like this:

```
$ esxcfg-vswitch -l
Switch Name     Num Ports   Used Ports  Configured Ports  MTU     Uplinks
vSwitch0        64          5           64                1500    vmnic3,vmnic0

  PortGroup Name      VLAN ID  Used Ports  Uplinks
  Service Console     0        1           vmnic0,vmnic3

Switch Name     Num Ports   Used Ports  Configured Ports  MTU     Uplinks
vSwitch2        64          3           64                1500    vmnic1

  PortGroup Name      VLAN ID  Used Ports  Uplinks
  SpecialZone         0        0           vmnic1

Switch Name     Num Ports   Used Ports  Configured Ports  MTU     Uplinks
vSwitch1        64          4           64                1500    vmnic2

  PortGroup Name      VLAN ID  Used Ports  Uplinks
  vMotion             0        1           vmnic2

Switch Name     Num Ports   Used Ports  Configured Ports  MTU     Uplinks
vSwitch4        64          3           64                1500    vmnic5

  PortGroup Name      VLAN ID  Used Ports  Uplinks
  GenLAN              0        0           vmnic5
```

As you can see in this example, we have four virtual switches: *vSwitch0* contains our "Service Console" portgroup, *vSwitch1* contains our "vMotion" portgroup, *vSwitch2* contains the "SpecialZone" virtual machine network, and *vSwitch4* contains a portgroup called "GenLAN" that connects to the general LAN.

Using the -a option, you can add more virtual switches to your ESX Server:

```
esxcfg-vswitch -a vSwitch5
```

 Check your options carefully before entering each of these commands. If you enter incorrect options, you risk being disconnected from your ESX Server.

Using the -l option again will show you that the new virtual switch has been added but doesn't have a portgroup or an uplink:

```
$ esxcfg-vswitch -l
Switch Name     Num Ports   Used Ports  Configured Ports  MTU     Uplinks
vSwitch5        64          1           64                1500

  PortGroup Name      VLAN ID  Used Ports  Uplinks
```

To configure a portgroup on your new virtual switch, use the `-A` (uppercase) option:

```
esxcfg-vswitch -A "Backup Network" vSwitch5
```

Again using the `-l` option to verify the changes, you will notice that the backup network portgroup has been added under *vSwitch5* but that it has not yet been assigned to an uplink:

```
$ esxcfg-vswitch -l
Switch Name     Num Ports    Used Ports  Configured Ports  MTU     Uplinks
vSwitch5        64           1           64                1500

   PortGroup Name       VLAN ID  Used Ports  Uplinks
   Backup Network       0        0
```

The `-L` option (uppercase) allows us to assign the PNIC (physical NIC) to the virtual switch:

```
esxcfg-vswitch -L vmnic4 vSwitch5
```

Verify your configuration change again, noticing this time that the uplinks on the vSwitch and the portgroup have been assigned to *vmnic4*:

```
$ esxcfg-vswitch -l
Switch Name     Num Ports    Used Ports  Configured Ports  MTU     Uplinks
vSwitch5        64           3           64                1500    vmnic4

   PortGroup Name       VLAN ID  Used Ports  Uplinks
   Backup Network       0        0           vmnic4
```

And finally, to remove a *vmnic* from a vSwitch and portgroup, use the `-U` switch:

```
esxcfg-vswitch -U vmnic4 vSwitch5
```

5.13 Generating a Logfile for VMware Support

Problem

VMware support may require you to send in a configuration dump of your ESX Server for troubleshooting specific issues.

Solution

Use `vm-support` to gather the data needed for troubleshooting.

Discussion

If you open a ticket with VMware support, VMware might request you to send a *support bundle*. This is an archive package filled with logs and other information about your ESX Server. Luckily, there is a very simple and powerful command that will generate a tar file that includes everything necessary. The `vm-support` command is also useful for your own troubleshooting:

```
$ vm-support -h
Usage: /usr/bin/vm-support [-n] [-N] [-a] [-s] [-S] [-d duration_in_seconds] [-i
interval] [-x] [-X wid] [-q] [-w] [-h] [-f] [-Z wid] [-t wid]
    -n causes no cores to be tar'ed up
    -N causes no service console cores to be tar'ed up
    -a causes all cores to be tar'ed up - even those from previous
       runnings of this script
    -c gather schedtrace snapshots (only if performance snapshots are enabled)
    -s take performance snapshots in addition to other data
    -S take only performance snapshots
    -d<s> set performance snapshot duration to <s> seconds [default 300]
    -i<s> sleep <s> seconds between snapshots [default autodetect]
    -x lists wids for running VMs
    -X <wid> grab debug info for a hung VM
    -q runs in quiet mode
    -w <dir> sets the working directory used for the output files
    -f allows you to force vm-support to use a VMFS working directory
    -l print list of files being collected
    -Z <wid> suspends a VM and grabs debug info
    -r causes all vmfs3 volumes' volume headers to be tar'ed up
    -t <wgid> takes a scsi command trace for I/O from a VM (specify world group id)
       Note:- this option consumes a noticeable amount of cpu so enabling it
              can negatively impact the performance of the system
            - limited to one VM at a time
            - trace contains NO customer sensitive data
            - only information recorded is:
              - serialnumber, timestamp, length of command
              - command type, block number
            - Therefore, actual data/payload of commands is not stored
    -v prints out vm-support version
    -h prints this usage statement

See man page for more information on vm-support version 1.29
```

The -x option displays all the running virtual machines on the ESX Server:

```
$ vm-support -x

VMware ESX Server Support Script 1.29

Available worlds to debug:

vmid=1104      TEST01
vmid=1116      TEST02
vmid=1124      TEST03
```

To bundle up all your logs on the ESX Server, just run vm-support without arguments. This process will take about 5–15 minutes and will produce a *.tgz* file in the same directory where the command is run. You will see something similar to this while the tarball is being generated:

```
$ vm-support

VMware ESX Server Support Script 1.29

Preparing files: /
```

When the command completes, it will give you detailed information on the location of the file and how to submit it to VMware support:

```
Waiting up to 300 seconds for background commands to complete:
sssssssssssssssssssssssssssssssssssssssssssssssssssssssssssssssssssss
Waiting for background commands: -
Creating tar archive ...


File: /root/esx-2008-12-08--20.23.15766.tgz
Please attach this file when submitting an incident report.
To file a support incident, go to http://www.vmware.com/support/sr/sr_login.jsp


To see the files collected, run: tar -tzf /root/esx-2008-12-08--20.23.15766.tgz

Done
```

You can do a lot of other things with this command, such as collect performance data or run an SCSI trace on a virtual machine. Use the -h option to see the available options.

5.14 Checking ESX Patches

Problem

You want to see what patches are applied to your ESX Server.

Solution

Run the *esxupdate* utility.

Discussion

A typical run of this command produces output like:

```
$ esxupdate -l query
Installed software bundles:
  ------ Name ------ --- Install Date --- --- Summary ---
        3.5.0-64607    10:59:37 12/11/07 Full bundle of ESX 3.5.0-64607
  ESX350-200802303-SG 11:35:59 03/31/08 util-linux security update
  ESX350-200802305-SG 11:36:17 03/31/08 openssl security update
  ESX350-200802408-SG 11:40:53 03/31/08 Security Updates to the Python Package.
  ESX350-200803209-UG 08:05:38 04/16/08 Update to the ESX Server Service Console
  ESX350-200803212-UG 08:06:54 04/16/08 Update VMware qla4010/qla4022 drivers
  ESX350-200803213-UG 08:07:52 04/16/08 Driver Versioning Method Changes
  ESX350-200803214-UG 08:08:30 04/16/08 Update to Third Party Code Libraries
     ESX350-Update01    08:11:00 04/16/08 ESX Server 3.5.0 Update 1
  ESX350-200804405-BG 10:45:18 05/01/08 Update to VMware-esx-drivers-scsi-megara
  ESX350-200805504-SG 09:17:06 06/13/08 Security Update to Cyrus SASL
  ESX350-200805505-SG 09:17:45 06/13/08 Security Update to unzip
  ESX350-200805506-SG 09:18:26 06/13/08 Security Update to Tcl/Tk
  ESX350-200805507-SG 09:19:04 06/13/08 Security Update to krb5
  ESX350-200805514-BG 09:21:09 06/13/08 Update to VMware-esx-drivers-net-e1000
```

```
ESX350-200808203-UG    11:43:37 08/19/08 Update to Backup Tools
ESX350-200808206-UG    11:45:04 08/19/08 Update to vmware-hwdata
ESX350-200808210-UG    11:46:51 08/19/08 Update to VMware-esx-drivers-net-ixgbe
ESX350-200808211-UG    11:47:26 08/19/08 Update to the tg3 Driver
ESX350-200808212-UG    11:48:01 08/19/08 Update to the MegaRAID SAS Driver
ESX350-200808215-UG    11:49:44 08/19/08 Update to the Emulex SCSI Driver
ESX350-200808218-UG    11:51:24 08/19/08 Security Update to Samba
   ESX350-Update-02    11:51:40 08/19/08 ESX Server 3.5.0 Update 2
    ESX350-Update02    11:51:55 08/19/08 ESX Server 3.5.0 Update 2
ESX350-200808405-SG    09:48:15 09/23/08 Security Update to Net-SNMP
ESX350-200808406-SG    09:49:00 09/23/08 Security Update to Perl
ESX350-200808407-BG    09:49:41 09/23/08 Updates Software QLogic FC Driver
ESX350-200808409-SG    09:50:16 09/23/08 Security Update to BIND
ESX350-200808412-BG    09:52:05 09/23/08 Updates lnxcfg
ESX350-200810201-UG    14:57:55 11/13/08 Updates VMkernel, Service Console, hostd
ESX350-200810203-UG    15:08:37 11/13/08 Updates MPT SCSI Driver
ESX350-200810204-UG    15:09:18 11/13/08 Updates bnx2x Driver for Broadcom
ESX350-200810205-UG    15:10:14 11/13/08 Updates CIM and Pegasus
ESX350-200810206-UG    15:10:55 11/13/08 Updates ATA PIIX SCSI Driver
ESX350-200810208-UG    15:12:09 11/13/08 Updates esxupdate documentation
ESX350-200810209-UG    15:12:49 11/13/08 Updates bnx2 Driver for Broadcom
ESX350-200810210-UG    15:23:32 11/13/08 Updates HP Storage Component Drivers
ESX350-200810212-UG    15:24:13 11/13/08 Updates VMkernel iSCSI Driver
ESX350-200810214-UG    15:24:48 11/13/08 Updated Time Zone Rules
ESX350-200810215-UG    15:25:38 11/13/08 Updates Web Access
    ESX350-Update03    15:25:59 11/13/08 ESX Server 3.5.0 Update 3
ESX350-200811402-SG    09:15:13 12/08/08 Updates ESX Scripts
ESX350-200811401-SG    09:16:57 12/08/08 Updates VMkernel, hostd, and Other RPMs
ESX350-200811405-SG    09:17:37 12/08/08 Security Update to libxml2
ESX350-200811406-SG    09:18:15 12/08/08 Security Update to bzip2
ESX350-200811409-BG    09:20:32 12/08/08 Updates Kernel Source and VMNIX
ESX350-200811408-BG    09:21:18 12/08/08 Updates QLogic Software Driver
```

As you can see, we have an extensive history of patches that have been applied to our server. This command is useful for confirming that specific patches have been applied, or learning about the history of a machine that has been running for a while but for which you have just been given responsibility.

5.15 Enabling NTP in vCenter

Problem

You want to enable NTP on your ESX host.

Solution

By using vCenter, you can easily configure NTP on your ESX host.

Discussion

Keeping your ESX Servers and virtual machines in sync is crucial to your virtual environment. Using NTP to manage time on your ESX Server and the virtual machines ensures that your virtual machines are not losing CPU cycles due to mismatched time synchronization.

This example shows you how to configure time via vCenter, the preferred method of for your ESX Server. However, if you are feeling brave, you can refer to Recipe 5.16 to configure NTP via the command line.

To get started, log into vCenter with your administrator account. Then follow these steps:

1. Click on the ESX Server on which you want to configure NTP. Under Configuration, select Time Configuration. You will then see a brief overview of your NTP configuration and NTP client stats, as shown in Figure 5-9.

Figure 5-9. The default timeserver configuration page

2. Continue by clicking the Properties link in the upper-right corner of the Time Configuration overview screen. You will be presented with a new window with options to configure NTP, as shown in Figure 5-10.

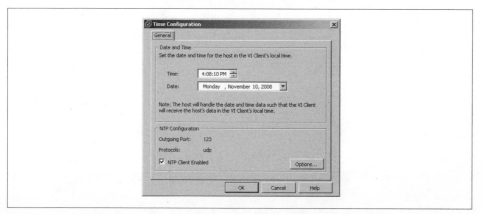

Figure 5-10. The Time Configuration page showing various information

3. Click the Options button near the bottom-right corner. You will be presented with a new window where you can select the appropriate startup policy. In our example, we chose "Start automatically if any ports are open, and stop when all ports are closed" (Figure 5-11). Note: if you are running ESXi, your first choice will read "Start automatically."

When you press OK, vCenter will change the firewall rules for you automatically and allow traffic through this port.

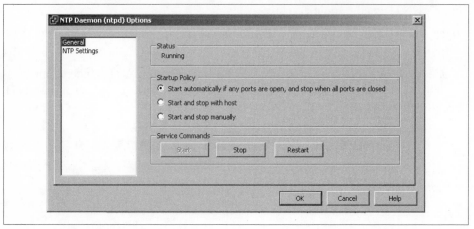

Figure 5-11. Selecting a startup NTP policy

4. Click on the NTP Settings link, and you will be shown the list of active NTP servers (Figure 5-12). If you are setting up NTP for the first time, there will be nothing listed here.

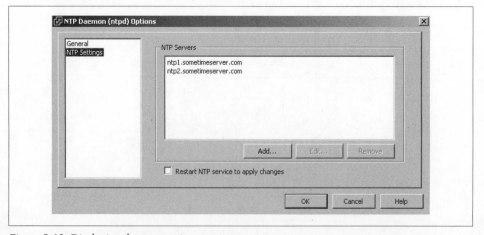

Figure 5-12. Displaying the current time servers

5. Click the Add button to add your NTP servers. If you have a default of 127.0.0.1, you can safely remove that entry by clicking it and then clicking the Remove button. Press OK to apply the changes and start the NTP service.

   ESX will automatically provision the correct firewall rules, allowing connections on port 123. You will notice that the system time is synchronized shortly after the NTP service is started.

See Also

Recipes 5.16 and 5.17

5.16 Enabling NTP via the Command Line

Problem

You want to enable NTP on your ESX host using the command line.

Solution

Using the service console, you can configure NTP services on your ESX host.

Discussion

While Recipe 5.15 showed you how to enable NTP interactively, you may want to do it in a script. All the steps shown in Recipe 5.15 can also be performed through shell commands:

1. To get started, edit the */etc/ntp.conf* file. This file holds the main configuration for NTP. We've created a default template that you can use to configure your *ntp.conf* file:

   ```
   restrict kod nomodify notrap noquery nopeer
   restrict 127.0.0.1
   # Replace these with your time servers.
   server npt1.timeserverdomain.com
   server ntp2.timeserverdomain.com
   driftfile /var/lib/ntp/drift
   ```

2. Next, modify the */etc/ntp/step-tickers* file. We have again created a template for you:

   ```
   # Replace these with your timeservers that you specified in ntp.conf
   server npt1.timeserverdomain.com
   server ntp2.timeserverdomain.com
   ```

3. The following command will open the firewall port to ensure all NTP-related traffic is allowed through:

   ```
   esxcfg-firewall –enableService ntpClient
   ```

4. Now restart the ntpd daemon:

```
service ntpd restart
```

You will see something similar to this:

```
Shutting down ntpd:                               [FAILED]
ntpd: Synchronizing with time server:             [  OK  ]
Starting ntpd:                                    [  OK  ]
```

You will probably receive a [FAILED] warning when the **restart** command tries to stop the ntpd daemon. This is OK, because you didn't have NTP configured or running previously.

5. Next, set the local hardware clock to the local system time:

```
hwclock --systohc
```

6. Finally, make sure that *ntpd* is set to start up on a system reboot. This can be accomplished by running the following command:

```
chkconfig --level 345 ntpd on
```

Alternatively, you can use the remote command-line interface (RCLI) utilities and the vicfg-ntp command to configure NTP. This also works with ESXi. For more information and downloads, visit *http://www.vmware.com/go/remotecli*.

See Also

Recipes 5.15 and 5.17

5.17 Changing the ESX Server's Time

Problem

You want to change the time on your ESX Server manually.

Solution

Use the date and hwclock commands to change the time.

Discussion

Run these two commands to manually change the time on the ESX Server:

```
date 120715002009
hwclock -systohc
```

The first command is the standard Linux date command, which allows us to manipulate the current date and time. In our example, we've used the date command to set the time as 3:00 p.m. on 12/07/2009 in the format MMDDhhmmYYYY. Next, we use the hwclock command to temporarily sync the system's hardware clock to the operating system.

While this method is good for some scenarios, it's good practice to make sure your ESX Servers are set up using NTP, as we've mentioned in Recipes 5.15 and 5.16.

See Also

Recipes 5.15 and 5.16

5.18 Using TCP Wrappers

Problem

You want to define a group of servers that can connect to wrapped services.

Solution

Set up configuration files for TCP wrappers.

Discussion

Using TCP wrappers, you can allow certain IP addresses to connect to specific services running on your ESX Server.

When an application is wrapped using TCP wrappers, the */etc/hosts.allow* and */etc/hosts.deny* files are used to determine whether the client is allowed to connect to the service you are specifying. Unless you have previously configured a different location, logs will be stored in */var/log/messages* on your ESX Server by default.

You can use the ldd command to verify whether a specific command is being wrapped. Wrapped services are linked to the libwrap.so library, so you'll see output like the following:

```
$ ldd /usr/sbin/sshd | grep libwrap
libwrap.so.0 => /usr/lib/libwrap.so.0 (0x00817000)
```

If no output is given, the service is not being wrapped.

As we mentioned earlier, the */etc/hosts.allow* and */etc/hosts.deny* files are used to manage the wrapped services' connection rules. These files follow a specific syntax, which we will outline for you next.

Both files follow the same format, which ensures maximum compatibility and saves you the trouble of figuring out two different syntaxes:

```
daemon: client [: option: option: ........]
```

The fields are:

daemon
> A comma-separated list of process names

client
> A comma-separated list of IP addresses and hostnames or the ALL wildcard

option
> The action that will be performed when the rule is triggered

An example entry in the *hosts.allow* file might look similar to the following, which is set to allow SSH access from a specific IP address, or a complete class of IP addresses:

```
sshd:172.20.45.10:allow
sshd:172.20.45.0/24:allow
```

An example entry in the *hosts.deny* file might look similar to this:

```
sshd:172.20.46.0/24:deny
```

You can use the ALL wildcard in either *hosts.allow* or *hosts.deny* to allow or deny all access to the specified service:

```
/etc/hosts.deny
sshd:ALL:deny
```

```
/etc/hosts.allow
sshd:ALL:allow
```

5.19 Restarting the vCenter Agent

Problem

You want to restart the vCenter agent on your ESX Server.

Solution

You can restart the agent from the command line.

Discussion

From time to time, you may have to restart the virtual center agent on your ESX Server. For example, vCenter may not see changes made with command-line utilities until you restart the agent. You can do this with the following command:

```
/etc/init.d/vmware-vpxa restart
```

While the agent is restarting, you may see your ESX Server become disconnected from vCenter. Don't worry, your virtual machines will continue to run, and the ESX Server will reconnect once the agent and the vCenter server reestablish a connection.

5.20 Unregistering a Virtual Machine via the Command Line

Problem

You wish to unregister a virtual machine.

Solution

You can unregister virtual machines via the command line.

Discussion

Running the following command will stop the virtual machine from showing up in the inventory of your ESX Server. It will not delete the virtual machine, which will be left intact:

```
vmware-cmd -s unregister /vmfs/volumes/datastore/NAME/NAME.vmx
```

Remember to replace *datastore* with your correct datastore name. The virtual machine must be powered off in order for this to work.

5.21 Registering a Virtual Machine via the Command Line

Problem

You wish to register a virtual machine via the command line.

Solution

Registering a virtual machine via the command line is as easy as unregistering one.

Discussion

Running the following command will add the virtual machine to the inventory of your ESX Server (remember to replace *datastore* with your correct datastore name):

```
vmware-cmd -s register /vmfs/volumes/datastore/NAME/NAME.vmx
```

This can also be done within vCenter, and this is the recommended method of registering a virtual machine.

5.22 Finding Virtual Machine Snapshots

Problem

You need to find snapshots for your virtual machines.

Solution

You can list all the snapshots via the command line.

Discussion

This command will list all the snapshots in your virtual machine's directories:

```
ls -Ral /vmfs/volumes/* |grep .vmsn
```

This is helpful if you need to track down which virtual machines currently have snapshots associated with them.

Snapshots will consume a lot of disk space if left unattended and should be reverted when possible.

5.23 Renaming a Virtual Machine via vCenter

Problem

You need to rename a virtual machine.

Solution

You can rename virtual machines in vCenter.

Discussion

Log into your vCenter server and follow these quick steps:

1. Power off the virtual machine you want to rename.
2. Rename the virtual machine by right-clicking and choosing Rename.
3. Migrate the virtual machine to another datastore.

This method requires you to have more than one datastore available to your ESX Servers. However, it is the quickest method available to rename a virtual machine, because it will actually copy the virtual machine's files to the new datastore and rename them accordingly.

See Also

Recipe 5.24

5.24 Renaming a Virtual Machine via the Command Line

Problem

You want to change a virtual machine's name via the command line.

Solution

Following these steps will ensure you correctly rename your virtual machine.

Discussion

You will need to be logged into your ESX Server to run the following commands, replacing *OLDNAME* with the virtual machine's current name and *NEWNAME* with the new name that you wish to give it. These names are case sensitive, and we've used capitals to help with the presentation of the commands:

1. Power off your virtual machine.
2. Unregister the virtual machine from the ESX host:

   ```
   vmware-cmd -s unregister /vmfs/volumes/datastore/OLDNAME/OLDNAME.vmx
   ```

3. Change the name of the virtual machine to reflect the new name:

   ```
   mv /vmfs/volumes/datastore/OLDNAME/vmfs/volumes/datastore/NEWNAME
   ```

4. Rename the virtual machine's files from the old name to the new name using the following command:

   ```
   cd /vmfs/volumes/datastore/NEWNAME
   vmkfstools -E OLDNAME.vmdk NEWNAME.vmdk
   ```

5. Next, do a mass find and replace to rename the virtual machine. Replace the *OLDNAME* with the current virtual machine's current name and *NEWNAME* with the new name of the virtual machine:

   ```
   find . -name '*.vmx*' -print -exec sed -e 's/OLDNAME/NEWNAME/g' {} \;
   mv OLDNAME.vmx NEWNAME.vmx
   ```

6. Reregister the virtual machine with its new name:

   ```
   vmware-cmd -s register /vmfs/volumes/datastore/NEWNAME/NEWNAME.vmx
   ```

See Also

Recipe 5.23

5.25 Using Host Files

Problem

In order to locate your hosts, ESX needs the hostnames to be listed in */etc/hosts*.

Solution

Add entries in */etc/hosts* with the IP addresses and names of your ESX Servers.

Discussion

Configuring your */etc/hosts* file is one of the more important things to do after setting up a new ESX Server. Typically, you should list all of your ESX Servers and vCenter servers in your */etc/hosts* file.

ESX will use the */etc/hosts* file for functions such as high availability, VMotion, and internal communications. Using this file also ensures that you are protected within your ESX environment in the event of a DNS failure.

A typical */etc/hosts* file might look like this:

```
127.0.0.1 localhost.localdomain localhost
172.20.33.1 esxserver01.youdomain.com esxserver01
172.20.33.2 esxserver02.youdomain.com esxserver02
```

Make sure you leave the line with the local IP address of 127.0.0.1; otherwise, you will run into problems further down the road.

5.26 Setting ESX Options Using the Command Line

Problem

You want to set advanced configuration variables on your ESX Server, but you can't use vCenter (or you want to automate the process by using command-line tools).

Solution

Run the esxcfg-advcfg command on the ESX Server.

Discussion

The esxcfg-advcfg command allows you to adjust advanced configuration values from the command line. These values can also be changed inside vCenter, which is much easier; however, if vCenter isn't available, this command will allow you to make the needed adjustments. Options you can change are:

```
Usage: esxcfg-advcfg <options> [<adv cfg Path>]
  -g|--get              Get the value of the config option
  -s|--set <value>      Set the value of the config option
  -d|--default          Reset Config option to default
  -q|--quiet            Suppress output
  -k|--set-kernel       Set a VMkernel load time option value.
  -j|--get-kernel       Get a VMkernel load time option value.
  -m|--set-message      Set DCUI welcome message.
  -u|--uuid             Ensure the VMkernel system UUID is set and print it.
  -h|--help             Show this message.
  -r|--restore          Restore all advanced options from the configuration
                        file. (FOR INTERNAL USE ONLY).
```

To get an idea of what is configurable via the command line, look in the */proc/vmware/config* directory. It contains the following subdirectories:

```
BufferCache
COW
Cpu
DirentryCache
Disk
FileSystem
Irq
LPage
LVM
Mem
Migrate
Misc
Net
NFS
Numa
Scsi
User
VMFS3
World
```

Inside these directories are text files that contain configurable values. For example, the *Misc* subdirectory has a file named *HostName* that contains a value like the following:

```
$ esxcfg-advcfg -g /Misc/HostName
Value of HostName is esx2cluster1.testdomain.com
```

The -g switch allows you to retrieve the value of the configuration parameter you wish to see or change.

The -s switch lets you set a specific parameter. For instance, the following command changes the hostname of the ESX Server:

```
esxcfg-advcfg -s esx2cluster2.testdomain.com /Misc/HostName
```

5.27 Configuring Authentication Choices Using the Command Line

Problem

You want to use the command line to set authentication parameters such as the type of authentication, the authentication server, and password aging.

Solution

Run the `esxcfg-auth` command on the ESX Server.

Discussion

The `esxcfg-auth` command allows you to configure different authentication methods on your ESX Server. We won't go into detail on the configurable options here, as we discuss setting up Active Directory in Chapter 6. However, here's a list of those options:

```
$ esxcfg-auth -h
usage: esxcfg-auth [options]

options:
  --enablemd5              Enable MD5 password storage
  --disablemd5             Disable MD5 password storage
  --enableshadow           Enable Shadow password storage
  --disableshadow          Disable Shadow password storage
  --enablenis              Enable NIS Authentication
  --disablenis             Disable NIS Authentication
  --nisdomain=domain       Set the NIS domain
  --nisserver=server       Set the NIS server
  --enableldap             Enable LDAP User Management
  --disableldap            Disable LDAP User Management
  --enableldapauth         Enable LDAP Authentication
  --disableldapauth        Disable LDAP Authentication
  --ldapserver=server      Set the LDAP Server
  --ldapbasedn=basedn      Set the base DN for the LDAP server
  --enableldaptls          Enable TLS connections for LDAP
  --disableldaptls         Disable TLS connections for LDAP
  --enablekrb5             Enable Kererbos Authentication
  --disablekrb5            Disable Kererbos Authentication
  --krb5realm=domain       Set the Kerberos Realm
  --krb5kdc=server         Set the Kebreros Key Distribution Center
  --krb5adminserver=server
                           Set the Kerberos Admin Server
  --enablead               Enable Active Directory Authentication
  --disablead              Disable Active Directory Authentication
  --addomain=domain        Set the Active Directory Domain
  --addc=server            Set the Active Directory Domain Controller
  --usepamqc=values        Enable the pam_passwdqc module
  --usecrack=values        Enable the pam_cracklib module
  --enablecache            Enables caching of login credentials
  --disablecache           Disables caching of login credentials
```

```
--passmaxdays=days      Set the maximum number of days a password remains valid.
--passmindays=days      Set the minimum number of days a password remains valid.
--passwarnage=days      Set the number of days a warning is given before a
                        password expires.
--maxfailedlogins=count
                        Sets the maximum number of login failures before the
                        account is locked out, setting to 0 will disable this
-p, --probe             Print the settings to the console
-v, --verbose           Enable verbose logging
-h, --help              show this help message and exit
```

5.28 Manipulating the Bootloader

Problem

You need to change GRUB boot options or preserve changes made to the boot options on a currently running system.

Solution

Run the esxcfg-boot command on the ESX Server.

Discussion

Generally, you will not need to make changes using this command unless you are loading special drivers or need to make modifications to the default bootloader that VMware provides. The configurable options are shown here:

```
$ esxcfg-boot -h
esxcfg-boot -h --help
            -q --query boot|vmkmod
            -p --update-pci
            -b --update-boot
            -d --rootdev UUID=<uuid>
            -a --kernelappend <kernel append>
            -r --refresh-initrd
            -g --regenerate-grub

    Queries cannot be combined with each other or other options.
    Passing -p or -d enables -b even if it is not passed explicitly.
    -b implies -g plus a new initrd creation.
    -b and -r are incompatible, but -g and -r can be combined.
```

Changes to configuration files are usually made by editing them directly, but you can also use the esxcfg-boot command to view or change kernel device drivers, without having to edit files.

Running esxcfg-boot with the -q option queries either the boot or the vmkmod entry and displays the relevant information.

The `-q boot` option displays the kernel and initial RAM disk (*initrd*) image being used when the ESX Server boots:

```
$ esxcfg-boot -q boot
272 0:*; UUID=38baf5c7-6682-4d0a-8892-b38980d45334 /vmlinuz-2.4.21-57.ELvmnix
/initrd-2.4.21-57.ELvmnix.img
```

The output from `-q vmkmod` displays which drivers are currently loaded and the ones that will be loaded when the ESX Server boots. For example, the following modules load on our ESX Server when it boots:

```
vmklinux
megaraid_sas.o
bnx2.o
e1000.o
qla2300_707_vmw.o
lvmdriver
vmfs3
etherswitch
shaper
tcpip
cosShadow.o
migration
nfsclient
deltadisk
vmfs2
iscsi_mod.o
```

With the `-g` option, you can regenerate the */boot/grub/grub.conf* file. This method is a safe way to ensure that your grub file is correctly built against your ESX Server's setup.

The `-r` option rebuilds the *initrd*vmnix.img* file. The *initrd* is an initial root filesystem that gets mounted before the real server's filesystem. It works alongside the server's kernel to ensure that all modules and drivers are loaded when the system boots. You should also run the command with this option if you manually add a new device driver to your ESX Server, as the *initrd* needs to be rebuilt to reflect this at boot time.

5.29 Manipulating the Crash Dump Partition

Problem

You wish to manage the VMkernel crash dump partition. Normally, this is set up during the installation of your ESX Server and will not require any further maintenance. However, a tool is available if you need to look at it or manipulate it.

Solution

Run the `esxcfg-dumppart` command on the ESX Server.

Discussion

A dump partition is a section of your hard drive that is set aside as a place for information from crashes to be automatically stored for later retrieval and use in troubleshooting.

Here is the output from the `esxcfg-dumppart` command that we will be discussing in this recipe:

```
$ esxcfg-dumppart -h
esxcfg-dumppart <options> [<partition>]
 -l|--list              List the partitions available for Dump Partitions.
                        WARNING: This will scan all LUNs on the system.
 -t|--get-active        Get the active Dump Partition for this system,
                        returns the internal name of the partition
                        (vmhbaX:X:X:X) or 'none'.
 -c|--get-config        Get the configured Dump Partition for this
                        system, returns the internal name of the partition
                        (vmhbaX:X:X:X) or 'none'.
 -s|--set               Set the Dump Partition for this system and activate it,
                        either vmhbaX:X:X:X or 'none' to deactivate
                        the active dump partition.
 -f|--find              Find usable Dump partitions and list in order of
                        preference.
 -S|--smart-activate    Activate the configured dump partition or find
                        the first appropriate partition and use it
                        (same order as -f).
 -a|--activate          Activate the configured dump partition.
 -d|--deactivate        Deactivate the active dump partition.
 -h|--help              Show this message.
```

Running the command with the -l option lists the ESX Server's crash dump partition, which is normally set up when ESX is installed. Typical output will look similar to this:

```
$ esxcfg-dumppart -l
VM Kernel Name Console Name                 Is Active   Is Configured
vmhba0:0:0:7   /dev/sda7                    yes         yes
```

In this case the output shows that we are using */dev/sda7*, or the seventh partition of the disk, for the ESX dump partition on controller *vmhba0*. It also shows that the partition is active and configured.

You'll notice that the partition will not show in a normal df or vdf command. However, the partition can be validated using the fdisk command:

```
# fdisk /dev/sda

The number of cylinders for this disk is set to 8844.
There is nothing wrong with that, but this is larger than 1024,
and could in certain setups cause problems with:
1) software that runs at boot time (e.g., old versions of LILO)
2) booting and partitioning software from other OSs
   (e.g., DOS FDISK, OS/2 FDISK)

Command (m for help): p
```

```
Disk /dev/sda: 72.7 GB, 72746008576 bytes
255 heads, 63 sectors/track, 8844 cylinders
Units = cylinders of 16065 * 512 = 8225280 bytes

   Device Boot    Start      End    Blocks   Id  System
/dev/sda1   *         1       13    104391   83  Linux
/dev/sda2            14      650  5116702+   83  Linux
/dev/sda3           651     8508 63119385   fb  Unknown
/dev/sda4          8509     8844  2698920    f  Win95 Ext'd (LBA)
/dev/sda5          8509     8577   554211   82  Linux swap
/dev/sda6          8578     8831  2040223+   83  Linux
/dev/sda7          8832     8844   104391   fc  Unknown

Command (m for help):
```

You will probably never need to make changes to this partition, but the tools are available in case you do.

5.30 Configuring a Firewall on the Command Line

Problem

You want to configure the firewall on your ESX Server using the command line.

Solution

Run the `esxcfg-firewall` command on the ESX Server.

Discussion

VMware makes it easy to configure the firewall on your ESX hosts with the **esxcfg-firewall** command. Generally, the firewall is configured via the vCenter client. However, it is important to understand how to do this via the command line as well. The configuration options are listed here:

```
$ esxcfg-firewall -h
esxcfg-firewall <options>
-q|--query                               Lists current settings.
-q|--query <service>                     Lists setting for the
                                         specified service.

-q|--query incoming|outgoing             Lists setting for non-required
                                         incoming/outgoing ports.

-s|--services                            Lists known services.
-l|--load                                Loads current settings.
-r|--resetDefaults                       Resets all options to defaults
-e|--enableService <service>             Allows specified service
                                         through the firewall.
-d|--disableService <service>            Blocks specified service
-o|--openPort <port,tcp|udp,in|out,name> Opens a port.
-c|--closePort <port,tcp|udp,in|out>     Closes a port previously opened
                                         via --openPort.

  --blockIncoming                        Block all non-required incoming
```

```
                                    ports (default value).
    --blockOutgoing                 Block all non-required outgoing
                                    ports (default value).
    --allowIncoming                 Allow all incoming ports.
    --allowOutgoing                 Allow all outgoing ports.
   -h|--help                        Show this message.
```

We won't go into detail on the configuration options here because we discuss configuring your firewall in Chapter 6.

See Also

Recipe 6.11

5.31 Managing ESX Driver Modules

Problem

You wish to manage modules that are loaded in the VMkernel on system boot.

Solution

Run the `esxcfg-module` command on the ESX Server.

Discussion

The `esxcfg-module` command provides you with a way to adjust the driver modules that are loaded during the ESX Server's startup sequence. Here's a list of the configurable options:

```
$ esxcfg-module -h
Usage: esxcfg-module <options> <module>
   -g|--get-options    Get the options for a given module and whether it is loaded
                       on boot.
   -s|--set-options    Set the options for a given module.
                       WARNING this may be overwritten by per device options.
   -e|--enable         Enable a given module, indicating it should be loaded on
                       boot.
   -d|--disable        Disable a given module, indicating it should not be loaded on
                       boot.
   -q|--query          Query enabled modules options.
   -l|--list           List all modules and whether they are enabled.
   -h|--help           Show this message.
```

Use the `-l` option to find out which modules are loaded on boot and whether any modules are disabled. In our example, we have no modules disabled (modules that are disabled will display as `false`):

```
$ esxcfg-module -l
Device Driver Modules
Module          Enabled Loaded
vmklinux        true    true
```

```
bnx2              true    true
qla4022           true    true
qla2300_707_vmwtrue       true
e1000             true    true
megaraid_sas      true    true
lvmdriver         true    true
vmfs3             true    true
etherswitch       true    true
shaper            true    true
tcpip             true    true
cosShadow         true    true
migration         true    true
nfsclient         true    true
deltadisk         true    true
vmfs2             true    true
```

The -g option allows you to view information specific to a module. In this example, the 1 informs us that the module is enabled and that we have not set any specific options for it:

```
$ esxcfg-module -g iscsi_mod
iscsi_mod enabled = 1 options = ''
```

5.32 Configuring Storage Multipathing

Problem

You want to manage the paths between the ESX Server and its storage devices via the command line instead of using the vCenter client.

Solution

By running the esxcfg-mpath command on the ESX Server, you can configure the pathing information for your SAN storage.

Discussion

The easiest way to manage your storage's paths is using vCenter. However, VMware also provides the esxcfg-mpath command to enable you to manage them via the command line.

Let's take a look at the options available for the esxcfg-mpath command:

```
$ esxcfg-mpath -h
esxcfg-mpath <options> [--lun=<LUN>] [--path=<path>]
 -l|--list                    List all LUNs and their paths.
 -p|--policy <type>           Set the policy for a specific LUN.  Requires
                              a --lun flag.  Type must be one of mru, rr, fixed or
                              custom.
 -H|--custom-hba-policy       Set the custom HBA policy value.  Must be one of
                              mru, preferred, any, minq.
 -T|--custom-target-policy    Set the custom target policy value. Must be one of
```

```
                              mru, preferred, any
    -C|--custom-max-commands   Set the custom policy value for max commands
    -B|--custom-max-blocks     Set the custom policy value for max blocks
    -s|--state <on|off>        Set the state for a specific LUN Path.  Requires
                               both --lun and --path flags.
    -f|--preferred             Set the given path to be preferred for the
                               given LUN.  Requires both --path and --lun flags.
    -q|--query                 Query the information on a specific LUN.
                               Requires a --lun flag.
    -P|--path=vmhbaX:X:X       Used to specify a path for setting the
                               path state or preferred path.  Uses the
                               VMkernel internal path name.
    -L|--lun=vmhbaX:X:X        Indicate which LUN to operate on.  This can be
                               either the internal VMkernel vmhba name for
                               this LUN (vmhbaX:X:X) or the vml name as
                               found in /vmfs/devices/disks.
    -v|--verbose               Show all information about the LUNs and
                               paths, otherwise a minimal set of data
                               is displayed to conserve space.
    -b|--bulk                  Bulk path listing suitable for parsing.
    -a|--hbas                  List HBAs on the system with a unique ID
                               if one is available.
    -h|--help                  Show this message.
    -r|--restore               Restore path setting to configured values
                               on system start. (INTERNAL USE ONLY)


NOTE vmhba names are not guaranteed to be valid across reboots.  Use vml LUN
names to be sure of consistency.

Examples:

  To see all paths
      esxcfg-mpath -l

  To see paths for disk vml.123456
      esxcfg-mpath -q --lun=vml.123456

  To set policy for disk vmhba0:0:1 to mru
      esxcfg-mpath --policy=mru --lun=vmhba0:0:1

  To set preferred path for disk vmhba0:0:1
      esxcfg-mpath --preferred --path=vmhba1:0:1 --lun=vmhba0:0:1

  To enable a path for disk vmhba0:0:1
      esxcfg-mpath --path=vmhba1:0:1 --lun=vmhba0:0:1 --state=on

  To disable a path and set policy to fixed for disk vmhba0:0:1
```

Using the -l option, you can get the output of your current paths, mounts, etc. The following output on our development system shows our current paths to the local disk, */dev/sda*, and our three Fibre connections on */dev/sdb*, */dev/sdc*, and */dev/sdd*. It shows that the local disk has a set policy of Fixed, while the Fibre connections are each set to MRU (Most Recently Used):

```
$ esxcfg-mpath -l
Disk vmhba1:0:0 /dev/sdb (418505MB) has 2 paths and policy of Most Recently Used
  FC 14:3.0 210000e08b9c9ee4<->202700a0b8117546 vmhba1:0:0 On active
  FC 14:3.1 210100e08bbc9ee4<->201700a0b8117546 vmhba2:0:0 On  preferred

Disk vmhba0:0:0 /dev/sda (69376MB) has 1 paths and policy of Fixed
  Local 2:14.0 vmhba0:0:0 On active preferred

Disk vmhba1:0:2 /dev/sdd (1142360MB) has 2 paths and policy of Most Recently Used
  FC 14:3.0 210000e08b9c9ee4<->202700a0b8117546 vmhba1:0:2 On active preferred
  FC 14:3.1 210100e08bbc9ee4<->201700a0b8117546 vmhba2:0:2 On

Disk vmhba1:0:1 /dev/sdc (512000MB) has 2 paths and policy of Most Recently Used
  FC 14:3.0 210000e08b9c9ee4<->202700a0b8117546 vmhba1:0:1 On active
  FC 14:3.1 210100e08bbc9ee4<->201700a0b8117546 vmhba2:0:1 On  preferred
```

5.33 Managing NFS Mounts

Problem

You want to manage the remote storage mounted over NFS.

Solution

Run the esxcfg-nas command on the ESX Server.

Discussion

Using this tool, you can list, mount, and unmount NFS exports from the VMkernel.

Let's take a look at the options available for the esxcfg-nas command:

```
$ esxcfg-nas -h
esxcfg-nas <options> [<label>]
-a|--add                Add a new NAS filesystem to /vmfs volumes.
                        Requires --host and --share options.
                        Use --readonly option only for readonly access.
-o|--host <host>        Set the host name or ip address for a NAS mount.
-s|--share <share>      Set the name of the NAS share on the remote system.
-y|--readonly           Add the new NAS filesystem with readonly access.
-d|--delete             Unmount and delete a filesystem.
-l|--list               List the currently mounted NAS file systems.
-r|--restore            Restore all NAS mounts from the configuration file.
                        (FOR INTERNAL USE ONLY).
-h|--help               Show this message.
```

The -l option displays the current NFS mounts on your ESX Server:

```
$ esxcfg-nas -l
NFSMOUNT01 is /NFS from 172.20.44.100 mounted
```

One of the most important requirements of NAS and software-based iSCSI is that you need to have a VMkernel port configured on the ESX Server's network. Assuming the VMkernel port is already configured, you can add a new mount as follows:

```
$ esxcfg-nas -a -o 172.20.44.101 -s /nfs02 NFSMOUNT02
Connecting to NAS volume: NFSMOUNT02
NFSMOUNT02 created and connected.
```

5.34 Managing Disk Volumes with ESX4

Problem

You want to use the command line to manage snapshots or replica volumes.

Solution

Run the esxcfg-volume command on the ESX Server.

Discussion

VMware added a new command-line tool in ESX4 to enable management of disk snapshot/replica volumes. This new command allows you to:

- Find these resources and view information about them.
- Mount or unmount a volume.
- Change the signature on a volume (resignaturing).
- Make the mounting of a volume persistent across reboots.

This command can come in handy if you need to mount a snapshot of your LUN because of corruption on the original LUN.

Let's take a look at the options available for the esxcfg-volume command:

```
$ esxcfg-volume -h
esxcfg-volume <options>
-l|--list                              List all volumes which have been
                                       detected as snapshots/replicas.
-m|--mount <VMFS UUID|label>           Mount a snapshot/replica volume, if
                                       its original copy is not online.
-u|--umount <VMFS UUID|label>          Unmount a snapshot/replica volume.
-r|--resignature <VMFS UUID|label>     Resignature a snapshot/replica volume.
-M|--persistent-mount <VMFS UUID|label> Mount a snapshot/replica volume
                                       persistently, if its original copy is
                                       not online.
-h|--help                              Show this message.
```

5.35 Configuring Ethernet Adapters

Problem

You want to manage and set specific variables on the physical Ethernet adapters in the ESX Server.

Solution

Run the esxcfg-nics command on the ESX Server.

Discussion

Let's take a look at the options available for the esxcfg-nics command:

```
$ esxcfg-nics -h
esxcfg-nics <options> [nic]
-s|--speed <speed>     Set the speed of this NIC to one of 10/100/1000/10000.
                       Requires a NIC parameter.
-d|--duplex <duplex>   Set the duplex of this NIC to one of 'full' or 'half'.
                       Requires a NIC parameter.
-a|--auto              Set speed and duplexity automatically. Requires a NIC
                       parameter.
-l|--list              Print the list of NICs and their settings.
-r|--restore           Restore the nics configured speed/duplex settings
                       (INTERNAL ONLY)
-h|--help              Display this message.
```

To list all Ethernet ports in the server, use the -l option. The output will give you a variety of information about the interface, including the driver, PCI, speed, duplex, and MTU, along with a description. Multiple interfaces will be displayed as *vmnic0*, *vmnic1*, and so on. For example:

```
$ esxcfg-nics -l
Name    PCI       Driver      Link Speed     Duplex MTU    Description
vmnic0  02:01.00  e1000       Up   1000Mbps  Full   1500   Intel Corporation 82545EM
Gigabit Ethernet Controller (Copper)
```

You can also set the speed of your interface using the -s option. The following example sets the speed to 100Mbps and the duplex mode to full duplex on the *vmnic0* interface (note that if you are changing the speed, you must also specify a duplex mode):

```
esxcfg-nics -s 100 -d full vmnic0
```

Changing the adapter to use the maximum speed can be accomplished using the -a option. Remember, you can use the -l option to verify your changes.

5.36 Rescanning Host Bus Adapters

Problem

You wish to rescan the host bus adapters in your ESX Server. This is useful if you add new LUNs or need to troubleshoot HBAs. To view a list of HBAs in your ESX Server, you can use the `esxcfg-vmhbadevs` command referenced in Recipe 5.43.

Solution

Run the `esxcfg-rescan` or `esxcfg-advcfg` command on the ESX Server.

Discussion

Use these commands to rescan a single adapter, or all the adapters on your ESX Server:

```
esxcfg-rescan adapter_name # single adapter (use VMkernel name)
esxcfg-advcfg -s 1 /Scsi/ScsiRescanAllHbas # all the adapters on the ESX Server
```

The following example rescans the specified HBA card for new LUNs. A typical scan, without adding any new LUNs, will look like this:

```
$ esxcfg-rescan vmhba2
Rescanning vmhba2...done.
On scsi3, removing:.
On scsi3, adding:.
```

5.37 Managing ESX4 Add-ons from the Command Line

Problem

You wish to manage available add-ons via the command line using ESX4.

Solution

Run the `esxcfg-addons` command on the ESX Server.

Discussion

VMware added a new command in ESX4, called `esxcfg-addons`, that you can use to enable, disable, and list all the available add-ons (perhaps better understood as "modules"):

```
$ esxcfg-addons -h
usage: esxcfg-addons [action] [parameter(s)]
   help        display this help message
   list        list addons
   enable      enable disabled addon
   disable     disable enabled addon
   version     display version information
```

The command is easy to use and pretty self-explanatory. If you have already installed ESX4, you may have noticed during the installation a new option to load add-ons. By default, your ESX4 installation will get a preloaded list of add-ons. The ones loaded by default on our Dell 1950 are shown in the following listing:

```
$ esxcfg-addons list
*   [01] base
*   [02] vmware-aacraid
*   [03] vmware-adp94xx
*   [04] vmware-ahci
*   [05] vmware-aic79xx
*   [06] vmware-ata_piix
*   [07] vmware-bnx2
*   [08] vmware-bnx2x
*   [09] vmware-cciss
*   [10] vmware-cdc_ether
*   [11] vmware-e1000e
*   [12] vmware-e1000
*   [13] vmware-enic
*   [14] vmware-fnic
*   [15] vmware-forcedeth
*   [16] vmware-hpsa
*   [17] vmware-igb
*   [18] vmware-ipmi_devintf
*   [19] vmware-ipmi_msghandler
*   [20] vmware-ipmi_si_drv
*   [21] vmware-ips
*   [22] vmware-iscsi_linux
*   [23] vmware-ixgbe
*   [24] vmware-libata
*   [25] vmware-lpfc820
*   [26] vmware-megaraid2
*   [27] vmware-megaraid_mbox
*   [28] vmware-megaraid_sas
*   [29] vmware-mptsas
*   [30] vmware-mptspi
*   [31] vmware-nx_nic
*   [32] vmware-pata_amd
*   [33] vmware-pata_atiixp
*   [34] vmware-pata_cmd64x
*   [35] vmware-pata_hpt3x2n
*   [36] vmware-pata_pdc2027x
*   [37] vmware-pata_serverworks
*   [38] vmware-pata_sil680
*   [39] vmware-qla2xxx
*   [40] vmware-qla4xxx
*   [41] vmware-random
*   [42] vmware-s2io
*   [43] vmware-sata_nv
*   [44] vmware-sata_promise
*   [45] vmware-sata_sil
*   [46] vmware-sata_svw
*   [47] vmware-tg3
*   [48] vmware-tpm_tis
```

```
*  [49] vmware-usbnet
*  [50] vmware-vmklinux
```

Disabling add-ons is simple:

```
esxcfg-addons disable vmare-usbnet
```

Enabling add-ons is also very simple:

```
esxcfg-addons enable vmware-usbnet
```

Only one add-on can be enabled or disabled in each command.

In a listing, when the star preceding the add-on is red, the associated add-on is installed but disabled. Enabled modules (add-ons) are displayed next to a green star.

5.38 Managing Resource Groups from the Command Line

Problem

You want to add or manage resource groups from the command line. The vCenter client makes it easy to do the same tasks and offers a wider variety of options, but the ESX Server does contain a command with some useful options.

Solution

Run the `esxcfg-resgrp` command on the ESX Server.

Discussion

This command is largely undocumented, and as far as we can tell it is not used much. Perhaps in the future VMware will expand its options.

The currently available options are listed here:

```
$ esxcfg-resgrp -h
Usage: esxcfg-resgrp [options] [resgrp path]
  -a, --add rgname     Add a new group under the path
  -d, --delete         Delete the resource group
  -l, --list           List all the resource groups
                       Or stats about a specific resource group
      --restore        Restore all resource groups from configuration
                       file (FOR INTERNAL USE ONLY).
  -h, --help           Show this message
```

Typical usage scenarios are:

```
esxcfg-resgrp -a testgroup host/user
esxcfg-resgrp -d host/user/testgroup
```

5.39 Managing VMkernel Network Routes

Problem

You want to set or change the routes the VMkernel uses to reach networks.

Solution

Run the esxcfg-route command on the ESX Server.

Discussion

VMware gives you the ability to modify the network routes via the command line using the esxcfg-route command. Alternatively, you can configure the routes using the vCenter client.

Let's take a look at the options available for the esxcfg-route command:

```
$ esxcfg-route -h
esxcfg-route <options> [<network> [<netmask] <gateway>] | <default gateway>
    <network> can be specified in 3 ways:
      * As a single argument in <Network>/<Mask> format
      * Or as a <Network> <Netmask> pair.
      * Or as 'default'

    -a|--add        Add route, to the VMkernel,
                    requires <network> (described above)
                    and gateway IP address
    -d|--del        Delete route from VMkernel.
                    Requires <network> (described above)
    -l|--list       List configured routes for the VMkernel
    -r|--restore    Restore route setting to configured values
                    on system start. (INTERNAL USE ONLY)
    -h|--help       Show this message.

If no options are specified then it will print the default gateway.
The default gateway can be set directly as : esxcfg-route <gateway>

Examples:

Add a route to 192.168.100.0 network through 192.168.0.1
esxcfg-route -a 192.168.100.0/24 192.168.0.1
or
esxcfg-route -a 192.168.100.0 255.255.255.0 192.168.0.1

Set the VMkernel default gateway of 192.168.0.1
esxcfg-route 192.168.0.1
or
esxcfg-route -a default 192.168.0.1

Delete a 192.168.100.0 route from the VMkernel:
esxcfg-route -d 192.168.100.0/24 192.168.0.1
```

As you can see, VMware provides some nice usage examples for the esxcfg-route command. Let's take a look at using the -1 option to display the current routes on our ESX Server. Your display might be similar to the following:

```
$ esxcfg-route -l

VMkernel Routes:
Network          Netmask           Gateway
172.20.44.0      255.255.252.0     Local Subnet
default          0.0.0.0           Local Subnet
```

To add a route to the 172.20.44.0 network using the gateway of 172.20.44.254, we would do something like this:

```
esxcfg-route -a 172.20.46.0/24 172.20.44.254
```

or this:

```
esxcfg-route -a 172.20.44.0 255.255.255.0 172.20.44.254
```

To set the default gateway for the VMkernel, issue the following command:

```
esxcfg-route -a default 172.20.44.254
```

And finally, to delete a route, use the -d option. For example:

```
esxcfg-route -d 172.20.46.0/24 172.20.44.254
```

You can also use vCenter to manage your ESX Server's routes.

5.40 Configuring Software iSCSI Options

Problem

You need to manage your software-based iSCSI connections on your ESX Server.

Solution

Run the esxcfg-swiscsi command on the ESX Server.

Discussion

Although vCenter provides access to all the options you can manipulate on iSCSI devices, you might want to manage them through command-line tools. Let's take a look at a few of the options available to the esxcfg-swiscsi command:

```
$ esxcfg-swiscsi -h
Usage: esxcfg-swiscsi options
  -e, --enable        Enable sw iscsi
  -d, --disable       Disable sw iscsi
  -q, --query         Check if sw iscsi is on/off
  -s, --scan          Scan for disk available through sw iscsi interface
  -k, --kill          Try to forcibly remove iscsi sw stack
  -r, --restore       Restore sw iscsi configuration from file
```

```
                    (FOR INTERNAL USE ONLY)
   -h, --help           Show this message
```

Running the `esxcfg-swiscsi` command with the `-q` switch will query the server to let you know whether software-based iSCSI is enabled. In our case, it is not enabled:

```
$ esxcfg-swiscsi -q
Software iSCSI is not enabled
```

Using the `-e` option, we can enable software-based iSCSI and open the firewall ports it requires:

```
$ esxcfg-swiscsi -e
Allowing software iSCSI traffic through firewall...
Enabling software iSCSI...
```

Finally, using the `-d` switch, we can disable software-based iSCSI on the ESX Server. Note that if you do this, you will need to manually restart the firewall to ensure the ports are closed for iSCSI:

```
$ esxcfg-swiscsi -d
Disabling software iSCSI for next boot
Software iSCSI traffic set to be blocked
Run firewall utility to set effect now (this may affect existing sw iscsi traffic)
```

If you choose to manage your software-based iSCSI via the command line, these changes might not be immediately reflected in vCenter; you will want to issue a `service mgmt-vmware restart` command to refresh vCenter.

See Also

Recipe 5.41

5.41 Configuring Hardware iSCSCI Options

Problem

You want to configure and display basic information for the hardware iSCSI cards used by an ESX Server.

Solution

Run the `esxcfg-hwiscsi` command on the ESX Server.

Discussion

VMware provides a command-line utility you can use to list and configure a few options for hardware iSCSI. However, you may also find additional options that can be configured on your iSCSI HBA; check with the manufacturer to see if it offers a Linux command-line configuration tool.

Let's take a look at the options available with the `esxcfg-hwiscsi` command:

```
$ esxcfg-hwiscsi -h
Usage: /usr/sbin/esxcfg-hwiscsi [-l] [-a allow|deny] [-j enable|disable] [-h]
<vmkernel SCSI adapter name>
   -l: list current configuration (overrides setting options)
   -a: allow or deny ARP redirection on adapter
   -j: enable or disable jumbo frame support
       (enabled: MTU = 9000, disabled: MTU = 1500)
   -h: print this message
```

You can display a small set of configurable values for your hardware-based iSCSI adapters using this command. For instance, in the following example we specified *vmhba19*, one of our iSCSI ports, in the -l option to learn about its configured values (keep in mind that your device ID will probably be different from ours):

```
$ esxcfg-hwiscsi -l vmhba19
DHCP Configuration Disabled
ARP Redirection Enabled
MTU Size = 9000
```

In this case, we have DHCP disabled, ARP redirection enabled, and the MTU size set to 9,000.

The -a option allows you to enable or disable ARP redirection on the adapter's interface. For example, the following command disables ARP redirection on *vmhba19*:

```
esxcfg-hwiscsi -a deny vmhba19
```

The -j option allows you to enable or disable jumbo frames:

```
esxcfg-hwiscsi -j enable vmhba19
```

See Also

Recipe 5.40

5.42 Upgrading Your Version of VMware

Problem

You want to upgrade a server from VMware ESX 2.x to ESX 3.x.

Solution

Run the `esxcfg-upgrade` command on the ESX Server.

Discussion

This command is not for general use. However, it offers the ability to assist you in upgrading your ESX 2.x servers to ESX 3.x. A few options are available:

```
$ esxcfg-upgrade -h
            -h --help
            -g --convert-grub
            -f --convert-fstab
            -r --upgrade-pre-vmkernel
            -o --upgrade-post-vmkernel
```

The -g option may only be used with the -r option.

For more information, refer to the VMware website's documentation on upgrading from ESX 2.x to ESX 3.x.

5.43 Displaying vmhba Names with Associated Mappings

Problem

You want to see which Linux device, service console partition, or VMFS volume is associated with each *vmhba*.

Solution

Run the esxcfg-vmhbadevs command on the ESX Server.

Discussion

The esxcfg-vmhbasdev command shows how *vmhba* adapters are mapped on the server to physical Linux devices. Let's take a look at the available options:

```
$ esxcfg-vmhbadevs -h
esxcfg-vmhbadevs <options>
Print the mappings between vmhba names and /dev names
-m|--vmfs               Print mappings for VMFS volumes to their
                        Service Console partitions and vmhba names.
-f|--vfat               Print mappings for VFAT volumes to their
                        Service Console partitions and vmhba names.
-q|--query              Print mapping in 2.5 compatibility mode to mimic
                        vmkpcidivy -q vmhba_devs.
-a|--all                Print all devices, regardless of whether they have
                        console device or not.
-h|--help               Show this message.
```

The -a option displays all devices, regardless of whether a console device is connected. The *vmhba* adapter is displayed along with the associated Linux mount point:

```
$ esxcfg-vmhbadevs -a
vmhba19:0:0    /dev/sda
vmhba19:1:0    /dev/sdb
vmhba19:2:0    /dev/sdc
vmhba19:3:0    /dev/sdh
vmhba21:0:0    /dev/sdd
vmhba21:0:1    /dev/sde
```

```
vmhba21:0:2    /dev/sdf
vmhba23:0:0    /dev/sdg
```

The -m option adds VMFS volume mappings. For example, instead of looking in */volumes/vmfs* to see the symlink connections from */dev/sdX* to the VMFS mapping, you can use this option:

```
$ esxcfg-vmhbadevs -m
vmhba19:0:0:1    /dev/sda1              48a588ed-b2021a45-7f93-001e4f1e7175
vmhba19:1:0:1    /dev/sdb1              48b5a2f4-92606cbf-7dfc-0015175b82be
vmhba21:0:1:1    /dev/sde1              4766e976-80ec4aa8-0ade-001b210caf2e
vmhba19:2:0:1    /dev/sdc1              48bedde1-02750777-b10f-0015175b82be
vmhba19:3:0:1    /dev/sdh1              492c0819-1419a85c-0be1-0015175b82be
vmhba21:0:0:1    /dev/sdd1              47668165-05f97e46-5570-001b210cb31c
vmhba23:0:0:3    /dev/sdg3              47cbf46d-44f3d18a-25ec-001e4f1e5402
vmhba21:0:2:1    /dev/sdf1              47cd6dd2-31a2a254-a6a1-001e4f1e7171
```

 This command has been eliminated in ESX4 vSphere and has been replaced with the esxcfg-scsidevs command.

See Also

Recipe 5.44

5.44 Managing SCSI Device Mappings with ESX4 vSphere

Problem

You want to manage your SCSI device mappings via the command line with ESX4 vSphere.

Solution

Run the esxcfg-scsidevs command on the ESX Server.

Discussion

In ESX4, VMware retired the old esxcfg-vmhbadevs command and replaced it with a similar but more feature-rich command called esxcfg-scsidevs:

```
$ esxcfg-scsidevs -h
esxcfg-scsidevs <options>
Print the mappings between vmhba names and /dev names
-l|--list                    List all Logical Devices known on this
                             system with device information.
-c|--compact-list            List all Logical Devices each on a
                             single line, with limited information.
-u|--uids                    List all Device Unique Identifiers with their
```

```
                            primary name.
       -d|--device          Used to filter the --list, --compact-list
                            and uids commands to limit output to a
                            specific device.
       -m|--vmfs            Print mappings for VMFS volumes to their
                            Service Console partitions and vmhba names.
       -f|--vfat            Print mappings for VFAT volumes to their
                            Service Console partitions and vmhba names.
       -a|--hbas            Print HBA devices with identifying information
       -A|--hba-device-list Print a mapping between HBAs and the devices it
                            provides paths to.
       -o|--offline-cos-dev Offline the COS device corresponding to this
                            vmkernel device.
       -n|--online-cos-dev  Bring online the COS device corresponding to
                            this vmkernel device.
       -h|--help            Show this message.
```

See Also

Recipe 5.43

5.45 Managing VMkernel Ports

Problem

You want to create, update, or delete entries in the VMkernel configuration for VMotion, NAS, and software iSCSI.

Solution

Run the `esxcfg-vmknic` command on the ESX Server.

Discussion

This command is used to configure the VMkernel ports on virtual switches. The VMkernel port is a special port that is used for VMotion, software-based iSCSI, and NFS access. Let's take a look at the available options:

```
$ esxcfg-vmknic -h
esxcfg-vmknic <options> [[<portgroup>]]
     -a|--add             Add a VMkernel NIC to the system,
                          requires IP parameters and portgroup name.
     -d|--del             Delete VMkernel NIC on given portgroup.
     -e|--enable          Enable the given NIC if disabled.
     -D|--disable         Disable the given NIC if enabled.
     -l|--list            List VMkernel NICs.
     -i|--ip <X.X.X.X> or DHCP  The IP address for this VMkernel NIC.
                          Setting an IP address requires that the
                          --netmask option be given in same command.
                          Setting this to DHCP requires DHCP support
                          in the VMkernel
     -n|--netmask <X.X.X.X>  The IP netmask for this VMkernel NIC.
```

```
                              Setting the IP netmask requires that the --ip
                              option be given in the same command.
      -P|--peerdns            Set peer dns. If set the system
                              will use the HostName, HostIPAddress
                              Domain returned by DHCP. Valid only for DHCP
      -t|--tso                Disable TSO for the vmknic being created.
      -m|--mtu MTU            MTU for the interface being created.
      -r|--restore            Restore VMkernel TCP/IP interfaces from
                              Configuration file (FOR INTERNAL USE ONLY).
      -h|--help               Show this message.
```

The -l option shows the ports that are already created on our virtual switches. In our case, we have a VMotion port on *vmk0* (the lines are wrapped here to fit on the page):

```
$ esxcfg-vmknic -l
Interface  PortGroup        IP Address      Netmask       Broadcast
MAC Address        MTU    TSO MSS   Enabled
vmk0       vMotion          172.20.47.2     255.255.252.0  172.20.47.255
00:50:56:74:f1:b9 1500    40960     true
```

The -a option allows you to add a new VMkernel NIC to the ESX Server. However, you must have a portgroup present before adding a new NIC to the system. You can create a new portgroup using the esxcfg-vswitch command, as discussed in Recipe 5.12. The command to add the port is:

```
esxcfg-vmknic -a -i 172.20.47.3 -n 255.255.255.0 vMotion
```

The -d option allows you to remove the VMkernel NIC from the system:

```
esxcfg-vmknic -d vMotion
```

You can also use the -e option to enable a disabled port or the -D (uppercase) option to disable an enabled port. When a port is disabled, you must enable it before you can delete it.

Another important option is -m, which allows you to set an MTU speed for the VMkernel NIC port. This is important for NFS or iSCSI connections, where you might use something similar to the following:

```
esxcfg-vmknic -a -i 172.20.47.5 -n 255.255.255.0 -m 9000 iSCSI
```

If you use the -l option to verify the results, you will notice that the MTU speed is now set to 9,000 instead of the default 1,500.

5.46 Managing vswif Console Network Settings

Problem

You want to create, update, and delete *vswif* service console network settings.

Solution

Run the esxcfg-vswif command on the ESX Server.

Discussion

The `esxcfg-vswif` command allows you to configure, add, and delete *vswif* interfaces on your ESX Server. This command is useful if you cannot manage your ESX Server through the vCenter client.

Let's take a look at the available options:

```
$ esxcfg-vswif -h
esxcfg-vswif <options> [<vswif>]
 -a|--add                    Add vswif, requires IP parameters.
                             Automatically enables interface.
 -d|--del                    Delete vswif.
 -l|--list                   List configured vswifs.
 -e|--enable                 Enable this vswif interface.
 -s|--disable                Disable this vswif interface.
 -p|--portgroup              Set the portgroup name of the vswif.
 -i|--ip <X.X.X.X> or DHCP   The IP address for this vswif or specify
                             DHCP to use DHCP for address.
 -n|--netmask <X.X.X.X>      The IP netmask for this vswif.
 -b|--broadcast <X.X.X.X>    The IP broadcast address for this vswif
                             (not required if netmask and ip are set).
 -c|--check                  Check to see if a virtual NIC exists.
                             Program outputs a 1 if the given vswif
                             exists and is enabled, 0 otherwise.
 -D|--disable-all            Disable all vswif interfaces.
                             (WARNING: This may result in a loss of network
                             connectivity to the Service Console).
 -E|--enable-all             Enable all vswif interfaces and bring them up.
 -A|--autoNet                Setup one DHCP vswif per vSwitch.
 -r|--restore                Restore all vswifs from the configuration.
                             file (FOR INTERNAL USE ONLY).
 -h|--help                   Show this message.

!!!WARNING!!!
Loss of network connectivity may result if invalid parameters are passed to
Add, Delete, Portgroup or IP operations.
```

Like most of VMware's command-line tools, this one has the -l option available to list the current settings:

```
$ esxcfg-vswif -l
Name      PortGroup        IP Address      Netmask         Broadcast
Enabled   DHCP
vswif0    Service Console  172.20.44.3     255.255.255.0   172.20.44.255
true      false
```

The lines are wrapped here to fit on the page. As you can see, we have one *vswif* interface assigned to our service console. The output also lists the IP address, the netmask, the broadcast address, whether the interface is enabled, and whether it got its address through DHCP.

Suppose we wish to create a backup service console group in our ESX environment. The first thing we need to do is make sure the portgroup is configured:

```
esxcfg-vswitch -A "Service Console Backup" vSwitch1
```

We can then create the backup group:

```
esxcfg-vswif -a -i 172.20.44.199 -n 255.255.255.0 -p "Service Console Backup" vswif1
```

Using the -l option to verify the changes will show us the new *vswif* interface:

```
$ esxcfg-vswif -l
Name     PortGroup              IP Address      Netmask         Broadcast
Enabled  DHCP
vswif0   Service Console        172.20.44.3     255.255.255.0   172.20.44.255
true       false
vswif0   Service Console Backup 172.20.44.199   255.255.255.0   172.20.44.255
true       false
```

## CHAPTER 6

General Security

In this chapter we will provide solutions to help you maintain a secure virtual environment, using technologies that are already available to you in your VMware implementation. This chapter will cover a lot of basic Linux-related material, since the ESX Server has Red Hat Linux as its base. We will also discuss increasing security with ESXi, VMware's console-less hypervisor.

This chapter will focus on using the command line for security and monitoring tasks. Most of the tasks we'll examine (apart from user-related tasks such as role management) can be performed using the vCenter client, and in fact that is VMware's suggested method. However, we feel that users should know how to use alternative ways to manage their ESX Servers, in case there are problems that prevent the use of the vCenter client. Thus, we have chosen to focus on the command line in this chapter. If you need details on performing any of these tasks via vCenter, we recommend that you familiarize yourself with a great document VMware provides on security, located at *http://www.vmware.com/files/pdf/vi35_security_hardening_wp.pdf*.

6.1 Enabling SSH on ESXi

Problem

You want to enable SSH on your server console.

Solution

Enable SSH. However, note that leaving direct *root* SSH disabled is the suggested configuration.

Discussion

SSH is a valuable service to have on your service console because it provides a way for an administrator to go behind the VMware GUI and issue commands directly to the operating system running on the server. By default, ESXi does not have SSH enabled;

in fact, VMware does not directly support running SSH on an ESXi server. If you need to enable it, however, you can do so by following these steps:

1. On your ESXi console, press Alt-F1 to open a command prompt. Next, enter **unsupported** along with your system's root password.

2. At the command line, edit the *inetd.conf* file, which maintains information for various services running on your ESXi console. The file is located at */etc/inetd.conf*. Look for the line that starts with #ssh and remove the pound sign (#). Save the file to finalize your changes.

3. You now need to restart the *inetd* service, because making the change in the configuration file does not do this automatically. To do so, enter the following command at the command line:

   ```
   /sbin/services.sh restart
   ```

   If you are running ESX 3.5 Update 4, you will instead need to issue the following command to restart SSH:

   ```
   kill - HUP inetd
   ```

Your SSH service is now enabled, and you can access your console by using your favorite SSH terminal program.

6.2 Enabling Direct root Logins on Your ESX Server

Problem

Though they are normally disallowed, you want to enable direct *root* logins on your ESX Server.

Solution

Edit the SSH configuration file to allow direct *root* logins.

Discussion

By default, ESX 3.x servers are set to deny remote *root* logins. Depending on your environment and personal preference, however, you may wish to enable such logins on your ESX Server consoles.

 To maintain a more secure environment, the best practice would be to implement a system administrator–type account and use **sudo** to perform these tasks. The suggested configuration by VMware leaves direct *root* SSH disabled.

To enable SSH on your ESX console, follow these steps:

1. Press Alt-F1 to open a command prompt and enter your system's *root* password.

2. Once you've logged in, edit the *sshd_config* file. This file contains multiple configuration variables for the SSHD daemon. We will be making only one change, to allow direct logins. Open the following file:

   ```
   /etc/ssh/sshd_config
   ```

3. Look for the line that says `PermitRootLogin`, most likely located toward the top of the file. Change it to:

   ```
   PermitRootLogin yes
   ```

4. Then save the configuration file and restart the SSHD daemon by entering one of the following at the command line:

   ```
   /etc/init.d/sshd restart
   ```

   or:

   ```
   service sshd restart
   ```

Your SSHD daemon is now set to permit direct *root* logins. Bear in mind that you are doing this at your own risk, as best practice suggests leaving direct *root* SSH capabilities turned off.

6.3 Adding Users and Groups

Problem

You need to be able to manage the accounts for each of your users.

Solution

You can set up users and groups using the console, according to your needs. ESXi users can use lockdown mode to help secure their user environments.

 While not discussed in this recipe, all aspects of user management can also be handled via the vCenter client, and this is VMware's preferred method.

Discussion

You'll make use of two commands in this recipe: `useradd` and `groupadd`. You'll use the `useradd` command to make modifications to the */etc/passwd* and */etc/shadow* files, which store user information such as the UID, GID, path, shell, and home directory. You'll also use the `groupadd` command to modify the /etc/group file, which stores the users' group information. To begin, log into the ESX Server as *root*, via SSH or the console.

For this example, we are going to assume that you need to set up two groups, a junior system administrator group and a senior system administrator group. We'll use the `groupadd` command to create the two groups from the command line:

```
groupadd jradmin
groupadd sradmin
```

Once you've created the groups, you will notice that they are listed in the /etc/group file. Now we'll add users to the groups by using the `useradd` command from the command line. The `useradd` command has many different options, but we will only use the -g option to set the group membership:

```
useradd -g jradmin rtroy
useradd -g sradmin mhelmke
```

We now have two users, one assigned to the *jradmin* group and one assigned to the *sradmin* group. By setting up groups, you allow yourself to limit the areas each user can access. For example, if you are using `sudo`, you can give the *jradmin* group a less complete set of options than the *sradmin* group.

Our example invokes a very simple `useradd` command to set group membership. Other options are available to further customize your users' accounts and groups. Here's some detailed information on the `useradd` command:

```
Usage: useradd [options] LOGIN

Options:
  -b, --base-dir BASE_DIR    base directory for the new user account
                  home directory
  -c, --comment COMMENT      set the GECOS field for the new user account
  -d, --home-dir HOME_DIR    home directory for the new user account
  -D, --defaults             print or save modified default useradd
                  configuration
  -e, --expiredate EXPIRE_DATE  set account expiration date to EXPIRE_DATE
  -f, --inactive INACTIVE    set password inactive after expiration
                  to INACTIVE
  -g, --gid GROUP            force use GROUP for the new user account
  -G, --groups GROUPS        list of supplementary groups for the new
                  user account
  -h, --help                 display this help message and exit
  -k, --skel SKEL_DIR        specify an alternative skel directory
  -K, --key KEY=VALUE        overrides /etc/login.defs defaults
  -m, --create-home          create home directory for the new user
                  account
  -o, --non-unique           allow create user with duplicate
                  (non-unique) UID
  -p, --password PASSWORD    use encrypted password for the new user
                  account
  -r, --system               create a system account
  -s, --shell SHELL          the login shell for the new user account
  -u, --uid UID              force use the UID for the new user account
```

Similarly, here is an overview of the groupadd command:

```
Usage: groupadd [options] GROUP

Options:
  -f, --forceforce        exit with success status if the specified
                    group already exists
  -g, --gid GID           use GID for the new group
  -h, --help              display this help message and exit
  -K, --key KEY=VALUE     overrides /etc/login.defs defaults
  -o, --non-unique        allow create group with duplicate
                    (non-unique) GID
```

Another important command is userdel, which allows you to remove a user from the system. You have the option of leaving her home directory intact, which will preserve any personal settings, scripts, or applications stored there.

The userdel command will remove entries from both the */etc/passwd* and */etc/shadow* files. However, if you are using sudo, the userdel command will not remove any entries from the *sudoers* file, so be sure to remove those as necessary.

To remove a user and simultaneously delete that user's home directory, use the -r option, as shown here:

```
userdel -r rtroy
```

To remove the user but leave her home directory intact, omit the -r switch:

```
userdel rtroy
```

Removing a group can be accomplished by using the groupdel command:

```
groupdel jradmin
```

This command removes the *jradmin* group from the server, deleting its entries in the */etc/group* and */etc/gshadow* files.

These commands offer many advanced features that you can find out about through their --help options or manpages.

See Also

Recipe 6.6

6.4 Allowing or Denying Users the Use of SSH

Problem

You want to control which users can access your ESX Server via SSH.

Solution

Configure individual account permissions to allow or deny SSH access to specific users.

Discussion

For security, it is generally better to create an individual account for each user and to avoid allowing multiple users to have access to the *root* account. This allows actions to be connected to the people performing them and is especially important for tracking problems in case an administrator "goes rogue." However, this approach does mean that you have to figure out how to allow these individual accounts to access the server securely.

By using the configuration options built into your SSH server, you can allow specific users to access your ESX Server directly, via SSH. To accomplish this, edit the SSH configuration file, located at */etc/ssh/sshd_config*. Look for the line that says `AllowUsers`. If this line is commented out with a #, remove the # sign. If you do not see a line containing this information, make a new line like the example below, making sure to change the usernames according to your needs.

In this example entry, we allow *tom*, *chris*, *bob* and any user whose username starts with the word *sysadmin* to have SSH access:

```
AllowUsers   tom    chris   bob    sysadmin*
```

Once you are satisfied, save the configuration (by pressing the `:wq!` keys in *vi*). At the command line, restart the *sshd* daemon to make your configuration changes take effect. To do this, enter either this command:

```
/etc/init.d/sshd restart
```

or this one:

```
service sshd restart
```

You can also deny specific users permission to access your ESX Server directly with SSH. To do this, look for a line in the */etc/ssh/sshd_config* file that says `DenyUsers`. If it is commented out with a #, remove the # sign. If you do not see a line containing this information, make a new line similar to the one below, remembering to change the usernames according to your needs.

In this example, we deny access to *george*, *todd*, *tim*, and any user whose username starts with *b*:

```
DenyUsers   george todd   tim    b*
```

Keep in mind when using the * wildcard character that, in our example, a user named *bob* would be denied access even if he is listed in the `AllowUsers` line like this (that is, the deny rules take precedence over the allow rules):

```
AllowUsers   tom    chris   bob    sysadmin*
```

Save the file and restart the daemon as before.

The users who have been denied will be barred from logging into the system via SSH, and any login attempts they make will show up in the */var/log/messages* file.

6.5 Turning on the MOTD for Console Users

Problem

You want to display a specific message to each of your users when they attempt to log into the server.

Solution

Edit the *sshd_config* file from the command line to enable the MOTD.

Discussion

The MOTD, or message of the day, allows you to display a note to users when they try to access your server via the console or SSH.

By default, the ESX Server is not set up to display the MOTD when users log in via SSH, so you need to change the *sshd_config* file to display it.

The first thing to do is navigate to your */etc/ssh* directory and open the *sshd_config* file with your favorite editor, as we do here using *vi*:

```
vi /etc/ssh/sshd_config
```

Change the following variable to enable SSH to display the MOTD by removing the # from the beginning of the line:

```
#PrintMotd yes
```

Save the file and restart the *sshd* services by issuing the following command:

```
service sshd restart
```

Now that the changes to the SSH configuration are in place, you can edit your */etc/ motd* file to include any information you wish to display to your users when they log in. This file comes standard with most Linux distributions and can be edited with your favorite editor. By default, the file is empty.

6.6 Changing the root Password via the Console

Problem

You want to change the *root* password.

Solution

Use the `passwd` command.

Discussion

Changing the *root* user's password on the ESX host requires to you be logged in either via SSH or via the console directly. You will need to be logged in as *root* or become the *root* user using sudo. You can then change the password by issuing the following command:

```
passwd
```

You will be asked to enter the current password, enter the new password, and then reenter the new password a second time to confirm that you have typed it correctly. The next time you log in, you will need to use the new password.

6.7 Recovering a Lost root Password

Problem

You lost or forgot your *root* password and you need to change it.

Solution

Log in as *root* via sudo and change the password, or edit the GRUB menu to boot in single-user mode.

Discussion

Because VMware uses a modified version of Red Hat Linux, recovering the *root* password is easy. We'll look at two different ways to recover the *root* password.

The first (and perhaps the easiest) method is by using sudo. If you have an account with full sudo su permissions, you can become the *root* user this way and change the *root* password.

For the second option, you will need to use the service console or be connected to a kernel-based virtual machine (KVM). To begin, use the GRUB menu, which is the menu you are first displayed when your ESX Server is booting, to boot into single-user mode.

You will notice three options in the GRUB menu (Figure 6-1): "VMware ESX Server," which boots your ESX Server normally; "VMware ESX Server (debug mode)," which turns on debugging options; and "Service Console only (troubleshooting mode)," which will drop you to the command line and not initiate any of the key services. There is also some descriptive text under the menu, giving you more advanced options to use within the GRUB menu.

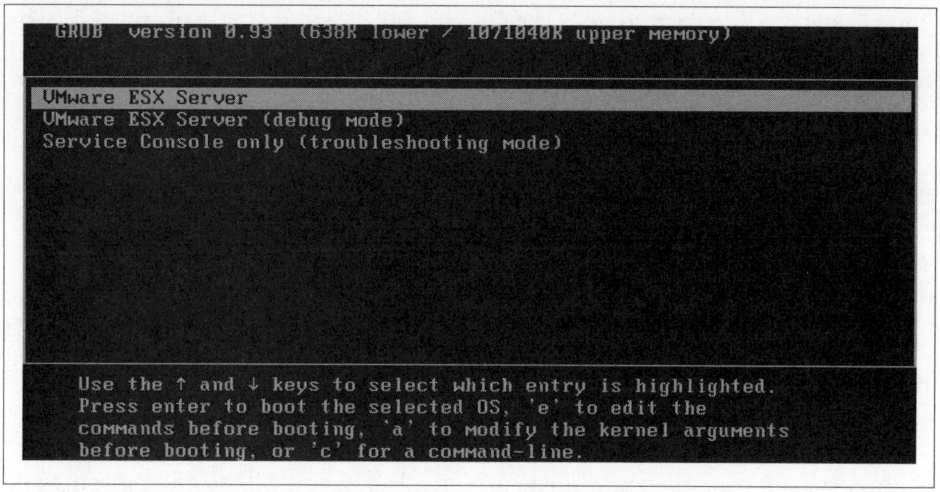

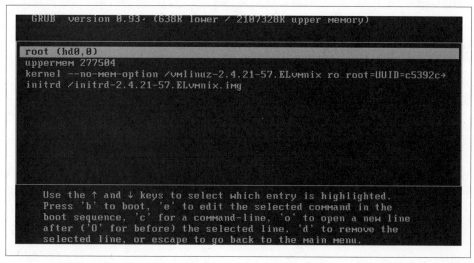

Figure 6-1. Boot menu for VMware ESX Server, showing boot selection

To begin the process of recovering your *root* password, you need to have the gray bar highlight the "VMware ESX Server" option on the menu. Press the letter **e** to bring up a more advanced menu, from which you will make a simple change to the kernel boot string. There are four menu options here, and you will use the line that starts with kernel (Figure 6-2). Highlight this line and press **e** again to enter edit mode.

Figure 6-2. Advanced boot options

Once in edit mode, go to the end of the line and add the word `single` (Figure 6-3). This tells the server to boot into single-user mode, allowing you to change the *root* password. Press Enter to return to the previous menu. Highlight the line starting with `kernel` and press the **b** key to initiate the single-user boot mode.

```
[ Minimal BASH-like line editing is supported.  For the first word, TAB
  lists possible command completions.  Anywhere else TAB lists the possible
  completions of a device/filename.  ESC at any time cancels.  ENTER
  at any time accepts your changes.]

<=UUID=96cfae68-fd3d-4944-86c1-9ee3548021a9 mem=272M single_
```

Figure 6-3. Adding single-user mode to the boot line

The system will be booted into single-user mode, and you will be given a command prompt from which you can type the `passwd` command to change your *root* password.

When the password change is complete, issue the `reboot` command to reboot the server in its original mode. Once rebooted, you can log in with the new *root* password.

6.8 Disabling Direct root Console Logins

Problem

Remote users can log in as *root* via the console, and you wish to prevent this for greater security.

Solution

Edit the configuration to prevent direct *root* login, even from the console.

Discussion

By default, remote users cannot log in to an ESX Server as *root*. However, they can log in as *root* on the console that is directly connected to the server. If you wish to lock down your ESX Servers even further, you can disable the ability to log in directly as *root* on that console. Users to whom you give *root* privileges can still become *root* through the `sudo` command, but you can use techniques discussed in Recipe 6.4 to restrict the commands they can execute. You cannot do this if they can log in directly as *root*.

In this example we will be modifying the */etc/securetty* file. When this file exists but is empty, direct *root* console logins are disabled. Follow these steps to implement this security measure:

1. Log into your ESX Server and run the following commands to back up the */etc/securetty* file, in case you wish to revert your changes at a later time:

    ```
    mv /etc/securetty /etc/securetty_backup
    ```

2. Now create an empty *securetty* file, by running the following command:

    ```
    touch /etc/securetty
    ```

3. You'll also want to ensure that the *securetty* file is readable and writable only by the *root* user. To accomplish this, run the following commands:

    ```
    chmod 400 securetty securetty_backup
    chown root :root securetty securetty_backup
    ```

Once complete, verify that you can no longer log into the console directly as the *root* user.

If you wish to revert your changes, simply copy the *securetty_backup* file to *securetty* using the following command:

```
cp /etc/securetty_backup securetty
```

If you try to log in from the console directly as the *root* user after restoring the *securetty* file, you should be able to do so.

For reference, your *securetty* file should contain lines such as the following, which list terminals and virtual terminals where *root* login is allowed:

```
console
vc/1
vc/2
vc/3
vc/4
vc/5
vc/6
vc/7
vc/8
vc/9
vc/10
vc/11
tty1
tty2
tty3
tty4
tty5
tty6
tty7
tty8
tty9
tty10
tty11
```

6.9 Securing the GRUB Bootloader Menu

Problem

The GRUB menu may be accessed during a reboot, and you wish to prevent knowledgeable users from changing the boot parameters and either damaging the server or accessing things they should not.

Solution

Require a password to access the GRUB boot menu.

Discussion

Setting a password for the ESX Server's GRUB boot menu ensures that your kernel boot parameters cannot be bypassed when the server is rebooting. For example, the parameters in the GRUB boot menu control which hard drive and kernel your ESX Server boots to. If these parameters are erroneously changed, your ESX Server may be unbootable.

To restrict access to this menu, you need to generate an encrypted password and put it in the */etc/grub.conf* configuration file.

Start by logging into your ESX Server with *root* permissions. From the command line, run the **grub** command. Next, at the grub prompt, enter **md5crypt**. You will be prompted for a password one time. Once your password has been validated, you will see an md5 hash text; copy this, as you will need to enter it in the */etc/grub.conf* file. When you have copied the md5 hash, exit the *grub* application by typing **quit**.

Now, edit this file with your favorite editor:

```
/etc/grub.conf
```

In order to set a password on your GRUB menu, you'll need to add a new variable to this file. Look for something similar to this:

```
...
default=1
timeout=10
```

Add the following line after the line that lists the **timeout** variable (keep in mind that, depending on your configuration, your timeout value may be slightly different). Substitute the hash string you saved for *hash_string*:

```
password --md5 hash_string
```

Save the file and exit. When you reboot your ESX Server, you will not be able to edit any of the boot options at the GRUB menu without first entering a password. By adding a GRUB password, you are removing the last trick, practically speaking, by which someone with physical access to the system can gain unauthorized access to your server.

About the only other things the attacker could do are boot from a CD or damage the system physically.

6.10 Disabling USB Drive Mounting

Problem

Allowing USB drives to be directly connected and mounted to your ESX Server may cause a security risk.

Solution

Disable the automatic mounting of USB devices on your ESX Server by editing the */etc/ modules.conf* file.

Discussion

To get started, log into your ESX Server as *root*. Then, edit the following file:

```
/etc/modules.conf
```

Search for the following entry and add a # sign at the beginning of the line:

```
alias usb-controller
```

After making the change, save the configuration file. You will need to reboot your server in order for the new settings to take effect.

 Disabling this might affect USB keyboards and mice in some configurations. It is suggested that you test thoroughly after making this change—if you are using a USB keyboard and/or mouse, you may not want to implement this solution.

6.11 Opening and Closing Firewall Ports via the Console

Problem

Although vCenter has an option called *Security Profile* that can help you maintain a large number of preset firewalls, you may encounter situations where you will need to maintain a custom rule specific to an application you wish to run.

Solution

ESX has a great tool called `esxcfg-firewall` that allows you to maintain your firewall from the command line.

Discussion

Before we get started, let's take a look at some of the configuration options the esxcfg-firewall command offers:

```
[root@esx6cluster2 log]# esxcfg-firewall -h
esxcfg-firewall <options>
-q|--query                          Lists current settings.
-q|--query <service>                Lists setting for the
                                    specified service.
-q|--query incoming|outgoing        Lists setting for non-required
                                    incoming/outgoing ports.
-s|--services                       Lists known services.
-l|--load                           Loads current settings.
-r|--resetDefaults                  Resets all options to defaults
-e|--enableService <service>        Allows specified service
                                    through the firewall.
-d|--disableService <service>       Blocks specified service
-o|--openPort <port,tcp|udp,in|out,name>    Opens a port.
-c|--closePort <port,tcp|udp,in|out>        Closes a port previously opened
                                    via --openPort.
   --blockIncoming                  Block all non-required incoming
                                    ports  (default value).
   --blockOutgoing                  Block all non-required outgoing
                                    ports (default value).
   --allowIncoming                  Allow all incoming ports.
   --allowOutgoing                  Allow all outgoing ports.
-h|--help                           Show this message.
```

Different levels of security—low, medium, and high—can be applied to the ESX firewall. The default setting is high, blocking all inbound traffic and allowing outbound communication only over ports 80, 443, 902, 427, 5988, 5989, 111, 2049, 27000–27010, and 22. These ports provide the basic foundation for the ESX Server to communicate over the network. You can verify your firewall security settings by running the following commands:

```
esxcfg-firewall -q incoming
esxcfg-firewall -q outgoing
```

Depending on the results of these commands, you can verify your ESX host's security level by using Table 6-1 as a reference.

Table 6-1. ESX host firewall levels

Configuration	Security level
Incoming ports blocked by default.	High
Outgoing ports blocked by default.	
Incoming ports blocked by default.	Medium
Outgoing ports not blocked by default.	
Incoming ports not blocked by default.	Low
Outgoing ports not blocked by default.	

Depending on the situation or your environment, you may wish to change the default security policy on your ESX hosts. It's recommended that you leave the security level set to its default and that you only open specific ports, but if you want to change the security level you can do so with the following commands:

- To set the security level to low:

```
esxcfg-firewall --allowIncoming --allowOutgoing
```

- To set the security level to medium:

```
esxcfg-firewall --blockIncoming --allowOutgoing
```

- To set the security level to high:

```
esxcfg-firewall --blockIncoming -blockOutgoing
```

After making these changes, you'll need to restart the VMware services in order for the new rules to take effect:

```
service mgmt-vmware restart
```

Other helpful commands to view your firewall ruleset are:

- To display all the firewall settings, inbound and outbound:

```
esxcfg-firewall -q
```

- To display known ESX Server firewall services by name:

```
esxcfg-firewall -s
```

Example output looks like this:

```
activeDirectorKerberos caARCserve CIMHttpServer CIMHttpsServer CIMSLP
commvaultDynamic commvaultStatic ftpClient ftpServer kerberos LDAP LDAPS
legatoNetWorker LicenseClient nfsClient nisClient ntpClient smbClient snmpd
sshClient sshServer swISCSIClient symantecBackupExec symantecNetBackup telnetClient
TSM updateManager VCB vncServer vpxHeartbeats
```

Enabling the firewall to allow or deny certain ports, both inbound and outbound, is relatively simple. To accomplish this, you'll again use the esxcfg-firewall command.

To open a firewall port, use the following syntax:

```
esxcfg-firewall -o port,protocol,direction,service_name
```

where *port* specifies the application ports, *protocol* is either tcp or udp, *direction* is either in or out, and *service_name* is the firewall service name (see Table 6-2).

To close a firewall port, use the following syntax. Notice that when closing a port, you don't specify a name:

```
esxcfg-firewall -c port,protocol,direction
```

You can also enable services within the firewall by using the following command, where the -e option specifies the name of the service:

```
esxcfg-firewall -e service_name
```

Alternatively, you can disable services using the same command with the the -d parameter:

```
esxcfg-firewall -d service_name
```

Table 6-2 lists the service names that can be used with the esxcfg-firewall command.

Table 6-2. Available firewall service names

aam	activeDirectorKerberos	caARCserve
activeDirectorKerberos	CIMHttpServer	CIMHttpsServer
CIMSLP	commvaultDynamic	commvaultStatic
ftpClient	ftpServer	kerberos
LDAP	LDAPS	legatoNetWorker
LicenseClient	nfsClient	nisClient
ntpClient	smbClient	snmpd
sshClient	sshServer	swISCSIClient
symantecBackupExec	symantecNetBackup	telnetClient
TSM	updateManager	VCB
vncServer	vpxHeartbeats	

Once you get familiar with the syntax, the esxcfg-firewall command will allow you to tweak and secure your environment. Remember, after making any changes to your firewall configuration, you will need to restart the firewall services using the following command:

```
service mgmt-vmware restart
```

6.12 Checking Default ESX Ports

Problem

One of the most common issues people have is making sure that the correct firewall ports are opened for the tasks they are trying to accomplish.

Solution

Adding or customizing ports can be done through the Security Profile option in vCenter or via the command line using the esxcfg-firewall command.

Discussion

Table 6-3 lists the essential ports you may have to adjust in your virtual environment when troubleshooting.

Table 6-3. Default ESX ports

Port	Incoming	Outgoing	Description
80	TCP		HTTP, VM console/Web access
427	UDP	UDP	3i service location (CIM client)
443	TCP		Secure HTTP access
902	TCP	UDP	ESX authentication traffic
903	TCP		Remote console traffic
2049	TCP	TCP	NFS devices
2050–5000	TCP, UDP	UDP	HA and autostart
3260	TCP		iSCSI
5900–5906	TCP	TCP	RFB for management tools
5988	TCP	TCP	CIM Server over HTTPS
5989	TCP	TCP	CIM Server over HTTP
8000	TCP	TCP	VMotion traffic
8042–8045	TCP, UDP	TCP, UDP	HA and EMC autostart manager
27000	TCP		License server inbound
27010	TCP		License server outbound

See Also

Recipe 6.11

6.13 Turning on SNMP for Remote Administration

Problem

You wish to monitor and administer your servers remotely.

Solution

Use a third-party application such as Cacti, MRTG, or a commercial solution.

Discussion

Turning on SNMP to monitor your ESX Servers using open source products like Cacti or MRTG, or commercial productions such as WhatsUp Pro, can provide many benefits for the health of your environment. Here's how to enable SNMP:

1. Log into your ESX Server as the *root* user. Navigate to the */etc/snmp* directory and edit the *snmpd.conf* file using your favorite editor (e.g., *vi*):

   ```
   vi snmpd.conf
   ```

2. Add the following lines to the configuration file. I normally add them toward the top:

```
syscontact you@yourdomain.com
syslocation location_of_server
rocommunity public
trapcommunity public
trapsink *.*.*.*

# VMware MIB modules. To enable/disable VMware MIB items,
# add/remove the following entries.
dlmod SNMPESX /usr/lib/vmware/snmp/libSNMPESX.so
```

3. Next, you will need to make a few more configuration adjustments to ensure that everything starts correctly if you need to reboot your server. Make sure the firewall ports are opened by running this command:

```
esxcfg-firewall -q
```

Look for the following information, which should be located toward the end of the output:

```
Enabled services: CIMSLP ntpClient VCB swISCSIClient CIMHttpsServer snmpd
vpxHeartbeats LicenseClient sshServer updateManager
```

If *snmpd* is not listed, open its port by running:

```
esxcfg-firewall -e snmpd
```

4. Enable the *snmpd* daemon to automatically start on system boot by running this command:

```
chkconfig snmpd on
```

5. Restart the *snmpd* service and the firewall to ensure all services are refreshed by running the following commands:

```
service snmpd restart
service mgmt-vmware restart
```

You will want to verify everything you've done by using the `snmpwalk` command. This will query the *snmpd* process on your server and will return basic information about the system, including the kernel version, hostname, uptime, and specific information set in the */etc/snmp/snmpd.conf* file, such as the Name, Contact, and Location:

```
snmpwalk -v 1 -c public localhost system
```

Output will generally appear similar to the following:

```
SNMPv2-MIB::sysDescr.0 = STRING: Linux localhost.localdomain 2.4.21-57.ELvmnix #1
Wed Oct 15 19:00:05 PDT 2008 i686
SNMPv2-MIB::sysObjectID.0 = OID: NET-SNMP-MIB::netSnmpAgentOIDs.10
SNMPv2-MIB::sysUpTime.0 = Timeticks: (13700) 0:02:17.00
SNMPv2-MIB::sysContact.0 = STRING: root@localhost (edit snmpd.conf)
SNMPv2-MIB::sysName.0 = STRING: localhost.localdomain
SNMPv2-MIB::sysLocation.0 = STRING: room1 (edit snmpd.conf)
SNMPv2-MIB::sysORLastChange.0 = Timeticks: (0) 0:00:00.00
```

```
SNMPv2-MIB::sysORID.1 = OID: IF-MIB::ifMIB
SNMPv2-MIB::sysORID.2 = OID: SNMPv2-MIB::snmpMIB
SNMPv2-MIB::sysORID.3 = OID: TCP-MIB::tcpMIB
SNMPv2-MIB::sysORID.4 = OID: IP-MIB::ip
SNMPv2-MIB::sysORID.5 = OID: UDP-MIB::udpMIB
SNMPv2-MIB::sysORID.6 = OID: SNMP-VIEW-BASED-ACM-MIB::vacmBasicGroup
SNMPv2-MIB::sysORID.7 = OID: SNMP-FRAMEWORK-MIB::snmpFrameworkMIBCompliance
SNMPv2-MIB::sysORID.8 = OID: SNMP-MPD-MIB::snmpMPDCompliance
SNMPv2-MIB::sysORID.9 = OID: SNMP-USER-BASED-SM-MIB::usmMIBCompliance
SNMPv2-MIB::sysORDescr.1 = STRING: The MIB module to describe generic objects for
network interface sub-layers
SNMPv2-MIB::sysORDescr.2 = STRING: The MIB module for SNMPv2 entities
SNMPv2-MIB::sysORDescr.3 = STRING: The MIB module for managing TCP implementations
SNMPv2-MIB::sysORDescr.4 = STRING: The MIB module for managing IP and ICMP
implementations
SNMPv2-MIB::sysORDescr.5 = STRING: The MIB module for managing UDP implementations
SNMPv2-MIB::sysORDescr.6 = STRING: View-based Access Control Model for SNMP.
SNMPv2-MIB::sysORDescr.7 = STRING: The SNMP Management Architecture MIB.
SNMPv2-MIB::sysORDescr.8 = STRING: The MIB for Message Processing and Dispatching.
SNMPv2-MIB::sysORDescr.9 = STRING: The management information definitions for the
SNMP User-based Security Model.
SNMPv2-MIB::sysORUpTime.1 = Timeticks: (0) 0:00:00.00
SNMPv2-MIB::sysORUpTime.2 = Timeticks: (0) 0:00:00.00
SNMPv2-MIB::sysORUpTime.3 = Timeticks: (0) 0:00:00.00
SNMPv2-MIB::sysORUpTime.4 = Timeticks: (0) 0:00:00.00
SNMPv2-MIB::sysORUpTime.5 = Timeticks: (0) 0:00:00.00
SNMPv2-MIB::sysORUpTime.6 = Timeticks: (0) 0:00:00.00
SNMPv2-MIB::sysORUpTime.7 = Timeticks: (0) 0:00:00.00
SNMPv2-MIB::sysORUpTime.8 = Timeticks: (0) 0:00:00.00
SNMPv2-MIB::sysORUpTime.9 = Timeticks: (0) 0:00:00.00
```

If you run into problems, double-check your *snmpd.conf* file for typos, and ensure that the *snmpd* process is running and that your firewall ports are opened. You may also look in the */var/log/messages* logfile for any errors that may have occurred.

6.14 Using SNMP Version 3

Problem

SNMPv3 is preferred over versions 1 and 2, for security reasons: version 3 allows for authentication between the agent and the management server, giving your SNMP traffic a more secure line of communication.

Solution

Enable SNMPv3 by editing the */etc/snmp/snmpd.conf* file.

Discussion

Follow these steps to enable version 3:

1. Log into your ESX Server and stop the *snmpd* daemon:

   ```
   service snmpd stop
   ```

2. Edit the */etc/snmp/snmpd.conf* file. You can create a user by adding a line like the following, replacing *yourusername* with the username you wish to add. This user will have read-only access; however, you can create a read/write user by using **rwuser** instead of the **rouser** variable:

   ```
   rouser yourusername auth system
   ```

3. Now you need to create a password for the user you just created by adding the following line to the */var/net-snmp/snmpd.conf* file. This will create an md5 password for the user:

   ```
   createUser yourusername MD5 secretpassword
   ```

4. After making the change, save your configuration and restart the *snmpd* service by issuing this command:

   ```
   service snmpd restart
   ```

5. Finally, verify that everything works correctly by issuing the following command:

   ```
   snmpwalk -v 3 -u yourusername -l authNoPriv -a MD5 -A secretpassword localhost
   ```

For detailed information on usage of SNMPv3, please refer to the *snmpd* website located at *http://net-snmp.sourceforge.net*.

6.15 Using sudo

Problem

You have a lot of users working on your servers and you want to keep track of who does what.

Solution

Using **sudo**, you can safely and effectively give users the ability to run certain predefined root commands with complete audit tracking.

Discussion

The **sudo** command allows users to run commands specified in the */etc/sudoers* file. Using this mechanism, you can allow normal non-*root* users to execute necessary commands to manage your ESX Server, without having to give them direct or complete *root* access.

To run a restricted command, or any command that tries to perform an activity limited to *root*, authorized users must preface the command with the word **sudo**. The first time a user does this, before the command is executed he will be asked for his regular user password. By default, **sudo** will automatically ask for the user's password again if he attempts to execute another restricted command after a timeout period of 5 minutes. You can modify this setting by adding this variable to your */etc/sudoers* file (where *XX* represents the value in minutes):

```
timestamp_timeout XX
```

By default, the ESX Server will use *syslog* to maintain logging for sudo. You can track users by looking in this file: all successful and failed sudo command attempts are logged here. However, if you want this information to be stored somewhere else, you can specify a different logfile location within the sudo configuration file by editing the */etc/sudoers* file and adding a line like this:

```
Default logfile=/var/log/sudo.log
```

To get started with sudo, you will need to configure the */etc/sudoers* file with the users, groups, and commands you wish to allow on your ESX Server. Although you can edit the file using your favorite editor, Linux systems also provide the visudo command specifically for that purpose. The visudo command launches *vi* to manage the configuration file and is the option we suggest.

When editing the *sudoers* file, there are a few guidelines you should follow to ensure that you use the correct syntax. We've compiled a short list to help you:

- Groups within the *sudoers* file must correspond to groups that reside in your */etc/group* file. For example, an *admin* group would be represented by using *%admin*.
- If you have multiple users on the same line, separate them with commas.
- Commands can also be separated by commas, but remember spaces are considered part of the command.
- You can use the word ALL to indicate that a line applies to all groups, usernames, commands, or servers, depending on where you insert the word.
- By using the NOPASSWD value, you can allow your users to bypass entering their passwords (this is not recommended).
- By using a backslash (\) at the end of a line, you can wrap it to a new line without breaking the syntax.

See Also

Recipe 6.16

6.16 Configuring sudo

Problem

Now that you have enabled sudo, you want to set it up according to your preferences.

Solution

Edit the */etc/sudoers* file.

Discussion

The nice thing about using sudo is that once you get a set of standards in place for your environment, adding new users, commands, or groups becomes a fairly quick process. However, setting it up initially may take some time and practice as you work out which command permissions to assign to your users.

Suppose we wanted to allow access to all *root* commands to a couple of users. We could do this with a line like the following:

```
ryan, matthew    ALL=(ALL) ALL
```

The real beauty of sudo, however, is its granular ability to allow users access to run only certain commands in specific locations on an ESX Server. For instance, if we wanted to grant *ryan* and *matthew* the ability to run only esxcfg commands and to restart the VMware management server, we could instead use a line like this:

```
ryan, matthew ALL= /usr/sbin/esxcfg-*, service mgmt-vmware restart
```

As mentioned in Recipe 6.15, you can also configure sudo to allow users to execute commands without having to enter their passwords. Here, we give *ryan* and *matthew* the ability to run all esxcfg commands, and restart the VMware management server, without having to enter a password by using the NOPASSWD variable:

```
ryan, matthew ALL= NOPASSWD: /usr/sbin/esxcfg-*, service mgmt-vmware restart
```

In this next example, we make *ryan*, *matthew*, and *bob* part of the *ADMINS* group and create a special *ESXCMD* group specifying which commands they can run. However, we disable the ability to use the su command:

```
Cmnd_Alias    ESXCMD = /usr/sbin/esxcfg-firewall,  /usr/bin/esxtop, \
                       /usr/sbin/esxcfginfo, /etc/init.d/mgmt-vmware


User_Alias    ADMINS = ryan, matthew, bob
ADMINS        ALL    = !/usr/bin/su, ESXCMD
```

This configuration is a reasonable attempt to ensure that these users cannot permanently become the *root* user by entering the su command. However, it doesn't prevent them from copying files to other locations. The goal is to create a policy that lets you track what your users are doing, while staying compliant with your company's security policies.

sudo is a very powerful tool, and we've only begun to see what it can do. For more detailed information on complex setups, check out *http://www.gratisoft.us/sudo/man/sudoers.html*.

See Also

Recipe 6.15

6.17 Tracking Users via the CLI

Problem

There are times when you may want to monitor what a user is doing when accessing the ESX Server via SSH or directly from the console.

Solution

There are many different commands and logfiles you can use to obtain information on what users are doing, who is logging into the system, and so on.

Discussion

First we'll take a look at the logfiles, their locations, and what information they contain. There is one primary logfile that contains information about user logins: */var/log/messages*. The *messages* logfile is a flat text file that can be searched using a command similar to the following:

```
grep sshd /var/log/messages
```

This command will search the logfile and display any lines containing the word *sshd*, thus telling you what your SSH users are up to. Depending on the size of your logfile, it might return a lot of information. Here is some example output from the preceding command:

```
Nov 10 08:25:32 esx6cluster2 sshd[30792]: Connection from 172.20.36.213 port 51085
Nov 10 08:25:35 esx6cluster2 sshd[30792]: Accepted password for root from
172.20.36.213 port 51085 ssh2
Nov 10 08:25:35 esx6cluster2 sshd(pam_unix)[30792]: session opened for user root by
(uid=0)
```

If you want to search for a specific user's login, you can do this by using the same command, but adapting it slightly:

```
grep sshd /var/log/messages | grep bob
```

You can also view the last 200 lines of the *messages* logfile by using the following command:

```
tail -200 /var/log/messages
```

and monitor the logfile for current activity by using the following command:

```
tail -f /var/log/messages
```

For more information on the egrep and tail commands, you can view their manpages by entering either man egrep or man tail at the command line.

Now let's take a look at some of the commands that are available to monitor users. Linux has inherited from Unix three useful commands for this purpose: w, who, and last. These commands allow you to monitor when and from where your users are connecting, what processes they are running, and other similar information.

Let's start with the who command. This tool allows an administrator to monitor who is connected to the system and to observe some of the characteristics relating to their connections. The who command has some useful options with which you should become familiar to help you identify users who are connected to your system.

To see a quick overview of how many users are connected to your ESX Server, run who with the -q option. If you want to see all the columns of information that the who command makes available, use the -a option (it is equivalent to specifying the options -b -d --login -p -r -t -T -u). By default, only files that are being accessed by at least one process are shown.

Example output when using the -a switch might look like this:

```
[ryan@esx1test1 ryan]$ who -a
                          Nov 12 17:30              616 id=si    term=0 exit=0
           system boot    Nov 12 17:30
           run-level 3    Nov 12 17:30                  last=S
                          Nov 12 17:30              824 id=l3    term=0 exit=0
   root      + tty1        Nov 12 20:53    .        1767
   LOGIN       tty2        Nov 12 17:30             1768 id=2
   LOGIN       tty3        Nov 12 17:30             1769 id=3
   LOGIN       tty4        Nov 12 17:30             1770 id=4
                          Nov 12 17:30             1771 id=5
                          Nov 12 17:30             1772 id=6
   ryan      + pts/0       Nov 13 13:55    .        9943 (10.0.1.200)
```

Looking at the output, you will see that the first four lines are related to system processes. The next line shows that the *root* user has logged in on the console using terminal *tty1*. The + character next to the username indicates that this user is able to use the write command. The following three lines, which begin with LOGIN, are login sessions that have yet to be established; they can be invoked by pressing Alt-F2, Alt-F3, and Alt-F4 at the ESX Server's terminal.

Running the who command without any switches will allow you to see a general overview of your connected users, displaying for each only the username, IP address, terminal, and connection time and date. The last line in the following output shows that *root* is logged in via SSH, hence the *pts/0* terminal notation:

```
[root@esx1cluster1 root]# who
root     pts/0        Nov 13 10:44 (172.20.36.213)
```

Now let's turn to the w command, an extension of the who command that displays more detailed information about the users who are connected and their current running processes. This commonly used user-tracking tool is available not only on your ESX Server, but on most Linux platforms.

The w command has a few options that provide valuable information. Here is the output if it is run without any switches:

```
[root@esx1cluster1 root]# w
 11:07:11  up 1 day, 45 min,  1 user,  load average: 0.23, 0.23, 0.17
USER     TTY      FROM             LOGIN@   IDLE   JCPU   PCPU  WHAT
root     pts/0    172.20.36.213    10:44am  0.00s  0.04s  0.00s  w
```

Notice that the w command displays more detailed information than the who command:

The first row contains the current time, the system's uptime, how many users are connected, and the system load average for the last 1, 5, and 15 minutes. The second row contains the following information:

- USER represents the connected users.
- TTY is the terminal to which the user is connected.
- FROM displays the source IP address from which the user has connected.
- LOGIN@ displays the time the user logged into the system.
- IDLE displays the elapsed time since the users' last activity.
- JCPU displays the currently running processes attached to the *tty*.
- PCPU displays the time used by the current process (listed in the WHAT column).
- WHAT displays what the user is currently doing on the system.

As you can see, the w command supplies a good amount of information on the state of your system; it is useful not just for monitoring users, but also the load and system uptime.

Finally, we'll look at the last command. This command searches the */var/log/wtmp* file and lists all of the users who have logged in and out since the file was created.

From the manpage:

> Names of users and tty's can be given, in which case last will show only those entries matching the arguments. Names of ttys can be abbreviated, thus last 0 is the same as last tty0.
>
> When last catches a SIGINT signal (generated by the interrupt key, usually control-C) or a SIGQUIT signal (generated by the quit key, usually control-\), last will show how far it has searched through the file; in the case of the SIGINT signal last will then terminate.
>
> The pseudo user reboot logs in each time the system is rebooted. Thus last reboot will show a log of all reboots since the logfile was created.

As you can see, by using a combination of commands, you have complete access to data on who is logging into your system and what they are doing.

6.18 Configuring Active Directory Authentication

Problem

You want to enable Microsoft Active Directory on your system.

Solution

Edit the authentication configuration to use Microsoft Active Directory.

Description

By using Microsoft Active Directory to allow your users to connect to your ESX Server via SSH, you establish a point of accountability for the user and create less work for yourself when managing users. Not all environments have a Microsoft Active Directory server, so this is an optional configuration.

To get started, log into the console on your ESX Server as the *root* user, or use the su command to become the *root* user. Then, you will need to prepare a few things in order to set up authentication.

First, make sure your ESX Server is synced to your NTP server. If you do not have an NTP server, we suggest setting one up, as it will make using ESX much easier. If you cannot set up an NTP server, use the date command on your ESX Server, and make sure the time and date match those on your Microsoft Active Directory server.

After you've verified that the time is correct on both servers, use the esxcfg-auth command to configure your ESX Server to authenticate from the Active Directory server, instead of using the native Linux */etc/passwd* file.

To get started, enter the following command, replacing *yourdomain.com* and *dc.yourdomain.com* with your respective Active Directory server names:

```
esxcfg-auth --enablead --addomain=yourdomain.com --addc=dc.yourdomain.com
```

As this command is run, it will automatically configure the necessary files and services to authenticate via your Active Directory server.

For your reference, the command will edit the */etc/krb5.conf* and */etcpam.d/system-auth* files and will open the necessary firewall rules. You should double-check each file by running the following commands, to ensure your variables were set correctly (if not, rerun esxcfg-auth to reconfigure):

```
more /etc/krb5.conf
```

Your output will look similar to this, but with your own domain:

```
[domain_realm]
.yourdomain.com = YOURDOMAIN.COM
yourdomain.com = YOURDOMAIN.COM

[libdefaults]
default_realm = YOURDOMAIN.COM

[realms]
YOURDOMAIN.COM = {
        admin_server = dc.yourdomain.com:464
        default_domain = yourdomain.com
        kdc = dc.yourdomain.com:88
}
```

```
more /etc/pam.d/system-auth
```

When you enable Active Directory, some extra variables will be added to your *system-auth* file. Here's what it looked like before:

```
account        required        /lib/security/$ISA/pam_unix.so

auth           required        /lib/security/$ISA/pam_env.so
auth           sufficient      /lib/security/$ISA/pam_unix.so  likeauth nullok
auth           required        /lib/security/$ISA/pam_deny.so

password       required        /lib/security/$ISA/pam_cracklib.so retry=3
password       sufficient      /lib/security/$ISA/pam_unix.so  nullok use_authtok
md5 shadow
password       required        /lib/security/$ISA/pam_deny.so

session        required        /lib/security/$ISA/pam_limits.so
session        required        /lib/security/$ISA/pam_unix.so
```

and what it looks like after enabling Active Directory:

```
account        sufficient      /lib/security/$ISA/pam_krb5.so
account        required        /lib/security/$ISA/pam_unix.so

auth           required        /lib/security/$ISA/pam_env.so
auth           sufficient      /lib/security/$ISA/pam_unix.so  likeauth nullok
auth           sufficient      /lib/security/$ISA/pam_krb5.so  use_first_pass
auth           required        /lib/security/$ISA/pam_deny.so

password       required        /lib/security/$ISA/pam_cracklib.so retry=3
password    sufficient /lib/security/$ISA/pam_unix.so  nullok use_authtok md5 shadow
password       sufficient      /lib/security/$ISA/pam_krb5.so      use_authtok
password       required        /lib/security/$ISA/pam_deny.so

session        required        /lib/security/$ISA/pam_limits.so
session        required        /lib/security/$ISA/pam_unix.so
session        sufficient      /lib/security/$ISA/pam_krb5.so
```

Ensure that the firewall rules are in place by issuing this command:

```
esxcfg-firewall -q
```

Essentially, when you run the `esxcfg-auth` command, it will add the following rules to your firewall ruleset:

```
esxcfg-firewall -openport 88,tcp,out,KerberosClient
esxcfg-firewall -openPort 464,tcp,out,KerberosPasswordChange
esxcfg-firewall -openport 749,tcp,out,KerberosAdm
```

The final step, and the only minor drawback to running authentication through your Active Directory server, is that you must create an account on the Linux server for the user who is authenticating via Active Directory. The username you add must match the username in Active Directory:

```
useradd bsmith
```

You do not need to set a password on this account; the system will pull the password from Active Directory. Essentially, the username on the Linux side assigns the UID and GID, which Linux requires.

To disable Active Directory authentication, use the following command:

```
esxcfg-auth --disablead
```

6.19 Setting a Maximum Number of Failed Logins

Problem

By default, the ESX Server does not explicitly set a login failure count.

Solution

Using the `esxcfg-auth` command, you can lock a user out of the system after too many failed login attempts.

Discussion

To begin, connect to the ESX Server as *root* and issue the following command. For this example we will set the password max login value to 10, but you may set this variable to any number that suits your specific environment:

```
esxcfg-auth --maxfailedlogins=10
```

Once the command has been run, you can verify it worked by running:

```
esxcfg-auth -p
```

You will see a line similar to the following in the output:

```
account      required    /lib/security/pam_tally.so    deny=10 no_magic_root
```

Notice that the `deny=10` and `no_magic_root` variables are now set. To revert to the default settings, run the same command but replace the 10 with a 0. This will remove the entry from your */etc/pam.d/system-auth* file.

6.20 Limiting Access to the su Command

Problem

You want to be certain that only certain user accounts have permission to acquire full *root* privileges using su.

Solution

Create a user group called *wheel* and configure it for access to su, adding to the group those users who need access.

Discussion

The *wheel* group is an operating system layer group that allows a limited number of specified users to use *root* commands, such as the su command. Using this method should be a second choice for implementing security on your ESX Server; the preferred method is implementing sudo, as discussed earlier in this chapter.

By default, only users who are part of the *wheel* group have the ability to run and execute the su command. By using a combination of Pluggable Authentication Modules (PAM) and the *wheel* user group, you can limit access to su by requiring users to use sudo to access *root* commands.

Navigate to the */etc/pam.d/* directory and look for the *su* file. Open this file in your preferred editor and search for the line that begins with `#auth required`. Remove the # character so the line reads like this:

```
auth required /lib/security/$ISA/pam_wheel.so use_uid
```

You will also need to make sure that any user you want to be able to use the su command is in the *wheel* group. Open up the */etc/group* file with your favorite editor and look for the following line:

```
wheel:*:0:root
```

Assuming we want to give the users *bob* and *tim* access to the *wheel* group, we would change the line to look like this:

```
wheel:*:0:root,bob,tim
```

6.21 Setting User Password Aging

Problem

You want user passwords to expire after a certain time, forcing users to create new ones.

Solution

Create a password aging policy.

Discussion

Since ESX is running a modified version of Red Hat Linux, we can take advantage of some of its tools to help manage users. By default, a password aging policy is set with the following parameters:

```
Maximum Days = 90 (default)
Minimum Days = 0 (Allows password changes to occur anytime)
Warning Time = 7 days
```

As you begin to look at your password aging strategy, you will most likely notice that some accounts will have no aging policy: for example, the *vpxuser* and *root* users are exempt.

The esxcfg-auth command allows you to globally set the password policy by using the --passmaxdays attribute, as you'll see momentarily. This command offers a wide variety of options for tweaking and modifying authentication-related tasks on your ESX Server:

```
usage: esxcfg-auth [options]

options:
    --enablemd5            Enable MD5 password storage
    --disablemd5           Disable MD5 password storage
    --enableshadow         Enable Shadow password storage
    --disableshadow        Disable Shadow password storage
    --enablenis            Enable NIS Authentication
    --disablenis           Disable NIS Authentication
    --nisdomain=domain     Set the NIS domain
    --nisserver=server     Set the NIS server
    --enableldap           Enable LDAP User Management
    --disableldap          Disable LDAP User Management
    --enableldapauth       Enable LDAP Authentication
    --disableldapauth      Disable LDAP Authentication
    --ldapserver=server    Set the LDAP Server
    --ldapbasedn=basedn    Set the base DN for the LDAP server
    --enableldaptls        Enable TLS connections for LDAP
    --disableldaptls       Disable TLS connections for LDAP
    --enablekrb5           Enable Kererbos Authentication
    --disablekrb5          Disable Kererbos Authentication
    --krb5realm=domain     Set the Kerberos Realm
    --krb5kdc=server       Set the Kebreros Key Distribution Center
    --krb5adminserver=server
                           Set the Kerberos Admin Server
    --enablead             Enable Active Directory Authentication
    --disablead            Disable Active Directory Authentication
    --addomain=domain      Set the Active Directory Domain
    --addc=server          Set the Active Directory Domain Controller
    --usepamqc=values      Enable the pam_passwdqc module
    --usecrack=values      Enable the pam_cracklib module
    --enablecache          Enables caching of login credentials
```

```
--disablecache          Disables caching of login credentials
--passmaxdays=days      Set the maximum number of days a password remains valid.
--passmindays=days      Set the minimum number of days a password remains valid.
--passwarnage=days      Set the number of days a warning is given before a
                        password expires.
--maxfailedlogins=count
                        Sets the maximum number of login failures before the
                        account is locked out, setting to 0 will disable this
-p, --probe             Print the settings to the console
-v, --verbose           Enable verbose logging
-h, --help              show this help message and exit
```

To change the password expiration policy, use the `--passmaxdays` switch. This will globally change the value for all new users on your system. Best practice is setting this value to 90 days. Alternatively, you can use "0" to disable the `passmaxdays` variable on your system, However, doing so will not change any current user's password aging policy:

```
esxcfg-auth --passmaxdays=90     Sets the expiration to 90 days
esxcfg-auth --passmaxdays=0      Disables system-wide
```

If you wish to change the password aging policy for existing users, you can do this using the `chage` command. For example:

```
chage -M -1 username     Disables aging
chage -M 0 username      Enables aging
chage -M 90 username     Sets to 90 days
```

To view the current settings for `esxcfg-auth`, use the `-p` switch. Doing so will display all the current authentication settings on your system that are managed by the `esxcfg-auth` command:

```
esxcfg-auth -p
```

Depending on the configuration you choose, one of seven files might be touched in the process of configuring `esxcfg-auth`. Let's take a look at the files that may be affected by the `esxcfg-auth` command and its function. First up is */etc/krb5.conf*, which contains information on your Kerberos setup:

```
/etc/krb5.conf


[domain_realm]
.yourdomain.com = YOURDOMAIN.COM
yourdomain.com = YOURDOMAIN.COM

[libdefaults]
default_realm = YOURDOMAIN.COM

[realms]
YOURDOMAIN.COM = {
        admin_server = dc.yourdomain.com:464
        default_domain = yourdomain.com
        kdc = dc.yourdomain.com:88
}
```

If you are connecting to an LDAP server, the */etc/openldap/ldap.conf* file contains information on the host, base, password model, SSL, and more:

```
/etc/openldap/ldap.conf


base dc=example,dc=com
host 127.0.0.1
pam_password md5
ssl no
```

Next up is the */etc/nscd.conf* file, which maintains the configuration for the name service cache daemon:

```
/etc/nscd.conf


        debug-level     0
        server-user     nscd

        auto-propagate group yes
        check-files     group yes
        enable-cache    group no
        negative-time-to-live   group       60
        positive-time-to-live   group       3600
        suggested-size group 211

        check-files     hosts   yes
        enable-cache    hosts   no
        negative-time-to-live   hosts       20
        positive-time-to-live   hosts       3600
        suggested-size          hosts       211

        auto-propagate passwd   yes
        check-files     passwd  yes
        enable-cache    passwd  no
        negative-time-to-live   passwd   20
        positive-time-to-live   passwd   600
        suggested-size passwd   211
```

The */etc/yp.conf* file is called by *ypbind* when you are using NIS; most people won't need to use this so we won't list its contents here.

The */etc/login.defs* file handles default permissions, group and user IDs, password expiration, and other important variables that will be used when creating a new user on your system:

```
/etc/login.defs


CREATE_HOME     yes
GID_MAX  60000
GID_MIN  500
MAIL_DIR /var/spool/mail
PASS_MAX_DAYS 0
PASS_MIN_DAYS 0
```

```
PASS_MIN_LEN  5
PASS_WARN_AGE 7
UID_MAX  60000
UID_MIN  500
```

The */etc/nsswitch.conf* file contains the configuration information that NIS and LDAP use to determine information such as hostnames, password files, and group files:

/etc/nsswitch.conf

```
aliases:     files nisplus
automount:   files nisplus
bootparams:  nisplus [NOTFOUND=return] files
ethers:      files
group:       files
hosts:       files dns
netgroup:    nisplus
netmasks:    files
networks:    files
passwd:      files
protocols:   files
publickey:   nisplus
rpc:         files
services:    files
shadow:      files
```

The */etc/pam.d/system-auth* file contains a central location for system-wide authentication settings:

/etc/pam.d/system-auth
#%PAM-1.0

```
account    required      /lib/security/$ISA/pam_unix.so

auth       required      /lib/security/$ISA/pam_env.so
auth       sufficient    /lib/security/$ISA/pam_unix.so        likeauth nullok
auth       required      /lib/security/$ISA/pam_deny.so

password   required      /lib/security/$ISA/pam_cracklib.so           retry=3
password   sufficient    /lib/security/$ISA/pam_unix.so               nullok
use_authtok md5 shadow
password   required      /lib/security/$ISA/pam_deny.so

session    required      /lib/security/$ISA/pam_limits.so
session    required      /lib/security/$ISA/pam_unix.so
```

Notice that the account, auth, password, and session strings are used. The meanings of the fields in these lines depend on the module being configured.

The passmaxday value, along with other important information regarding your password aging policy, is located in the */etc/login.defs* file. You should always use the esxcfg-auth command when you need to change a variable in this file. Editing it directly will result in lost settings because VMware maintains the files discussed here via esxcfg-auth and does not expect them to be modified any other way.

6.22 Disabling Copy and Paste

Problem

By default, copy and paste functionality is enabled between the guest and the host where the remote console is running. The remote console can be used via the web interface or the vCenter client. You want to prevent any applications that may be running on the host from accessing secure information stored on the guest's clipboard.

Solution

Disable copy and paste.

Discussion

Log into your vCenter client, which should be connected either directly to the ESX Server or to the vCenter server. Make sure the virtual machine on which you wish to change the settings is powered off.

Click the virtual machine, then click Edit Settings, followed by Options, and finally General, which is located under Advanced. From here, click Configuration Parameters, which will open a new dialog box containing advanced options.

Add the following parameters and set the values accordingly:

```
isolation.tools.copy.disable = true
isolation.tools.paste.disable = true
isolation.tools.setGUIOptions.enable = false
```

Once you've made these modifications, close the windows to save the configuration. Because these values get written to the virtual machine's *.vmx* file, they won't take effect until you restart the virtual machine.

6.23 Disabling Disk Shrinking on Virtual Machines

Problem

A default installation of the VMware tools will allow you to shrink a virtual machine's disk. The problem with leaving this option enabled is that any users, regardless of their permissions on the virtual machine, will be able to resize the virtual machine's disk.

Solution

By adding a few configuration parameters, you can ensure that your users cannot shrink the virtual machine's disk, thereby guaranteeing that it works at its maximum potential and limiting the possibility of the virtual machine becoming unavailable.

Discussion

To begin, log into your vCenter client, which should be connected either directly to the ESX Server or to the vCenter server. Your virtual machine will need to be powered off.

Click the virtual machine, then click Edit Settings, followed by Options, and finally General, which is located under Advanced. From here, click Configuration Parameters, which will open a new dialog box containing advanced options.

Add the following parameters and set the values accordingly:

```
isolation.tools.diskWiper.disable = True
isolation.tools.diskShrink.disable = True
```

Once you've added the new variables, restart the virtual machine so that they will become active. If you want to resize your disks in the future using the VMware tools, you can reset these values to `False` or remove them.

6.24 Disabling Unneeded Devices

Problem

When creating a new virtual machine, or doing a physical-to-virtual (p2v) conversion, you want to avoid adding unneeded devices that are not often used in a virtual environment, such as USB devices, floppy drives, parallel ports, and serial ports.

Solution

Edit the virtual machine settings as necessary.

Discussion

When you create a new virtual machine, you can choose whether or not to include these types of extra devices. However, when you do a p2v, any hardware on the physical server will be replicated to the new virtual machine. Before powering on your new p2v-converted server, you may wish to use vCenter to remove any unneeded devices.

Log into your vCenter server and select the virtual machine you wish to modify, right-click on it, and choose Edit Settings. You will be prompted with the devices that are currently attached to your virtual machine; adjust them as needed.

6.25 Preventing Unwanted Device Additions and Removals

Problem

By default, users can use the VMware tools to disconnect connected devices like CD-ROMs and Ethernet adapters. This can cause problems if the user has used the CD-ROM to install applications, or disconnects an Ethernet adapter and takes the virtual machine off the network.

Solution

To limit access to these features, set specific variables in the *.vmx* file. This can be accomplished using vCenter.

Discussion

To begin, log into your vCenter client, which should be connected either directly to the ESX Server or to the vCenter server. Make sure the virtual machine on which you wish to change the settings is powered off.

Click the virtual machine, then click Edit Settings, followed by Options, and finally General, which is located under Advanced. From here, click Configuration Parameters, which will open a new dialog box containing advanced options.

You will need to add the following parameters and set the values accordingly:

```
isolation.device.connectable.disable = TRUE
isolation.device.edit.disable = TRUE
Isolation.tools.connectable.disable = TRUE
```

Once the new variables have been added, you will need to restart the virtual machine for them to become active. You may disable these settings in the future by using the VMware tools to either set the parameters to `False` or remove them.

6.26 Disabling VMware Tools Settings Override

Problem

You wish to disable the option of allowing VMware tools to make overriding modifications to variables that are managed on the ESX Server, ensuring that users cannot make configuration changes or bypass rules you have already established.

Solution

Adjust the settings in the configuration file.

Discussion

To begin, log into your vCenter client, which should be connected either directly to the ESX Server or to the vCenter server. Make sure the virtual machine on which you wish to change the settings is powered off.

Click the virtual machine, then click Edit Settings, followed by Options, and finally General, which is located under Advanced. From here, click Configuration Parameters, which will open a new dialog box containing advanced options.

Look for the following value and set it to `false` if it's currently set to `true`. If it is not present, you can add it by clicking the Add Row option:

```
isolation.tools.setGUIOptions.enable = false
```

Restart the virtual machine so that your changes take effect.

## CHAPTER 7

Automating ESX Installation

On the occasions when an ESX Server fails—or more likely, when you have to restart it on another physical machine to reconfigure your site—the last thing you'll want is to have to step through the complex startup process manually. It's slow and error-prone, and practically negates the value of virtualizing your servers in the first place. Nearly every site, therefore, automates the startup. VMware uses a tool created by Red Hat named *Kickstart* to allow the bulk installation and startup of ESX. To run the Kickstart script you have to make some changes to ESX's configuration in VMware 3.5, however, because running scripts is disabled by default. This chapter therefore starts by showing you how to enable scripts, and then goes on to show what you can do with Kickstart.

 As of version 3.x, VMware does not support scripted installation with the ESXi version of its ESX product, so the recipes in this chapter will not work if you are using that version.

7.1 Enabling Scripted Install Support on ESX

Problem

VMware 3.5 ESX Server, by default, does not allow scripted installations and must be reconfigured before you can work through the other recipes in this chapter.

Solution

Edit your configuration file to enable scripted installations and restart your ESX Server.

Discussion

Scripted installations are controlled by a configuration file in the Tomcat web server. To change the default, power on your ESX Server, log into the console, and change to the *webapps/ui/WEB-INF* directory in your instance of Tomcat. If the system has multiple versions of Tomcat, you should usually work with the highest version. On our test system, we changed to the following directory; the pathname may be different on your system because it depends on the patch revisions you have installed:

```
cd /usr/lib/vmware/webAccess/tomcat/apache-tomcat-5.5.26/webapps/ui/WEB-INF
```

Look for a file called *struts-config.xml* and open it in your favorite editor, then look for the following line (broken to fit the width of the page):

```
<action path="/scriptedInstall" type="org.apache.struts.actions.ForwardAction"
parameter="/WEB-INF/jsp/scriptedInstall/disabled.jsp" />
```

Comment out this line by adding `<!--` at the beginning and `-->` at the end.

Directly under this, you will see the following entry:

```
<!--
<action path="/scriptedInstall" type="com.vmware.webcenter.scripted.ProcessAction">
<forward name="scriptedInstall.form1" path="/WEB-INF/jsp/scriptedInstall/form1.jsp" />
<forward name="scriptedInstall.form2" path="/WEB-INF/jsp/scriptedInstall/form2.jsp" />
<forward name="scriptedInstall.form3" path="/WEB-INF/jsp/scriptedInstall/form3.jsp" />
<forward name="scriptedInstall.form4" path="/WEB-INF/jsp/scriptedInstall/form4.jsp" />
<forward name="scriptedInstall.form5" path="/WEB-INF/jsp/scriptedInstall/form5.jsp" />
<forward name="scriptedInstall.form6" path="/WEB-INF/jsp/scriptedInstall/form6.jsp" />
<forward name="scriptedInstall.form7" path="/WEB-INF/jsp/scriptedInstall/form7.jsp" />
</action> -->
```

Uncomment this block of text by removing the opening `<!--` and closing `-->` strings, leaving the rest of the configuration untouched. Save the file and exit the editor.

Next, you need to restart Web Services in order to pick up the changes. This can be accomplished by entering the following command:

```
service vmware-webAccess restart
```

7.2 Using the Scripted Installer

Problem

To configure automated installation, you need a Kickstart installation file.

Solution

Use the scripted installer to generate a basic Kickstart configuration file. Recipe 7.3 will show you some useful customizations you can make to this file.

Discussion

VMware provides a basic wizard-style web interface you can use to create a simple Kickstart configuration file to automate scripted installations. Before you can access the scripted installer, you must first enable it, as discussed in Recipe 7.1.

Navigate to your ESX Server via a browser and choose the "Log in to the Scripted Installer" link, shown near the bottom right in Figure 7-1.

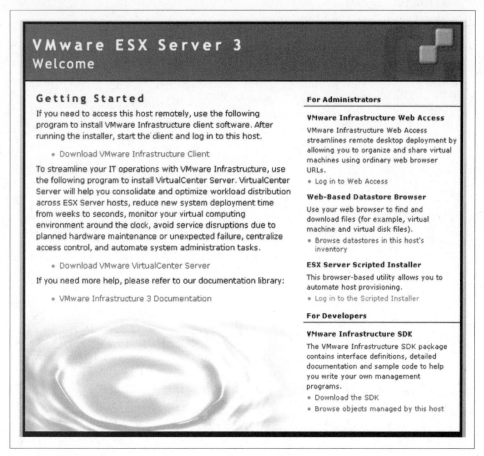

Figure 7-1. ESX web management screen

The first screen (Figure 7-2) is a basic configuration screen that allows you to set some variables, many of which are the same variables you would set on a normal installation off the CD-ROM.

A brief summary of the settings on this screen follows:

Installation Type

Select the type of installation you wish to create: choose from Initial Installation or Upgrade. Generally you will want to choose Initial Installation, as this option ensures that your ESX installation has all the required packages. The Upgrade option can be used to upgrade an existing ESX Server, but you're better off using the official VMware upgrade tools for that.

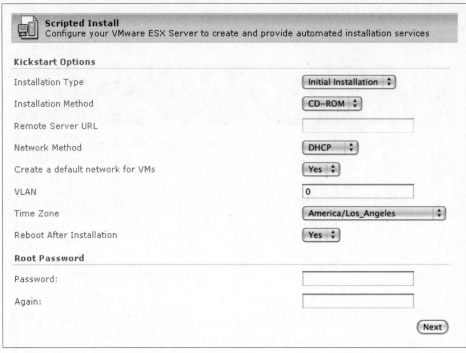

Scripted Install
Configure your VMware ESX Server to create and provide automated installation services

Kickstart Options

Installation Type	Initial Installation ⬍
Installation Method	CD-ROM ⬍
Remote Server URL	
Network Method	DHCP ⬍
Create a default network for VMs	Yes ⬍
VLAN	0
Time Zone	America/Los_Angeles ⬍
Reboot After Installation	Yes ⬍

Root Password

Password:	
Again:	

Next

Figure 7-2. Scripted installation configuration

Installation Method
Indicate the way you will install ESX when the process is automated. Choose between a CD-ROM, NFS mount, or a remote URL over FTP or HTTP.

Remote Server URL
Depending on the installation method you chose in the previous item, enter one of the following:

- For NFS: *nfs://servername.com/location_of_esx_files*
- For HTTP: *http://servername.com/location*
- For FTP: *ftp://servername.com/location*

Network Method
Indicate whether you will be using a static IP address for your ESX Server or assigning one automatically from DHCP. VMware suggests that all ESX Servers be configured with static IP addresses; however, you can leave this set to DHCP if you want and change the ESX Server's IP address at a later time.

"Create a default network for VMs"
This allows you to create a default network. This is not recommended for a normal installation or for Kickstart.

VLAN
If you wish to have your ESX Server in a specific VLAN, enter that information here.

Time Zone
Indicate the time zone in which your server will reside.

Reboot After Installation
Specify whether you wish to reboot your server after the installation has completed.

Password
Enter the password you wish to use on your new server.

When you are satisfied with your entries, click the Next button. If you chose to use a static IP address, you will be prompted to enter values in the Hostname, IP Address, Netmask, Gateway, and Name Servers fields. Clicking the Next button again will bring you directly to the terms and conditions.

Once you've accepted the license agreement, the next screen to appear will be the disk configuration screen (Figure 7-3). Here you will see some prepopulated disk entries with the / (*root*), */boot*, *swap*, */vmfs*, */var/log*, and *vmkcore* partitions.

Drive		Mount Point	Size	Type		Grow
SCSI Disk 1 (sda)	?	/boot	102	ext3		☐
SCSI Disk 1 (sda)	?	/	4997	ext3		☐
SCSI Disk 1 (sda)	?		544	swap		☐
SCSI Disk 1 (sda)	?	vmfs	10000	vmfs3		☑
SCSI Disk 1 (sda)	?		110	vmkcore		☐
SCSI Disk 1 (sda)	?	/var/log	1992	ext3		☐
SCSI Disk 1 (sda)	?			ext3		☐
SCSI Disk 1 (sda)	?			ext3		☐
SCSI Disk 1 (sda)	?			ext3		☐
SCSI Disk 1 (sda)	?			ext3		☐

Licensing Information

Licensing Mode	Use License Server

Figure 7-3. Disk selection and partitioning

The columns are:

Drive
The device on which the partition will be created.

Mount Point
The mount point for the partition (the directory to which you navigate to get access to its contents).

Size

The size of the partition in megabytes (MB).

Type

The type of filesystem in use. You have five options here: *vmfs2*, *vmfs3*, *vmkcore*, *ext3*, and *swap*.

Grow

Whether you want to allow the partition to grow to its maximum size or fill its partition. It's suggested that you disallow growing on your swap and boot volumes.

 To avoid possible data loss make sure to physically remove any attached storage, such as Fibre Channel, DAS, or iSCSI disks, before the initial installation of ESX.

The sizes shown on the disk configuration screen are defaults. For ESX Server installations, VMware suggests that you set up your partitions as outlined in Table 7-1.

Table 7-1. Suggested partitions for ESX Server installations

Mount point	Type	Size	Notes
None	*swap*	544MB	Allows the service console to use disk-based memory when the physical memory isn't available
/boot	*ext3*	100MB	Holds the ESX Server's kernel bootloader images (in ESX 3.x this is GRUB)
/	*ext3*	10GB[a]	Holds the operating system, configuration files, and third-party applications
/var	*ext3*	2GB[b]	Storage for logfiles
None	*vmkcore*	100MB	Holds the dump files for the VMkernel and is required when asking for support
/vmfs	*vmfs*	Varies[c]	Holds virtual machine *vdmk* files

[a] The / (*root*) partition should be at least 5GB in size.

[b] The /*var* partition should be at least 500MB in size, and we recommend 2GB to be safe.

[c] The /*vmfs* partition doesn't need to be configured on the local disk unless you have no attached SAN storage. However, it's convenient to have a local /*vmfs* partition in any case, for testing.

By default, these partitions will be created on the standard SCSI disk (*sda* on Dell systems and *cciss* on other systems, such as HP); however, this may vary depending on your hardware.

You will need to adjust the settings to fit the disk you are going to be using. Installation will fail if you put partitions on a nonexistent disk or one with insufficient space. VMware allows you to choose from a wide selection of disks for your ESX installation, but make sure to check the ESX manuals and your hardware manuals to ensure that your disk is supported.

The disk configuration screen also lets you select the license type for the installation. The options are:

Post Install
> Configure your license after installation.

Use License Server
> Retrieve the license from a license server.

Use Host License File
> Upload a license file.

To continue the installation, click Next. If you chose the Use License Server option, you will be presented with a dialog box where you can specify the server, port, and ESX license type; similarly, if you chose the Use Host License File option, you will be given the opportunity to upload your license file. When you're finished, click Next again.

You will now be prompted to download the Kickstart configuration file.

After downloading the Kickstart configuration file, you need either to put it on some removable media such as a floppy disk or CD-ROM, or store it on an NFS server that will be accessible from the server where you will later bring up ESX.

If you use removable media, you will load it on the physical server (which can be the same one you build it on or a different one) along with the ESX disk itself to run an automatic installation. For example, VMware suggests using the following command to initiate the installation from a floppy disk in ESX 3.x (ESX 4.x allows you to install via a USB device):

```
esx ks=floppy method=cdrom
```

This tells the installer to use the Kickstart file from the floppy disk and then use the CD-ROM to install ESX.

If you're installing from an NFS partition you'll use a similar command, but you instead specify the IP address of your NFS server and the path to your Kickstart file on that server. This file in turn lists the ESX files that should be loaded:

```
esx ks=nfs:1.1.1.2:/path/ks.cfg ksdevice=eth1
```

There are more advanced ways to automate your installation, such as using PXE boot; however, that is outside the scope of this recipe.

See Also

Recipes 7.1 and 7.3

7.3 Enhancing the Kickstart Configuration

Problem

You want to add some advanced features to your Kickstart installation.

Solution

Edit the Kickstart configuration file with a text editor to configure advanced installation options.

Discussion

Because VMware ESX is built upon Red Hat Enterprise Linux 3, it utilizes Anaconda to automate installations of ESX, just as Red Hat does for its Linux operating system.

Kickstart uses a simple text file that contains the variables, scripts, and items to be configured during the installation. In this section, we'll examine a sample Kickstart file that has been generated using the steps in Recipe 7.2 and discuss the meaning of each section and variable.

We'll also look at some more advanced configuration options that can further enhance your automated install of VMware ESX. Remember that, at the time of writing, VMware's ESXi product does not support automated installations using this method.

The Kickstart configuration file is limited to specific commands that control configuration, and does not allow general scripting. We'll discuss how to insert general Bash scripts with Linux commands in later recipes.

Example 7-1 shows the configuration file we ended up with after following the procedure in Recipe 7.2. This file can be edited with any text editor, because it's plain text.

Example 7-1. Sample Kickstart configuration file

```
# Installation method
cdrom

# root password
rootpw --iscrypted  $1$TNllmXJd$tSh9WvAEO/b4KlKBxncWX/

# Authconfig
auth --enableshadow --enablemd5

# Bootloader ( The user has to use GRUB by default )
bootloader --location=mbr

# Time zone
timezone America/Los_Angeles

# X Window System
skipx

# Install or upgrade
install

# Text mode
text

# Network install type
```

```
network --bootproto dhcp --addvmportgroup=1 --vlanid=0

# Language
lang en_US

# Language support
langsupport --default en_US

# Keyboard
keyboard us

# Mouse
mouse none

# Reboot after install?
reboot

# Firewall settings
firewall --disabled

# Clear partitions
clearpart --all --initlabel --drives=sda

# Partitioning
part /boot --fstype ext3 --size 102 --ondisk sda
part / --fstype ext3 --size 4997 --ondisk sda
part swap --size 544 --ondisk sda
part None --fstype vmfs3 --size 10000 --grow --ondisk sda
part None --fstype vmkcore --size 110 --ondisk sda
part /var/log --fstype ext3 --size 1992 --ondisk sda


# VMware-specific commands
vmaccepteula


%packages
@base
@everything
%pre
%post
```

The Kickstart file has the following sections:

General commands
> This part starts the file. It consists of a list of commands that always run during installation to set up the basic structure for your installation; these commands specify values such as the installation method, *root* password, bootloader configuration, time zone, network installation type, and language.

%packages
> This section is where you specify which packages will be configured during new installations. Example 7-1 installs everything in the @base and @everything packages, which contain all the required libraries, applications, and core ESX

components. This option does not apply to upgrades via Kickstart, because package selection is not available for upgrades.

%pre

In this section, you can list scripts to be run before installation to customize the system, install additional software, and so on. This section of the file is described in Recipe 7.5.

%post

This is like the %pre section, but it lets you specify scripts to be run after installation instead of beforehand. This section of the file is described in Recipe 7.6.

The rest of this recipe describes each of the major commands available in the general commands section, along with their most common options:

auth *(required)*

Sets the user authentication policy on your ESX Server. By default, ESX uses shadow passwords and md5 checksums. However, the auth command also supports a variety of other authentication methods. Options include:

--enablekrb5

Enables Kerberos 5 user authentication.

--enablemd5

Enables md5-encrypted passwords.

--enablenis

Enables NIS support. If you don't also specify --nisdomain, it uses whatever domain it finds on the network. If you don't specify --nisserver, it broadcasts to find the server.

--enableshadow *or* --usershadow

Enables the shadow password file.

--krb5realm=

Specifies the Kerberos realm in which your ESX will belong, in conjunction with the --enablekrb5 option.

--krb5kdc=

Specifies the KDCs that will serve the requests for the realm, in conjunction with the --enablekrb5 option. You can have multiple entries, separated by commas.

--krb5adminserver=

Specifies the KDC that runs the KADM5 administration server in your realm, in conjunction with the --enablekrb5 option.

--nisdomain=

Sets the NIS domain, in conjunction with the --enablenis option.

--nisserver=

Sets the NIS server, in conjunction with the --enablenis option.

bootloader *(required)*

Tells Kickstart where to install the bootloader. Example 7-1 tells Kickstart to put the bootloader on the master boot record (`--location=mbr`) of the primary drive. ESX version 3.x and higher utilize the GRUB bootloader rather than the older LILO bootloader. Options include:

--append=*kernel_options*

Allows you to specify advanced kernel features when the system boots.

--driveorder=

Specifies drives in the order you want the BIOS to check them to find a boot device.

--location=[mbr|*partition*|none]

Indicates the location of the bootloader. Normally it is on the MBR.

--md5pass=

Sets the encrypted password to use when running the GRUB bootloader.

--password=

Sets the cleartext password to use when running the GRUB bootloader.

--upgrade

Upgrades an existing bootloader, preserving all previous configuration options.

The following example installs the bootloader on the master boot record on the first SCSI device:

```
bootloader --location=mbr --driveorder=dev/sda
```

clearpart *(optional)*

Causes the indicated partitions to be deleted before creating the partitions specified in the configuration (via the `partition` command). This is not required when using the `upgrade` command, because that simply reloads existing partitions. Options include:

--all

Removes all partitions from the system. We strongly suggest that you physically disconnect any external SAN devices connected to the system before using this option.

--drives=

Specifies particular drives from which you wish to remove partitions. This is a good way to avoid disaster if you cannot remove your external disk.

--initlabel

Initializes the disk label to the default for the operating system you are installing.

--linux

    Removes all Linux partitions during the installation. If you have connections to any external SAN devices, it might be wise to disconnect them before using this option.

firewall *(optional)*

    Configures the ESX's firewall settings during the Kickstart installation. Options include:

--disabled

    Disables the firewall, allowing all traffic.

--enabled

    Enables the firewall, blocking all incoming connections unless they are in response to outgoing requests.

--ftp

    Allows all FTP traffic.

--http

    Allows all HTTP traffic.

--port=

    Allows you to specify which ports you wish to have opened in the firewall configuration.

--ssh

    Allows all SSH traffic.

--smtp

    Allows all SMTP traffic.

--telnet

    Allows all Telnet traffic through the firewall.

--trust=

    Lets you specify a particular device through which traffic will be allowed.

keyboard *(required)*

    Indicates the language setting for your keyboard.

install *(optional)*

    Tells Kickstart this is an install rather than an upgrade. Options include:

<cdrom|nfs|url>

    Installation variables.

--server

    Used in conjunction with the nfs command to specify the NFS server to connect to.

--dir=
> Used in conjunction with the `nfs` command to specify which directory to mount.

url
> The URL to be used (*http* or *ftp*); for example, `url --url http://<server>/<dir>`.

lang *(required)*
> Indicates the default language for the installation. Example 7-1 sets ours to U.S. English.

langsupport *(required)*
> Specifies the default language that will be installed on the ESX Server.

mouse *(required)*
> Indicates whether the console has a mouse. The default for ESX is no. Options include:

--device=
> Specifies which device the mouse will be used on.

--emulthree
> Lets you emulate a three-button mouse using a two-button mouse (clicking both of the mouse buttons simultaneously will simulate a third button).

network *(optional)*
> Configures network information for the ESX Server. Options include:

--addvmportgroup=[1|0]
> A VMware-specific command that allows you to create a default portgroup for virtual machines. Set this value to 0 if you do not want to create a default portgroup. The best practice is to disable this feature.

--bootproto=[dhcp|static]
> Specifies whether the IP address is assigned by DHCP or is statically assigned.

--device=
> Specifies the device to use for the installation.

--gateway=
> Specifies the gateway used by the ESX Server.

--hostname=
> Gives the hostname for the ESX Server.

--ip=
> Gives the IP address for the ESX Server.

--nameserver=
> Lists the primary DNS nameserver used by the ESX Server.

--netmask=
> Sets the netmask for the network interface.

--nodns
> Tells the installer to not configure DNS.

--vlanid=
> A VMware-specific command that allows you to specify the VLAN on which this ESX Server resides. The value can range from 0 to 4095.

nfs *(optional)*
> Specifies that the installation will take place over NFS. A typical command is:
>
> ```
> nfs --server=yourservername.com -dir=/somedirectory
> ```
>
> The --server option can specify either a hostname or an IP address.

partition *(required)*
> Creates a partition. These lines are generated by default from the screen shown in Figure 7-3, but you can modify them by hand. Options include:

--size=
> The minimum partition size in megabytes.

--grow
> Allows the partition to grow either to fill all available space, or up to the size specified in the --maxsize option.

--maxsize=
> The maximum size a partition can grow to, in megabytes.

--ondisk= *or* --ondrive=
> The disk on which the partition will be created.

--fstype=
> The filesystem type for the partition.

--badblocks
> Checks the partition for bad blocks during installation.

rootpw *(required)*
> Sets up the default *root* password on the system. As you can see, we are using an encrypted password in our installation (rootpw --iscrypted 1TNllmXJd $tSh9WvAEO/b4KlKBxncWX/); however, you can use a cleartext password if you wish. In the following example, changeme would be the cleartext password that would be passed to the ESX Server during configuration:
>
> ```
> rootpw changeme
> ```
>
> If you plan on using a cleartext password, we suggest that you change it when the installation has completed.

skipx *(optional)*
> If this value is present, the installation will not install X Windows.

timezone *(required)*

    Sets the system default time zone. This command has one option:

    `--utc`

        Use UTC time (formerly known as GMT).

url *(optional)*

    Specifies whether ESX will boot over a network using HTTP or FTP. Here are two examples using HTTP:

```
url --url http://servername.com/locationtoinstall
url --url http://1.1.1.1:8080/locationtoinstall
```

    And here are two examples using FTP:

```
url --url ftp://username:password@servername.com/locationtoinstall
url --url ftp://1.1.1.1/locationtoinstall
```

Along with the standard Kickstart commands, VMware also has some custom commands you can use in your Kickstart configuration file:

upgrade *(optional)*

    Tells Kickstart to start an upgrade to an ESX Server instead of an installation.

vmaccepteula *(required)*

    Automatically accepts the ESX license agreement.

vmlicense *(optional)*

    Allows you to set the license information during installation. You can download the license from a license server or store the license on the host itself.

    To download the license from another server, specify the `--server` option with the port on which the license server listens (27000 by default), followed by the IP address or hostname of the license server. The `--features` and `--edition` options can specify further information:

```
vmlicense --mode=server --server=27000@servername.com [--features=features]
[--edition=edition]
```

    In single-server mode, specify that the license is on the local server. Again, the `--features` and `--edition` options are available:

```
vmlicense --mode=file [--features=features] [--edition=edition]
```

    The contents of the license file must be included in the `%vmlicense_text` section of the Kickstart file.

zerombr *(optional)*

    Zeros out the MBR during installation. This can be useful if other installations are present and you want to ensure that any previous bootloaders are cleaned off.

See Also

Recipes 7.2, 7.5, and 7.6

7.4 Copying the CD-ROM to Facilitate NFS Installations

Problem

You want to create a local repository with the ESX installation so that physical media is not needed for installation on each server.

Solution

Use an NFS server, and copy the contents of the ESX CD-ROM to its hard drive.

Discussion

In our example, we'll create a directory called */data/kickstart* on our NFS server and copy the CD-ROM's contents there:

```
mount /dev/cdrom /mnt/cdrom
mkdir -p /data/kickstart
cd /mnt/cdrom
find . | cpio -pdmu /data/kickstart
```

The find command will locate all the files on the CD-ROM and copy them to the */data/kickstart* directory. In the cpio command, the p option copies the files from one place to another, the d option creates the directories that are needed, the m option maintains the original timestamps, and the u option replaces all the files unconditionally (in case any old ones are present).

You can also use the Linux cp command to copy files from the ESX installation CD-ROM, using the following method (the -ar options copy data recursively):

```
mount /dev/cdrom /mnt/cdrom
mkdir -p /data/kickstart
cp -ar /mnt/cdrom/* /data/kickstart
```

If you don't happen to have a CD-ROM available, you can download the ESX ISO file, then mount it and copy the data using the same methods we've shown. Replace the mount command with the following, where *XX* is the version number of the ISO you have downloaded:

```
mount -o loop vmare-esx-XX.iso /mnt/cdrom
```

7.5 Advanced Install Scripting Using %pre

Problem

You want to run additional scripts before the Kickstart configuration runs, or set up the environment in which it will run.

Solution

Put Kickstart-specific commands and Bash shell commands in the **%pre** section of the Kickstart configuration file.

Discussion

In the **%pre** section of Kickstart's configuration file, you can specify commands that you want to run just after the Kickstart configuration has been parsed. Using the **%pre** section, you can grab specific variables relating to your system, such as disk types, and create a partitioning schema based on the disks. For example, if you want to use the same Kickstart file on Dell servers and HP servers, you can check which type of disk is being used in the **%pre** section and partition the disk accordingly.

 You can access the network in the **%pre** section, but name resolution will not work.

Let's take a look at a simple possibility. The following commands will look for a USB drive, mount it, and copy some preconfigured scripts that you might want to run later in the installation, perhaps in the **%post** section of your Kickstart file:

```
%pre
if grep -iqE "ks=hd:[a-z]{2,3}[0-9]:" /proc/cmdline
then
    USBDISK=`cat /proc/cmdline | sed 's/.*ks=hd:\(.*\):.*/\1/'`
fi
mkdir -p /tmp/usbdisk/
mount /dev/$USBDISK /tmp/usbdisk/
mkdir -p /tmp/scripts
cp /tmp/usbdisk/scripts/* /tmp/scripts
```

For more detailed information on using scripts in the **%pre** section, see *http://www.red hat.com/docs/manuals/enterprise/RHEL-3-Manual/sysadmin-guide/s1-kickstart2-prein stallconfig.html*.

See Also

Recipe 7.3

7.6 Advanced Install Scripting Using %post

Problem

You wish to further enhance your ESX Servers' configuration after the ESX installation has completed, or do other initial tasks before applications start.

Solution

Put Kickstart-specific commands and Bash shell commands in the `%post` section of the Kickstart configuration.

Discussion

By including commands in the `%post` section of the Kickstart configuration file, you can customize your ESX configuration by creating virtual switches and network interfaces, making configuration file changes, and more. Recipe 7.3 discussed the advanced command-line options that are available to you. These can be combined in a rich manner in the `%post` section of your Kickstart configuration file. Let's look at a few common uses for that section:

Firewall configuration

This is one universal task that can be performed in the `%post` section. You can run the `firewall` command discussed in Recipe 7.3 during regular configuration, but it has limited options and flexibility. The following lines can be included in the `%post` section to open ports for the iSCSI software initiator, SSH client, NTP client, SNMP daemon, and SMB client:

```
esxcfg-firewall -e swISCSIClient
esxcfg-firewall -e sshClient
esxcfg-firewall -e ntpClient
esxcfg-firewall -e snmpd
esxcfg-firewall -e smbClient
```

Networking

Further customization might include network setup using the built-in ESX commands, which are not allowed in the general commands section because the commands in that section run before ESX is installed. Let's take a look at how to create a simple network.

First, we'll create a new virtual switch and assign the name *vmnic1* to that interface. Then we'll create the portgroup named *production_network* on *vSwitch0*. Finally, we'll restart networking:

```
esxcfg-vswitch -a vSwitch0
esxcfg-vswitch -L vmnic1 vSwitch0
esxcfg-vswitch -A production_network vSwitch0
service mgmt-vmware restart
```

Modifying system configuration files

This is also very easy to automate using built-in Linux commands. The following example uses the standard Linux `echo` command to modify the */etc/resolv.conf* file to configure the nameservers for your ESX Server:

```
echo "search yourdomain.com" > /etc/resolv.conf
echo "nameserver 10.1.1.1" >> /etc/resolv.conf
echo "nameserver 10.2.2.2" >> /etc/resolv.conf
```

Time synchronization

We can use the echo command again, along with other Linux commands, to enable the *ntpd* service:

```
chkconfig ntpd on
echo "ntp1.domain.com" > /etc/ntp/step-tickers
echo "ntp2.domain.com" >> /etc/ntp/step-tickers

echo "restrict 127.0.0.1" > /etc/ntp.conf
echo "restrict default kod nomodify notrap" >> /etc/ntp.conf
echo "server ntp1.domain.com" >> /etc/ntp.conf
echo "server ntp2.domain.com" >> /etc/ntp.conf
echo "driftfile /var/lib/ntp/drift" >> /etc/ntp.conf

service ntpd restart
hwclock --systohc
```

See Also

Recipe 7.3

7.7 Using the ESX Deployment Appliance

Problem

You wish to simplify your ESX installations even further by building them through a graphical interface.

Solution

The ESX Deployment Appliance (EDA) automates the complexities of editing Kickstart configuration files.

Discussion

The EDA is a premade virtual appliance based on Ubuntu Linux that is available for free download at *http://vmware.com/appliances/directory/1216*. Read *http://virtualappliances.eu/eda.html* for quick setup instructions.

EDA provides a straightforward user interface and uses a built-in script builder to automate the task of building Kickstart configuration files.

> The ESX Deployment Appliance is *not* an official VMware product and VMware cannot provide support for it. For technical support, visit *http://virtualappliances.eu*.

The EDA is built for use on VMware Server (free) or Workstation; however, you can run it in ESX using the VMware Converter product, which is available as a free download from the VMware website.

The EDA will grab an IP address via DHCP on first boot and direct you to that IP address to begin creating your Kickstart files, configure the deployment appliance, and much more. To use the EDA effectively, you will need to be familiar with the ESX command-line utilities and how ESX works. Although the appliance makes configuration a snap, you will still want to do some reading.

Index

A

Active Directory authentication, 238–240
%ACTV attribute (esxtop), 167
ADPTR attribute (esxtop), 168
affinity rules, defined, 146
anti-affinity rules, defined, 147
AQLEN attribute (esxtop), 169
auth command, 260
authentication
    Active Directory, 238–240
    configuring choices via command line, 188
automating installations
    copying CD-ROM, 266
    EDA support, 269
    Kickstart configuration, 257–265
    scripting, 251, 252–257
    scripting using %post, 267–269
    scripting using %pre, 266

B

ballooning, defined, 127
bandwidth, Ethernet traffic shaping, 109
bootloader
    Kickstart considerations, 261
    manipulating, 189
    securing GRUB menu, 224
bootloader command, 261
BusLogic driver, 158–160

C

cat command, 161
CCPU(%) attribute (esxtop), 163
CDP (Cisco Discovery Protocol), 91
chage command, 243

CHAP (Challenge Handshake Authentication
    Protocol), 62
Cisco Discovery Protocol (CDP), 91
clearpart command, 261
clusters
    adding hosts, 141–143
    creating, 138–140
    defined, 125
    enabling DRS, 144–147
    removing hosts, 147
    resource pool maximums, 10
    states and warnings overview, 148
command line, 103
    (see also specific commands)
    changing ESX Server time, 180
    changing Ethernet port speed, 121
    changing virtual disk SCSI driver, 158–160
    checking ESX patches, 175
    configuring authentication choices, 188
    configuring Ethernet adapters, 198
    configuring firewalls, 192
    configuring storage multipathing, 194–195
    creating service console network, 101
    creating VMFS volume, 80
    displaying associated mappings, 206
    displaying server information, 156
    emptying virtual machine logfile, 161
    enabling NTP, 179–180
    enabling NTP in vCenter, 176–179
    entering maintenance mode, 155
    generating logfiles, 173–175
    hardware iSCSI options, 204
    hiding VMware tools icon, 160
    host files, 186
    locating Ethernet adapters, 120

We'd like to hear your suggestions for improving our indexes. Send email to *index@oreilly.com*.

managing disk volumes, 197
managing ESX 4.x add-ons, 199–201
managing ESX driver modules, 193
managing NFS mounts, 196
managing resource groups, 201
managing virtual switches, 171–173
managing VMkernel ports, 208
manipulating bootloader, 189
manipulating crash dump partition, 190
monitoring CPU usage, 162–164
monitoring memory, 164–167
monitoring network usage, 169–171
monitoring storage performance, 168
registering virtual machines, 183
renaming virtual machines, 184, 185
renaming VMFS volume, 84
rescanning HBAs, 199
restarting vCenter agent, 182
restoring service console, 122
SCSI device mappings, 207
setting ESX Server options, 186
software iSCSI options, 203
TCP wrappers, 181
tracking users via, 235–238
unregistering virtual machines, 183
upgrading VMware version, 205
viewing disk partitions, 161
viewing ESX version, 157
virtual machine snapshots, 183
VMkernel network routes, 202
vswif console settings, 209–211
Converter application, 158
copy and paste function, 246
COS (see service console)
COSMEM attribute (esxtop), 166
cp command (Linux), 266
cpio command, 266
CPU
    configuration maximums, 8
    hotplug/hot add, 151
    monitoring usage, 162–164
CPU limits, 128–129
CPU reservations, 131
CPU shares, 129–131
crash dump partition, 190
%CSTP attribute (esxtop), 164

D

datastores

adding, 72, 77
creating port access, 74–76
determining location of, 88
removing storage volumes, 87
date command (Linux), 180
DAVG/cmd attribute (esxtop), 169
df command (Linux), 161
DHCP (Dynamic Host Configuration
        Protocol), 25
Disk Initialization wizard, 67
disk partitions
    crash dump partition, 190
    creating diagnostic partition, 86
    ESX 3.x considerations, 16
    ESX 4.x considerations, 48
    ESX Server considerations, 256
    viewing via console, 161
disk shrinking, disabling, 246
distributed resource scheduler (see DRS)
distributed switches (see virtual switches)
DNAME attribute (esxtop), 170
%DRPRX attribute (esxtop), 171
%DRPTX attribute (esxtop), 171
DRS (distributed resource scheduler)
    creating clusters, 140
    defined, 125
    enabling, 133
    enabling in clusters, 144–147
    resource pool maximums, 10
    vCenter server outage effects, 152
DTYP attribute (esxtop), 170
Dynamic Host Configuration Protocol
        (DHCP), 25

E

echo command (Linux), 268
EDA (ESX Deployment Appliance), 269
egrep command, 236
Enhanced VMotion Compatibility (EVC), 4
ESX 3.x
    configuration maximums, 5–11
    differences in support, 91
    disk partitioning sizes, 16
    installing, 12–20
    verifying hardware compatibility, 12
    version comparisons, 3
ESX 4.x
    configuration maximums, 5–11
    disk partitioning sizes, 48

host profiles, 4
installing, 12, 42–51
managing disk volumes, 197
storage improvements, 4
verifying hardware compatibility, 43
version comparisons, 3
virtual machine support, 151
virtual switch support, 5
VMFS Volume Grow feature, 5
vSphere support, 3
ESX Deployment Appliance (EDA), 269
ESX Server
    adding Fibre Channel storage, 72
    adding NFS datastore, 77
    adding VMFS datastore, 72
    checking patches, 175
    comparing storage options, 55
    components supported, 11
    configuring firewall, 92–95
    configuring ports, 92–95
    creating diagnostic partition, 86
    creating VMFS volume, 78, 80
    disk partitioning sizes, 16
    enabling direct root logins, 214
    enabling scripted installs, 251
    extending VMFS volume, 82–83
    hardware requirements, 12
    installing, 12–20
    managing add-ons, 199–201
    managing driver modules, 193
    manually changing time, 180
    monitoring CPU usage, 162–164
    monitoring memory, 164–167
    opening firewall ports, 68
    overview, 11
    removing storage volumes, 87
    restarting vCenter agent, 182
    setting options via command line, 186
    suggested partitions, 256
ESX server
    displaying information, 156
ESX, viewing version, 157
esxcfg-addons command, 199–201
esxcfg-advcfg command, 186, 199
esxcfg-auth command
    Active Directory authentication, 238
    configuring authentication methods, 188
    locking out users, 240
    setting password aging, 242–246

esxcfg-boot command, 189
esxcfg-dumppart command, 87, 190
esxcfg-firewall command, 93
    checking default ports, 228
    configuring firewalls, 192
    enabling NTP, 179
    ensuring rules, 239
    manipulating ports, 225–228
esxcfg-hwiscsi command, 204
esxcfg-info command, 156
esxcfg-module command, 193
esxcfg-mpath command, 85, 194–195
esxcfg-nas command, 196
esxcfg-nics command, 120, 122, 198
esxcfg-rescan command, 199
esxcfg-resgrp command, 201
esxcfg-route command, 202
esxcfg-scsidevs command, 207
esxcfg-swiscsi command, 203
esxcfg-upgrade command, 205
esxcfg-vmhbadevs command, 206
esxcfg-vmknic command, 116, 208
esxcfg-volume command, 197
esxcfg-vswif command, 119, 209–211
esxcfg-vswitch command, 117, 121, 171–173
ESXi
    adding hosts to clusters, 142
    benefits, 22
    compatibility considerations, 22
    configuring lockdown mode, 23
    configuring management network, 25–26
    configuring root password, 23
    differences in support, 91
    downloading ISO image, 12
    enabling SSH, 213
    hardware requirements, 22
    installing, 22–26
    license agreement, 16
    overview, 21
esxtop command
    monitoring CPU usage, 162–164
    monitoring memory, 164–167
    monitoring network usage, 170–171
    monitoring storage performance, 168
esxupdate command, 175
Ethernet adapters
    configuring, 198
    locating, 120
Ethernet ports

changing speed, 121
listing, 198
Ethernet traffic shaping, 109–111
EVC (Enhanced VMotion Compatibility), 4
expandable reservations, 136
extending VMFS volume, 82–83

F

failover, network adapters, 112–115
fdisk command, 85, 191
Fibre Channel
    adding storage in ESX, 72
    RDM support, 73
    storage maximums, 7
find command, 266
firewall command, 262, 268
firewall ports
    checking default, 228
    configuring, 92–95
    manipulating via console, 225–228
    opening, 68, 179
firewalls
    configuring on command line, 192
    network security elements, 105–106

G

gateways, multiple, 111
GAVG/cmd attribute (esxtop), 169
GID attribute (esxtop), 163
grep command, 88, 235
groupadd command, 215–217
groups, setting up, 215–217
GRUB menu, securing, 224

H

HA (high availability)
    creating clusters, 140
    defined, 125
    reconfiguring on hosts, 149
    resource pool maximums, 10
    vCenter server outage effects, 152
hardware iSCSI
    configuring initiators, 62–64
    configuring options, 204
    HBA support, 60, 63
    storage maximums, 8
HBAs (host bus adapters)
    hardware iSCSI support, 60, 63

rescanning, 199
storage device naming scheme, 56
high availability (see HA)
host bus adapters (HBAs)
    hardware iSCSI support, 60, 63
    rescanning, 199
    storage device naming scheme, 56
host files, 186
hosts
    adding to clusters, 141–143
    locating, 186
    reconfiguring HA, 149
    removing from clusters, 147
    vCenter server outage effects, 153
hot add/hotplug, 151
hwclock command, 180
hypervisors
    defined, 11
    ESXi support, 21

I

ID attribute (esxtop), 163
%IDLE attribute (esxtop), 163
initiators (see iSCSI initiators)
install command, 262
IP addresses, changing, 118–120
iSCSI, 69
    (see also hardware iSCSI; software iSCSI)
    jumbo frame interface, 116
    multipathing, 69–71
    RDM support, 73
iSCSI initiators
    configuring hardware iSCSI, 62–64
    configuring in virtual machines, 64–67
    creating networks for, 57–59
    defined, 60
    diagnostic partitions and, 87
    opening firewall ports, 68

J

jumbo frames
    enabling on virtual machines, 118
    enabling on vSwitch, 117
    VMkernel support, 116

K

KAVG/cmd attribute (esxtop), 169
keyboard command, 262

Kickstart tool
  automated installations, 252–257
  background, 251
  commands support, 260–265
  enhancing configuration, 257–265
  %post advanced scripting, 267–269
  %pre advanced scripting, 266
  sample configuration file, 258–260
kill command, 214
krb5.conf file, 243

L

lang command, 263
langsupport command, 263
last command, 236, 237
ldap.conf file, 244
ldd command, 181
license agreements
  accepting automatically, 265
  ESXi, 16
  iSCSI initiators, 65
license server
  installing, 37
  overview, 37
limits
  CPU, 128–129
  memory, 126
Linux platforms
  cp command, 266
  date command, 180
  df command, 161
  displaying associated mappings, 206
  echo command, 268
  installing vConverter, 41–42
  manipulating VMFS partitions, 85–86
  ping command, 103
  renaming VMFS volume, 84
ln command, 85
load balancing, network adapters, 112–115
lockdown mode
  configuring, 23
  defined, 142
logfiles
  emptying for virtual machines, 161
  generating, 173–175
  tracking users, 235–238
logical unit numbers (see LUNs)
login.defs file, 244
LQLEN attribute (esxtop), 169

ls command, 184
LSI Logic driver, 158–160
LUNs (logical unit numbers)
  configuring storage, 72
  diagnostic partitions and, 87
  ESX Server maximums, 64
  RDM support, 73
  storage device naming schemes, 56

M

maintenance mode, 155
management network, configuring, 25–26
MBREAD/s attribute (esxtop), 169
MbRX/s attribute (esxtop), 171
MbTX/s attribute (esxtop), 170
MBWRTN/s attribute (esxtop), 169
MCTLSZ attribute (esxtop), 167
MEMCTL attribute (esxtop), 167
memory
  configuration maximums, 8
  hotplug/hot add, 151
  monitoring, 164–167
  virtual machine considerations, 126
memory limits, 126
memory reservations, 126
memory shares, 126
MEMSZ attribute (esxtop), 167
message of the day (MOTD), 219
metadata, reading, 83
migration
  defined, 98
  enabling for virtual machines, 98–101
MKS (mouse-keyboard-screen) service, 92
%MLMTD attribute (esxtop), 164
monitoring
  CPU usage, 162–164
  memory, 164–167
  network usage, 169–171
  storage performance, 168
MOTD (message of the day), 219
mouse-keyboard-screen (MKS) service, 92
multipathing, configuring, 69–71, 194–195

N

N-Port ID Virtualization (NPIV), 74
NAME attribute (esxtop), 163
NAS (network attached storage), 7
network adapters

load balancing and failover, 112–115
modifying speed, 104
monitoring usage, 169–171
network attached storage (NAS), 7
network command, 263
networking
    changing Ethernet port speed, 121
    changing IP addresses, 118–120
    checking connectivity, 103
    choosing security elements, 105–106
    configuration maximums, 9
    configuring ports, 92–95
    creating service console network, 101
    differences in support, 91
    enabling jumbo frames, 117, 118
    enabling virtual machine migration, 98
    Ethernet traffic shaping, 109–111
    jumbo frame VMkernel interface, 116
    load balancing and failover, 112–115
    locating Ethernet adapters, 120
    managing VMkernel routes, 202
    modifying network adapter speed, 104
    multiple gateways, 111
    removing vSwitch, 97
    restoring service console, 122
    setting security policy, 106
    virtual machine support, 95
    vNetwork switch maximums, 9
nfs command, 262, 264
NFS datastore
    accessing, 74–76
    adding to ESX Server, 77
NFS installations, 266
NFS mounts, 196
NPIV (N-Port ID Virtualization), 74
nscd.conf file, 244
nsswitch.conf file, 245
NTP
    enabing in vCenter, 176–179
    enabling via command line, 179–180
ntpd service, 269
NWLD attribute (esxtop), 163

O

OVHD attribute (esxtop), 167
%OVRLP attribute (esxtop), 163

P

partition command, 261, 264
partitions (see disk partitions)
passwd command, 219, 222
password aging, 241–246
passwords, root
    changing via console, 219
    configuring, 23
    recovering, 220–222
PCPU(%) attribute (esxtop), 163
ping command (Linux), 103
PKTRX/s attribute (esxtop), 170
PKTTX/s attribute (esxtop), 170
PMEM attribute (esxtop), 165
PORT attribute (esxtop), 170
port groups
    adding, 102
    configuring properties, 58
    layer 2 security policy, 107
    listing, 172
ports, 74
    (see also firewall ports; VMkernel ports)
    accessing NFS datastore, 74–76
    changing speed, 121
    configuring, 92–95
    creating, 57
    Ethernet, 121, 198
    opening for iSCSI initiator, 68
PSHARE attribute (esxtop), 166

Q

QUED attribute (esxtop), 169

R

raw device mapping (RDM), 73–74
RCLI (remote command-line interface)
    configuring NTP, 180
    functionality, 23
RDM (raw device mapping), 73–74
%RDY attribute (esxtop), 163
READS/s attribute (esxtop), 169
registering virtual machines, 183
remote administration, 229–231
remote command-line interface (RCLI)
    configuring NTP, 180
    functionality, 23
renaming
    virtual machines, 184

virtual machines via command line, 185
VMFS volume, 84
replica volumes, managing, 197
rescanning
    host bus adapters, 199
    storage, 79
reservations
    CPU, 131
    expandable, 136
    memory, 126
resource groups, managing from command
        line, 201
resource management
    adding hosts to clusters, 141–143
    cluster states and warnings, 148
    CPU limits, 128–129
    CPU reservations, 131
    CPU shares, 129–131
    creating clusters, 138–140
    enabling DRS in clusters, 144–147
    expandable reservations, 136
    overview, 125
    reconfiguring HA on hosts, 149
    removing hosts from clusters, 147
    resource pool overview, 134
    setting up resource pools, 132–134
    vCenter server failure/outage, 151–153
    virtual machine considerations, 151
    virtual machine memory, 126
resource pools
    configuration maximums, 10
    DRS cluster maximums, 10
    expandable reservations, 136
    HA cluster maximums, 10
    overview, 134
    setting up, 132–134
    vCenter server outage effects, 152
restart command, 180
root user account
    changing password via console, 219
    configuring passwords, 23
    disabling direct logins, 222
    enabling direct logins, 214
    GRUB bootloader menu, 224
    recovering lost passwords, 220–222
    setting maximum for failed logins, 240
rootpw command, 264
%RUN attribute (esxtop), 163

S

SAN (storage area network)
    ESX improvements, 5
    virtual machine support, 65
SAS (Serial Attached SCSI), 4
scripted installations
    configuring automated, 252–257
    enabling, 251
    scripting using %post, 267–269
    scripting using %pre, 266
SCSI device mappings, 207
SCSI drivers, changing, 158–160
security
    Active Directory authentication, 238–240
    adding users and groups, 215–217
    changing root password, 219
    checking default ports, 228
    choosing network elements, 105–106
    configuring sudo, 233
    controlling SSH access, 217
    disabling copy and paste, 246
    disabling direct root logins, 222
    disabling disk shrinking, 246
    disabling unneeded devices, 247
    disabling USB drive mounting, 225
    disabling VMware tools override, 248
    enabling direct root logins, 214
    enabling SSH on ESXi, 213
    GRUB bootloader menu, 224
    limiting acces to su command, 241
    lockdown mode and, 23
    manipulating firewall ports, 225–228
    preventing device manipulation, 248
    recovering lost root passwords, 220–222
    setting layer 2 policy, 106
    setting maximum for failed logins, 240
    setting password aging, 241–246
    SNMP for remote administration, 229–231
    SNMP preferred version, 231
    sudo support, 232
    tracking users via CLI, 235–238
    turning on MOTD, 219
Serial Attached SCSI (SAS), 4
service console
    changing IP address, 118–120
    changing root password, 219
    creating network, 101
    disabling direct root logins, 222
    manipulating firewall ports, 225–228

overview, 11
restoring via CLI, 122
turning on MOTD, 219
viewing disk partitions, 161
vswif settings, 209–211
service mgmt-vmware restart command, 204, 228
service vmware-webAccess restart command, 252
shares
    CPU, 129–131
    memory, 126
SIGINT signal, 237
SIGQUIT signal, 237
skipx command, 264
snapshots
    managing, 197
    virtual machine, 183
SNMP
    preferred version, 231
    remote administration, 229–231
snmpd.conf file, 229–231
software iSCSI
    configuring, 59–62
    configuring options, 203
    creating separate networks, 57–59
    opening firewall ports, 68
    storage maximums, 8
SSH
    controlling access, 217
    enabling direct root logins, 214
    enabling on ESXi, 213
    MOTD support, 219
sshd_config file, 219
storage
    adding Fibre Channel in ESX, 72
    adjusting timeouts, 89
    comparing ESX options, 55
    configuring multipathing, 194–195
    device naming scheme, 56
    ESX improvements, 4
    Fibre Channel maximums, 7
    general maximums, 6
    hardware iSCSI maximums, 8
    managing NFS mounts, 196
    monitoring performance, 168
    NAS maximums, 7
    performing rescans, 79
    software iSCSI maximums, 8

VMFS2 maximums, 6, 7
storage area network (SAN)
    ESX improvements, 5
    virtual machine support, 65
su command, 234, 238, 241
subnets, configuring routes, 111
sudo command
    changing root password, 220
    configuring, 233
    enabling direct root logins, 214
    overview, 232
    recovering root password, 220–222
sudoers file, 232
SWAP attribute (esxtop), 166
SWCUR attribute (esxtop), 167
SWR/S attribute (esxtop), 167
SWW/S attribute (esxtop), 167
%SYS attribute (esxtop), 163
system-auth file, 245

T

tail command, 235
TCP wrappers, 181
templates, server outage effects, 153
timeouts
    adjusting, 89
    setting in Windows, 89
timezone command, 265
Tomcat web server, 251
top command (Unix), 168

U

Unix top command, 168
unregistering virtual machines, 183
upgrade command, 265
UPLINK attribute (esxtop), 170
url command, 265
USB drives, disabling mounting, 225
%USED attribute (esxtop), 163
USED BY attribute (esxtop), 170
user accounts
    controlling SSH access, 217
    MOTD support, 219
    setting up, 215–217
useradd command, 215–217

V

VCB (VMware Consolidated Backup), 73

vCenter agent, restarting, 182
vCenter client
    enabling NTP, 176–179
    installing, 36
    LSI Logic support, 158
    overview, 36
    ports supported, 92
    preventing device manipulation, 248
    VMotion support, 4
    vSphere support, 3
vCenter server, 125
    (see also resource management)
    adjusting timeouts, 89
    configuration maximums, 10
    creating VMFS volume, 78
    database requirements, 28–36
    downloading ISO image, 29
    installation requirements, 28
    installing, 27–36
    linked mode, 4
    overview, 27
    ports supported, 92
    renaming virtual machines, 184
    rescan feature, 79
    surviving failure/outage, 151–153
    vSphere support, 3
vCenter vConverter
    installing, 38–42
    installing on Linux, 41–42
    installing on Windows, 39
    overview, 38
vConverter (see vCenter vConverter)
vdf command, 161
versions
    SNMP preference, 231
    upgrading VMware, 205
    viewing, 157
VI3 (VMware Infrastructure 3), 3
vicfg-ntp command, 180
vicfg-user function, 23
vimsh command, 155
virtual disk file (VMDK), 73
Virtual Infrastructure (see ESX 3.x)
virtual machines
    affinity rules, 146
    apportioning memory, 126
    configuration maximums, 5
    configuring CPU limits, 128–129
    configuring CPU reservations, 131

configuring CPU shares, 129–131
configuring iSCSI initiators, 64–67
creating vSwitch, 95
disabling disk shrinking, 246
disabling unneeded devices, 247
emptying logfiles, 161
enabling jumbo frames, 118
enabling migration, 98–101
ESX 4.x support, 151
finding snapshots, 183
hardware improvements, 4
hot add support, 4
MKS support, 92
RDM support, 73–74
registering via command line, 183
renaming, 184
storage improvements, 5
unregistering via command line, 183
vCenter server outage effects, 153
virtual switches, 5
    (see also vSwitch)
    configuration maximums, 9
    ESX support, 5
virtualization
    defined, 1
    ESX Server support, 11
virtualization layer, 1
visudo command, 233
VLAN tagging, 106
vm-support command, 173–175
vmaccepteula command, 265
VMDK (virtual disk file), 73
VMFS datastore
    adding, 72
    determining location of, 88
VMFS partitions, 85–86
VMFS volume
    creating in vCenter, 78
    creating via command line, 80
    displaying associated mappings, 206
    extending, 82–83
    reading metadata, 83
    renaming from command line, 84
    viewing information about, 81–82
vmhba names, 206
VMkernel
    crash dump partition, 190
    ESX driver modules, 193
    jumbo frame interface, 116

managing network routes, 202
overview, 11
VMkernel ports
  accessing NFS datastore, 74–76
  creating, 57
  managing, 208
  VMotion support, 99
vmkfstools command, 80, 84
VMKMEM attribute (esxtop), 165
vmkping command, 103
vmlicense command, 265
vmmemctl driver, 127
VMotion
  distributed switch support, 5
  enabling migration, 98–101
  functionality, 4
  vCenter server outage effects, 152
  VMkernel support, 76, 208
VMware Consolidated Backup (VCB), 73
VMware ESX (see ESX)
VMware ESX Server (see ESX Server)
VMware ESXi (see ESXi)
VMware Fusion, 12
VMware Infrastructure 3 (VI3), 3
VMware Infrastructure client (see vCenter
  client)
VMware tools
  disabling disk shrinking, 246
  disabling settings override, 248
  hiding icon, 160
  preventing device manipulation, 248
VMware vCenter Converter (see vCenter
  Converter)
VMware vCenter server (see vCenter server)
VMware vSphere (see vSphere)
VMware Workstation, 12
VMware, upgrading version, 205
vmware-cmd command
  registering virtual machines, 183
  renaming virtual machines, 185
  unregistering virtual machines, 183
vmxnet driver, 116, 118
VMXNET Generation 3, 4
vNetwork switch maximums, 9
vSphere, 5
  (see also ESX 4.x)
  components, 3
  hardware support, 4
  new features, 4–5

SCSI device mappings, 207
vswif service console, 209–211
vSwitch
  creating, 95
  enabling jumbo frames, 117
  Ethernet traffic shaping, 109
  layer 2 security policy, 107
  listing, 123
  load balancing and failover, 112
  managing, 171–173
  removing, 97

W

w command, 236, 237
%WAIT attribute (esxtop), 163
who command, 236
Windows platform
  configuring iSCSI initiators, 64–67
  installing vConverter, 39
  setting disk timeouts, 89
Windows registry
  adjusting disk timeout value, 90
  hiding tools icon, 160
write command, 236
WRITES/s attribute (esxtop), 169

Z

zerombr command, 265

About the Authors

Ryan Troy has more than 12 years of Unix/Linux system administration experience in industries ranging from web hosting to newspapers. He serves as technical administrator and chairman of the Ubuntu Forum Council. He currently works for a Michigan-based consulting company and specializes in storage and virtualization.

Matthew Helmke has written articles for magazines such as *Linux+* and *Linux Identity*, and helped write Prentice Hall's *The Official Ubuntu Book*. He is an active member of the Ubuntu Linux community as an administrator and Forum Council member for the Ubuntu Forums (*ubuntuforums.org*), and a member of the membership approval committee for Ubuntu in Europe, the Middle East, and Africa.

Colophon

The animal on the cover of *VMware Cookbook* is a leatherback sea turtle (*Dermochelys coriacea*). At four to eight feet in length, the leatherback turtle is the fourth largest reptile, behind certain species of crocodile. Most sea turtles have bony shells; however, the leatherback's shell is made of skin and oily flesh.

Leatherback sea turtles live as far north as the Arctic Circle and as far south as the Cape of Good Hope in Africa and the southernmost tip of New Zealand. They inhabit all tropical and subtropical oceans.

The turtle's diet consists almost entirely of jellyfish, and ecologists theorize that the turtle plays a key role in controlling jellyfish populations. Scientists also note that the leatherback turtle continues to be important to local ecosystems even after it dies: decomposing leatherback turtles often wash ashore and host various species of flies and beetles.

As with other sea turtles, leatherbacks begin their lives on land as they burst forth from the sand of their nesting beaches. Yet their lives are in danger even before they are born: birds and humans eat leatherback turtle eggs (in Malaysia, where the leatherback turtle is nearly extinct, the eggs are considered a delicacy). The danger doesn't end, however, once leatherbacks are born: birds, crustaceans, reptiles, and people will often eat newborn turtles before they reach the water. Once they reach the sea, the turtles become prey for some species of fish and cephalopods. Given all of their predators, very few leatherbacks reach adulthood; those that do usually have a life span of 30 to 50 years.

The cover image is from *Dover's Animals*. The cover font is Adobe ITC Garamond. The text font is Linotype Birka; the heading font is Adobe Myriad Condensed; and the code font is LucasFont's TheSansMonoCondensed.